SPACEMAZES

By Aaron and Peter Landesman

Published by Mathmaze

Copyright © 2002 by Mathmaze.
All rights reserved. No part of this book may be reproduced or transmitted in any form or by any means, without prior written permission of the publisher.

Patents Pending for "N-Dimensional Mazes" and "Number Mazes".

ISBN 1-59196-152-1

Printed by Instantpublisher.com

Edited by Susan Landesman

Preface

Spacemazes takes advantage of children's natural desire to learn. While they explore the exciting new mazes, they acquire mathematical skills. Satisfied by every twist and turn, your child will learn how to move in 3 dimensional space.

Babies first learn how to crawl around the floor in 2 dimensions. As they explore, their curiosity leads them to venture toward the edge of a bed or sofa where they learn about the 3rd dimension(height). As babies grow into toddlers and young children, they learn to climb, jump, kick a soccer ball up into the air, or dive into a pool of deep water and gradually develop an intuition about moving in 3 dimensions. *Spacemazes* helps children learn useful skills that airplane pilots must know in order to fly, that submarine commanders and space captains must know in order to steer a ship in three dimensions, that doctors and biologists must know in order to understand the 3-dimensional pathways that chemicals travel in the body, and that visitors to New York City must know in order find their way through Grand Central Terminal, the Port Authority Bus Terminal or Macy's six-story store.

Aaron is an ordinary child who loves mazes. Looking for new challenges, he and his Daddy, Peter, developed the 3 dimensional mazes shown in this book. While Aaron was playing with mazes, his Dad, a mathematics teacher, was helping his son learn math. You can recreate the same enjoyable experiences when you read this book with your child: mazes + math = fun.

In this book, one learns about 3-dimensional space as well as related elementary mathematical concepts such as 3-dimensional size, coordinates, negative numbers and base 2 arithmetic. Introducing these ideas to children, when in pre-school and the early elementary grades, will enable them to understand these concepts more fully when they are formally presented at a later stage in school. Mathematics is a language with a specialized vocabulary that should be introduced to children at as early an age as possible. One's understanding of mathematical concepts grows over time through repeated exposure.

To order additional copies of *Spacemazes*, email the authors at mathmaze@yahoo.com.

Aaron and Peter

Table of Contents

Chapter 1	**Introduction to Mazes**	**5**
Chapter 2	**Introduction to 3 Dimensional Mazes**	**9**
Chapter 3	**Mazes Without Helping Ladders**	**30**
Chapter 4	**The Size of a Maze**	**37**
Chapter 5	**4 by 4 by 3 Mazes**	**47**
Chapter 6	**Number Mazes**	**55**
Chapter 7	**6 by 4 by 3 Mazes**	**74**
Chapter 8	**Subtraction Number Mazes**	**95**
Chapter 9	**4 by 4 by 4 Mazes**	**105**
Chapter 10	**Negative Number Mazes**	**112**
Chapter 11	**6 by 4 by 4 Mazes**	**124**
Chapter 12	**Coordinates in 3 Dimensions**	**142**
Chapter 13	**8 by 4 by 5 Mazes** (Practicing coordinates)	**152**
Chapter 14	**3 by 3 by 3 by 2 Mazes** (The only 4 dimensional maze in print)	**158**

Chapter 1

This is an easy 2 dimensional maze. If you can master these, you will be able to wind your way through a 3 dimensional maze.

START

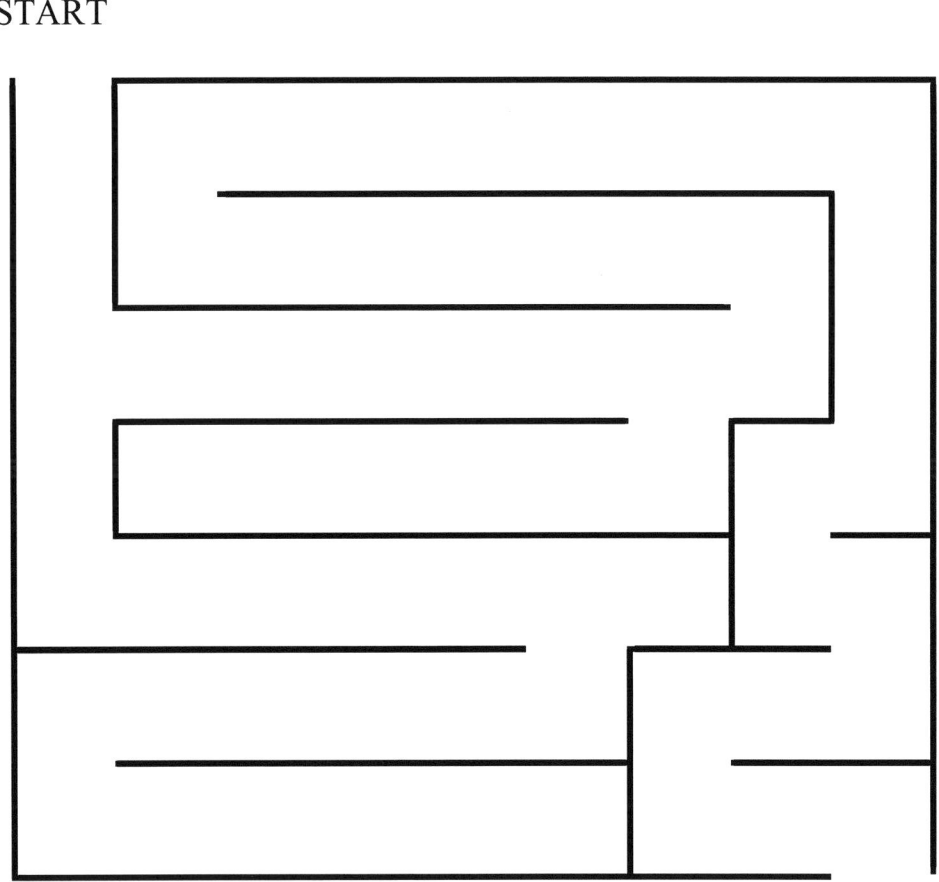

END

This is a harder 2 dimensional maze.

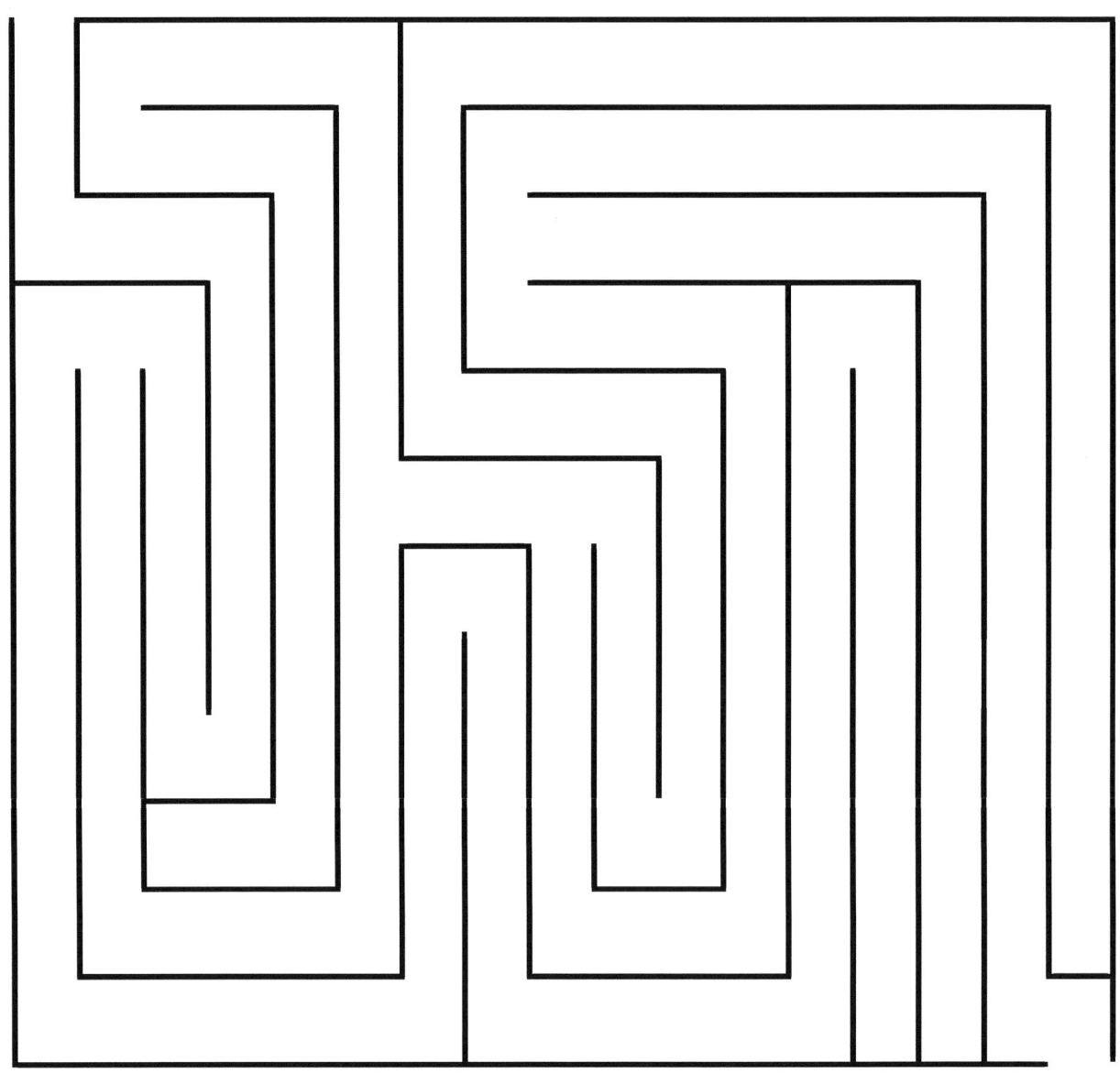

If you string two or more 2 dimensional mazes together, they almost become 3 dimensional mazes.

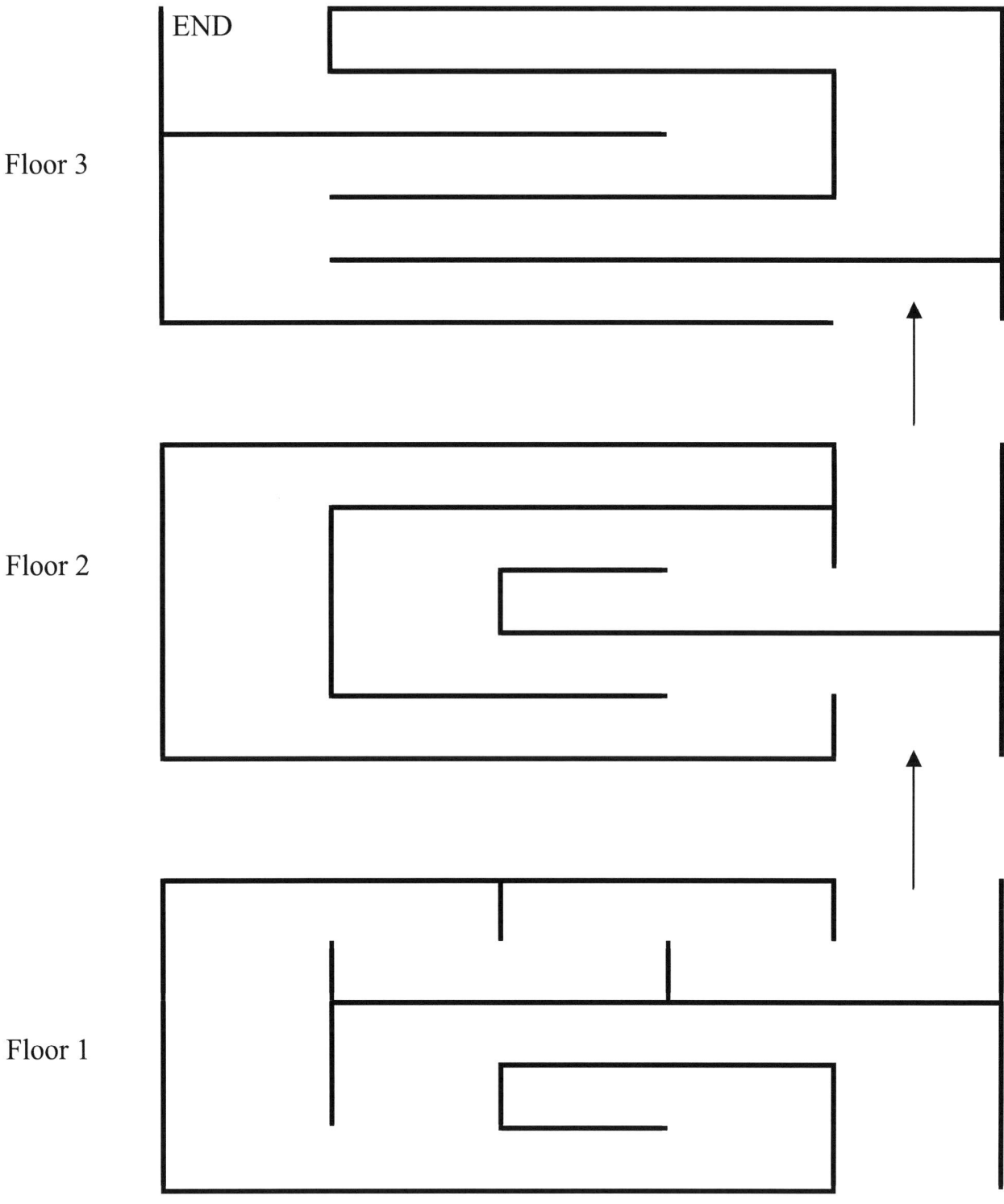

If you think of each 2 dimensional maze as a floor and can go up or down from floor to floor, then you will have a 3 dimensional maze.

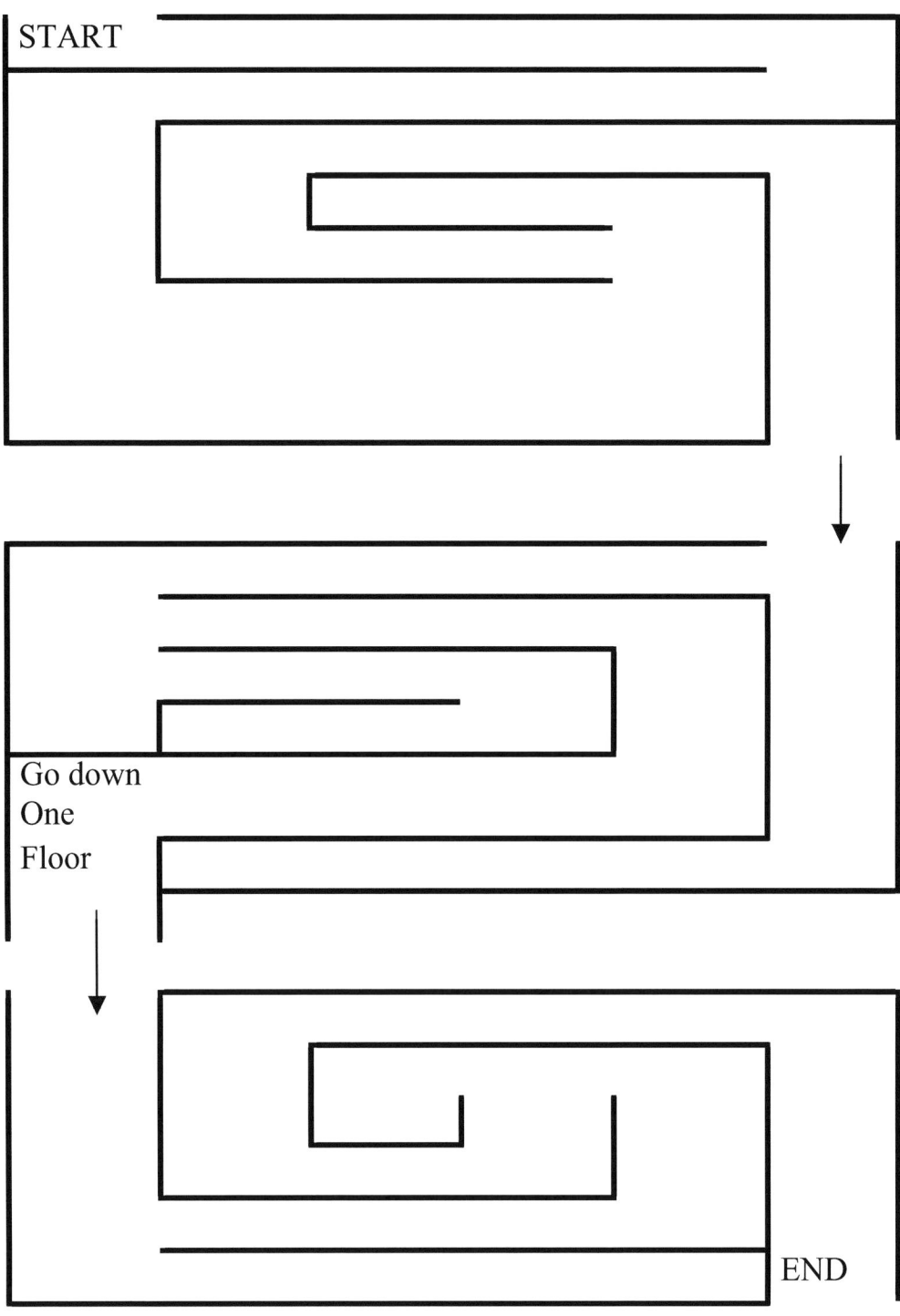

CHAPTER 2 Introduction to 3 Dimensional Mazes
(3 by 2 by 3 Mazes)

Directions for navigating through a 3 Dimensional Maze:
1. Imagine one floor placed on top of another.
2. Begin at the word "START".
3. Move through each floor as you would move through any 2 dimensional maze. (Do not cross the walls.)
4. At any shape such as a star ☆ or a triangle △ , you can move up or down a floor to the same shape directly above or below it on another floor. Imagine that you can go up or down a floor on stairs connecting one ☆ to another or connecting one △ to another.
5. Move up or down and through each floor until you reach the maze's "END".

EXAMPLE

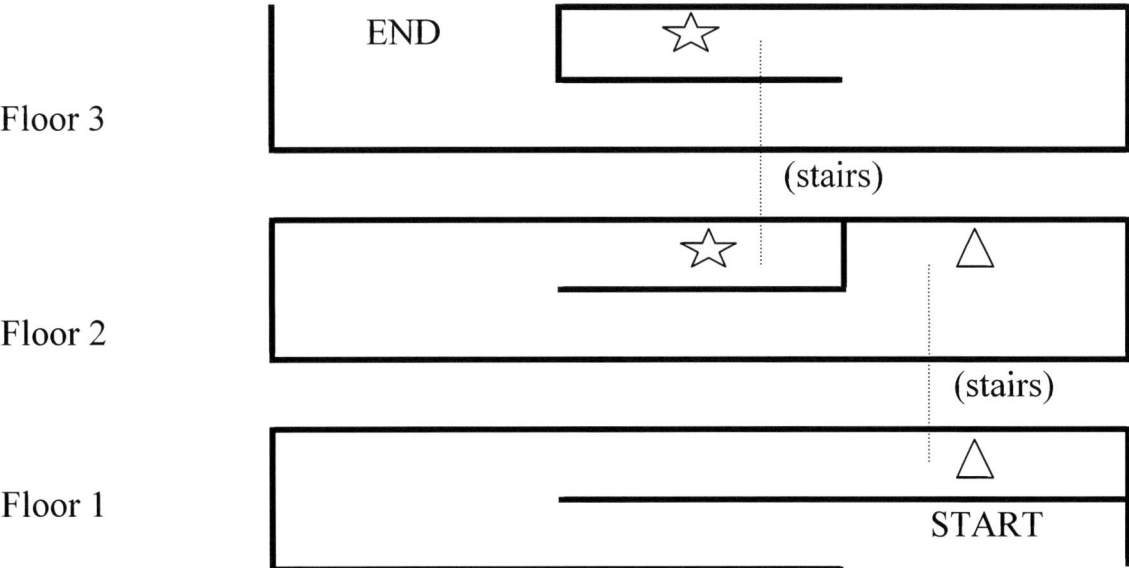

The vertical dotted lines seen in this picture indicate imaginary stairs.

How to do this Maze.

Imagine a house with 3 floors and stairs between the same shapes on different floors. Enter the front door and go up the stairs to the End.

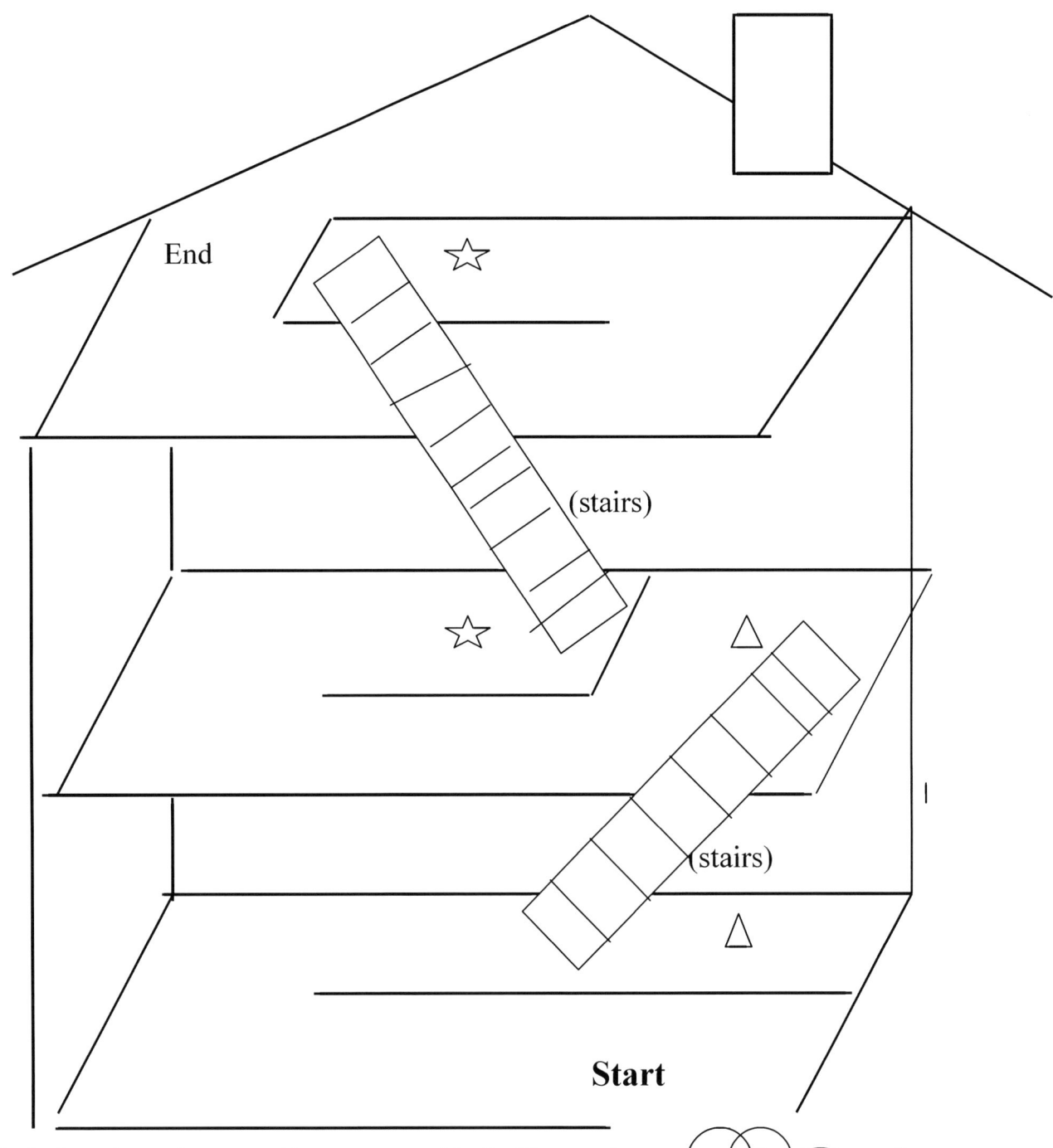

Stairs have been drawn on this page to graphically illustrate how to move from floor to floor.

You must imagine Stairs connecting the 2 triangles △ and the 2 stars ☆ .

The solution to the maze is shown below. Follow the arrows or the numbers from the Start to the End. This is called the "solution to the maze."

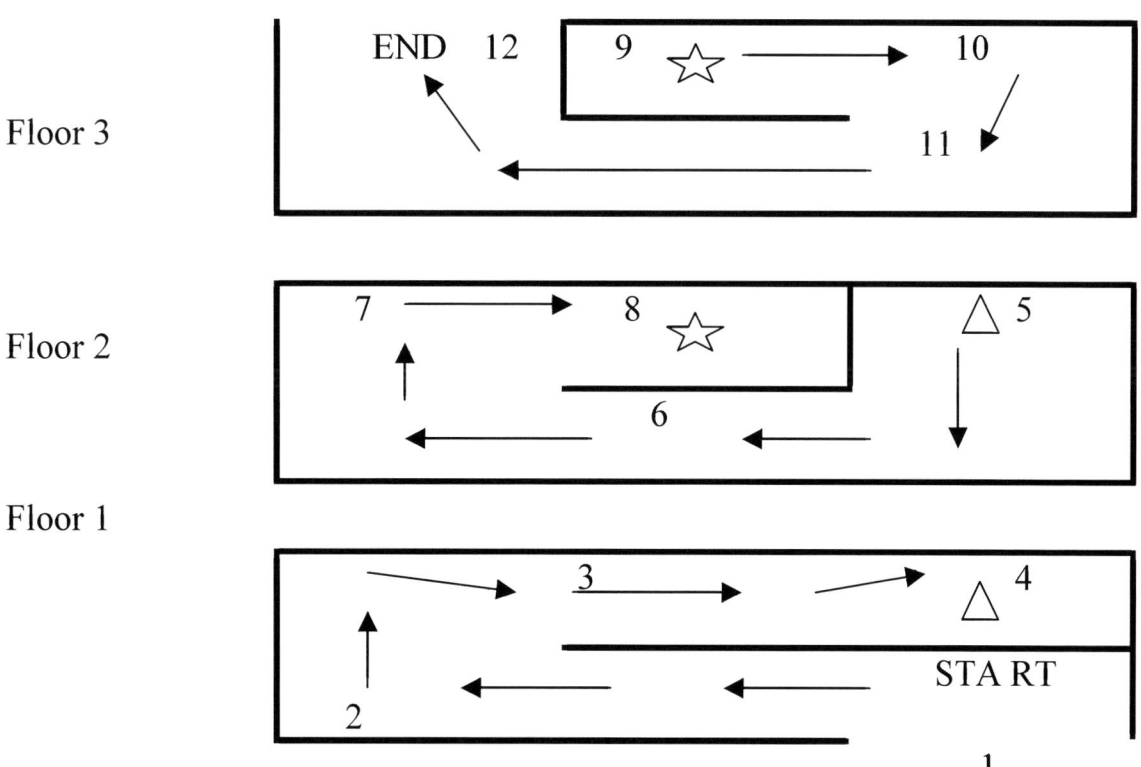

Sometimes you have to go up and then back down one floor before you reach the End at the top.

The shapes ☆, △, ◇ and ◎ are the tops or the bottoms of imaginary stairs connecting 2 different floors. To solve the Maze you have to go up or down these imaginary stairs.

Example

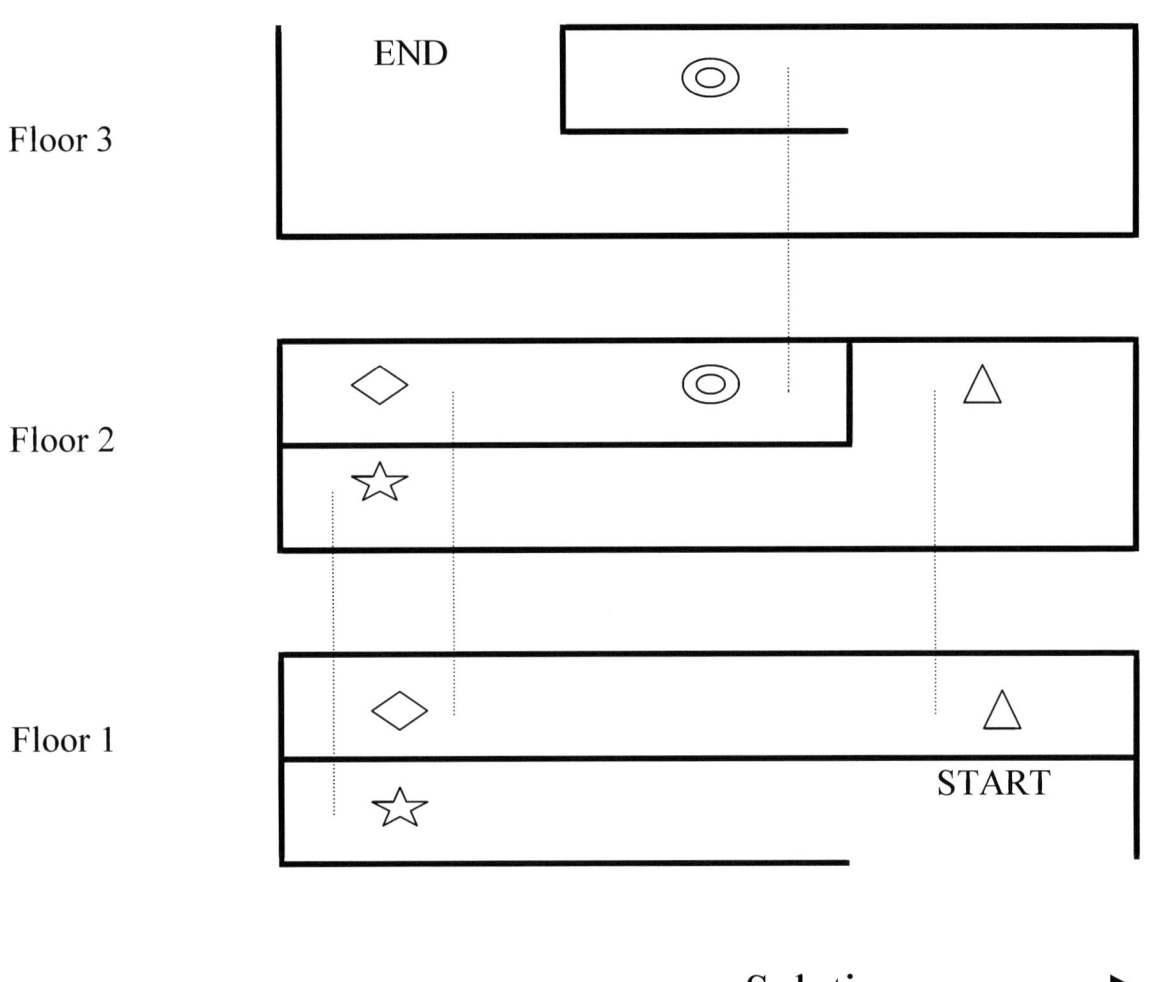

Solution ⟶

Solution - Follow the Numbers

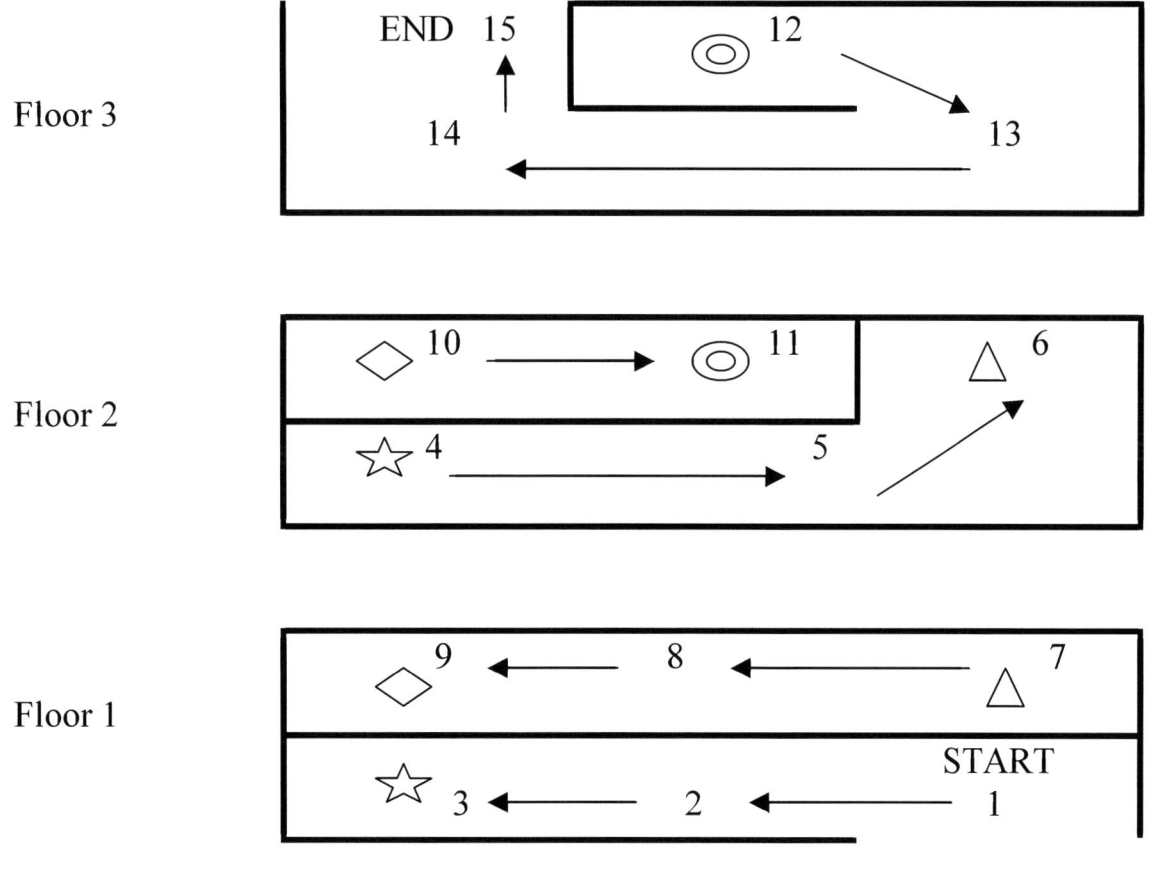

Sometimes you have to go up to Floor 3, then all the way down to Floor 1 and then back up to Floor 3 in order to get to the End.

Example

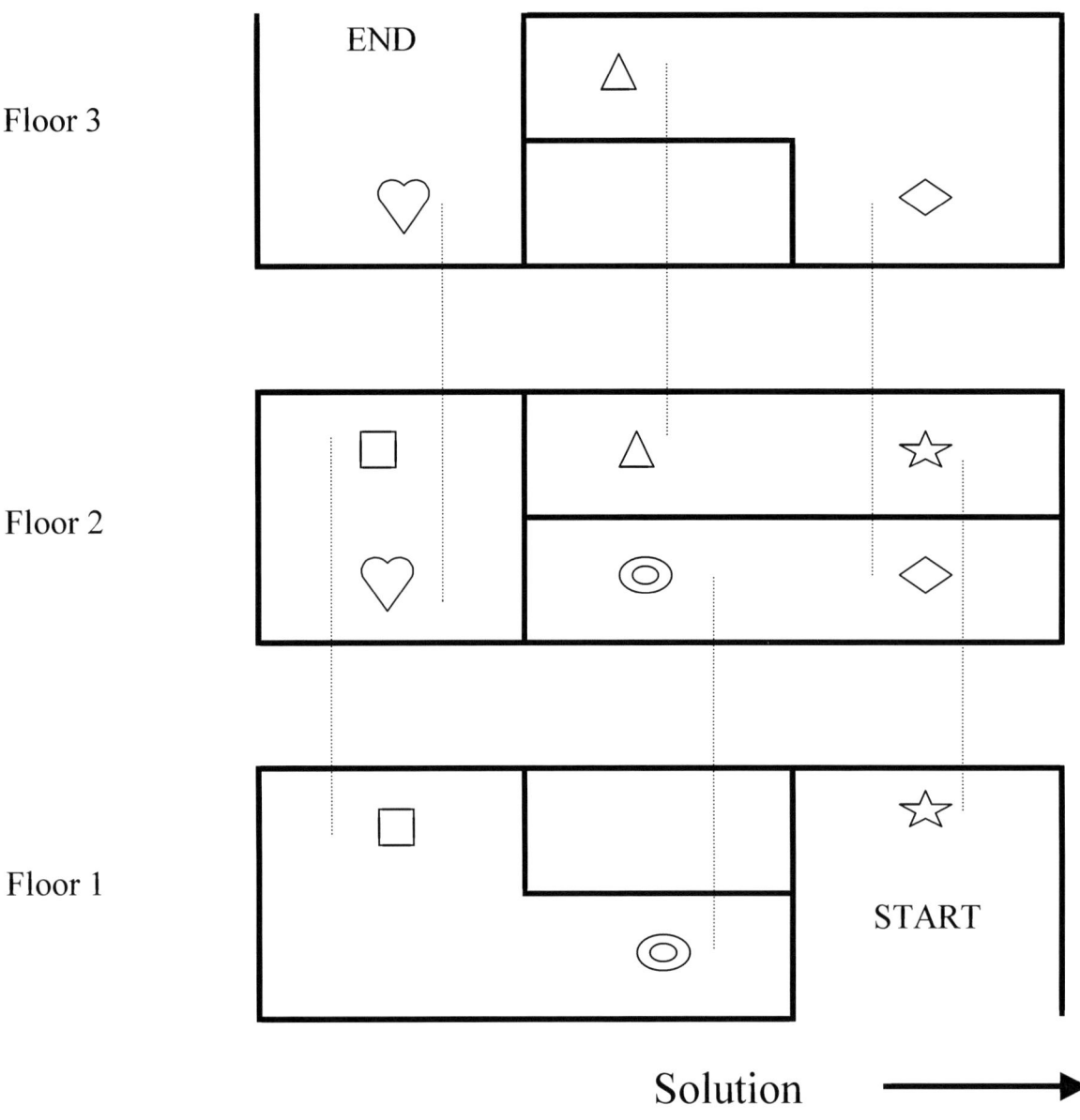

Floor 3

Floor 2

Floor 1

Solution →

Solution = Follow the Numbers

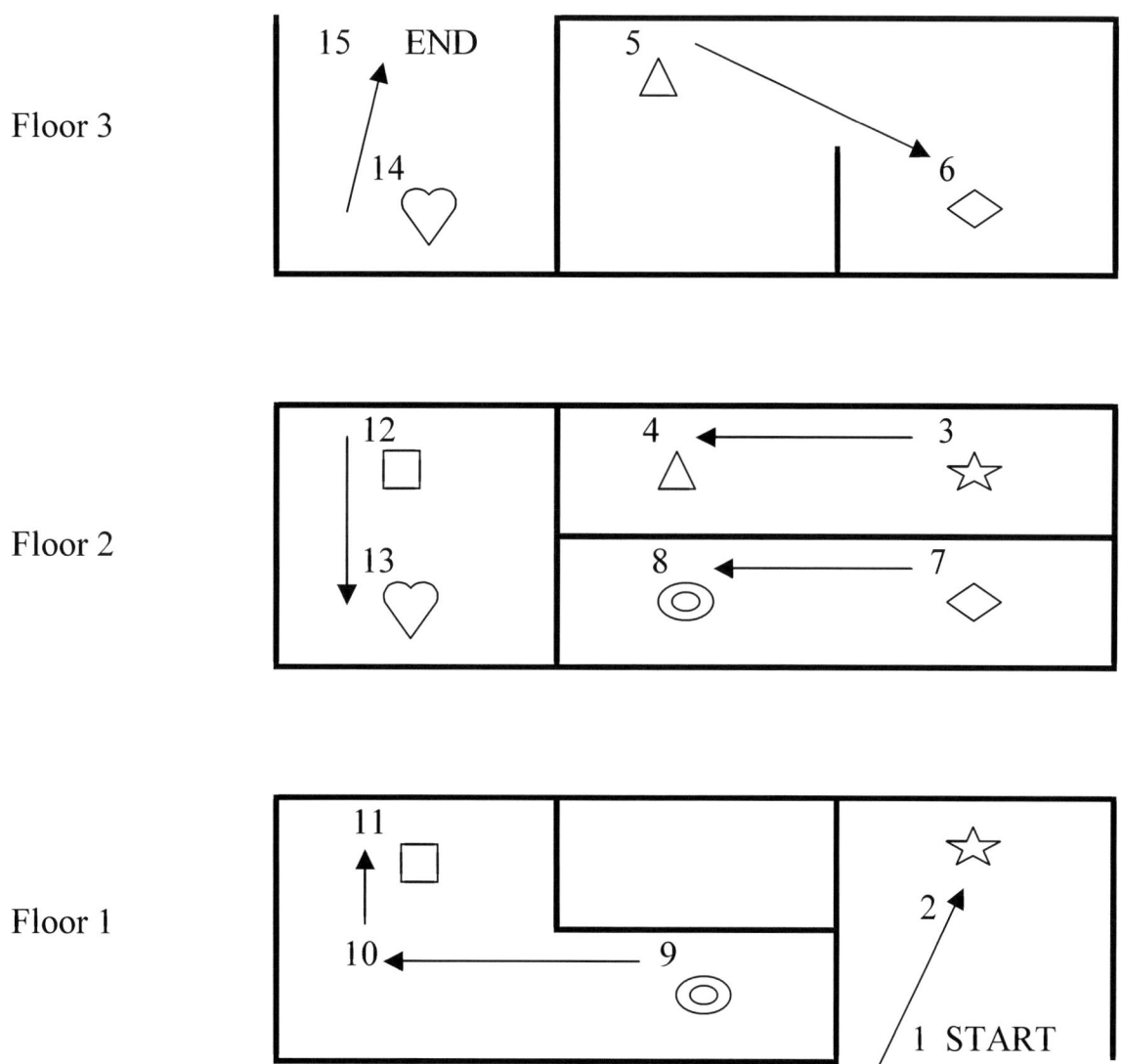

Dead Ends can be in many different places throughout the maze. Here is an easy example.

Example

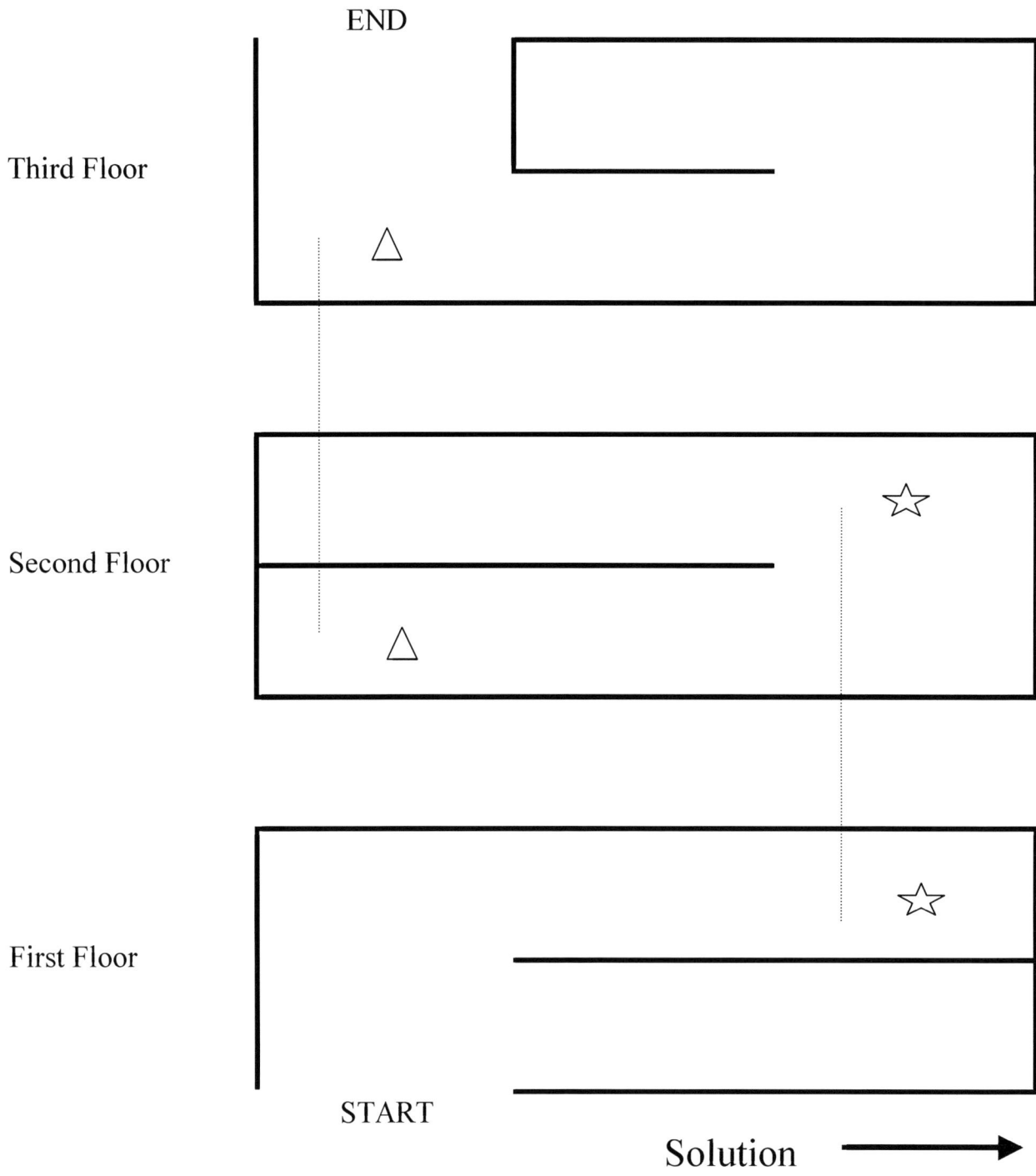

Solution = Follow the Numbers to see the solution of the maze.

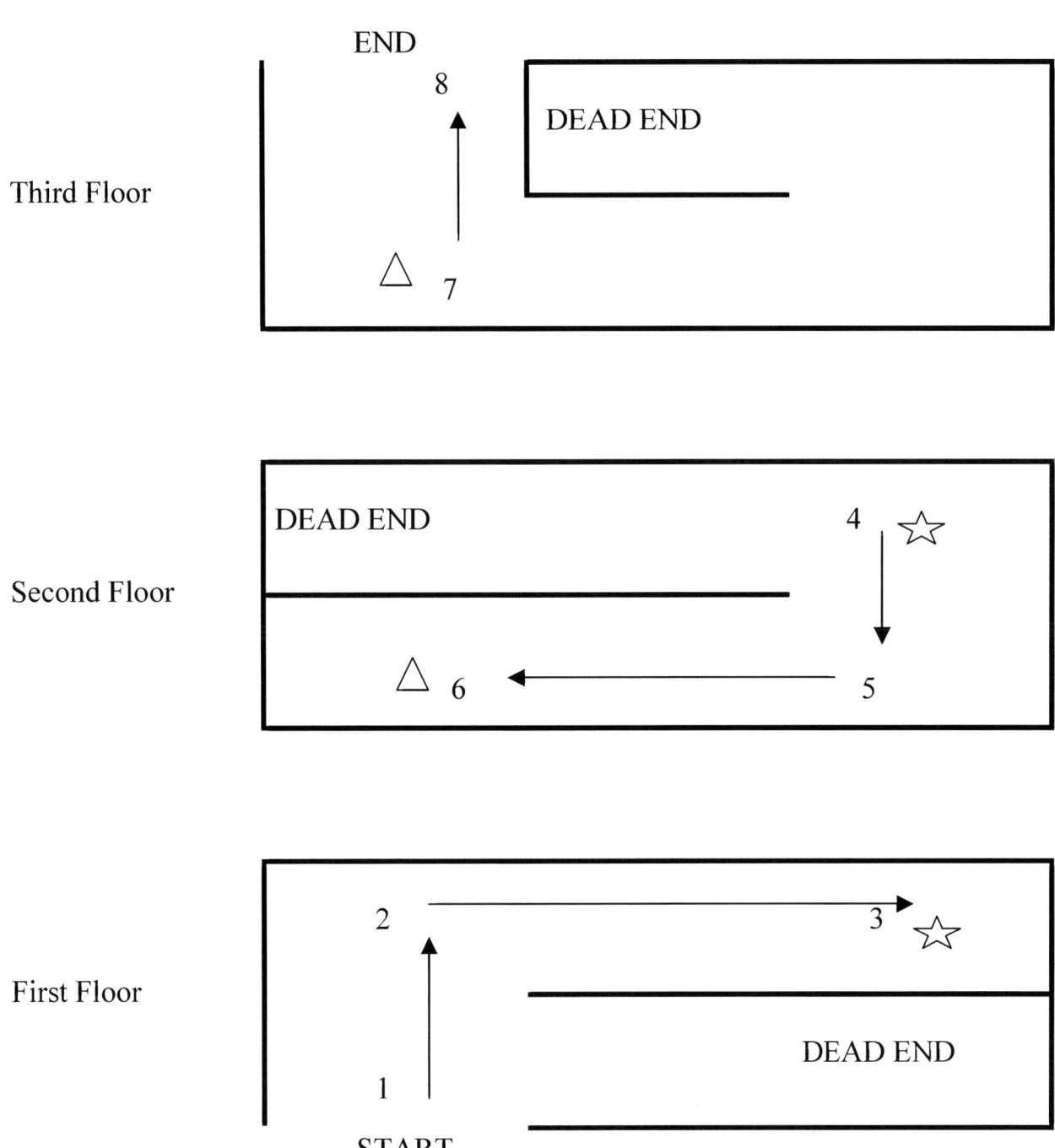

Sometimes Dead Ends take you to the wrong Floor. If so, you will have to retrace your path.

Example

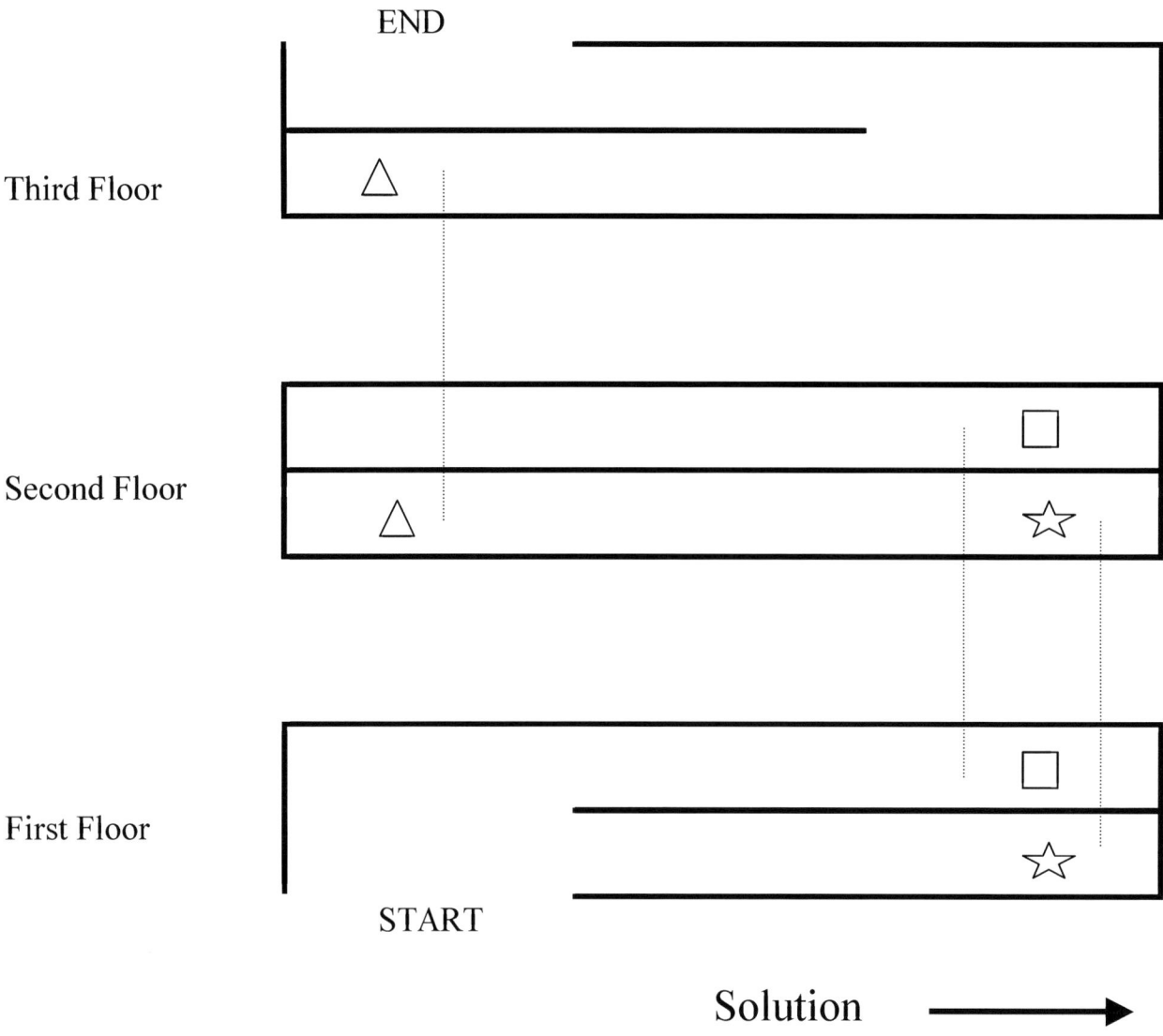

Solution →

Solution = Follow the Numbers.

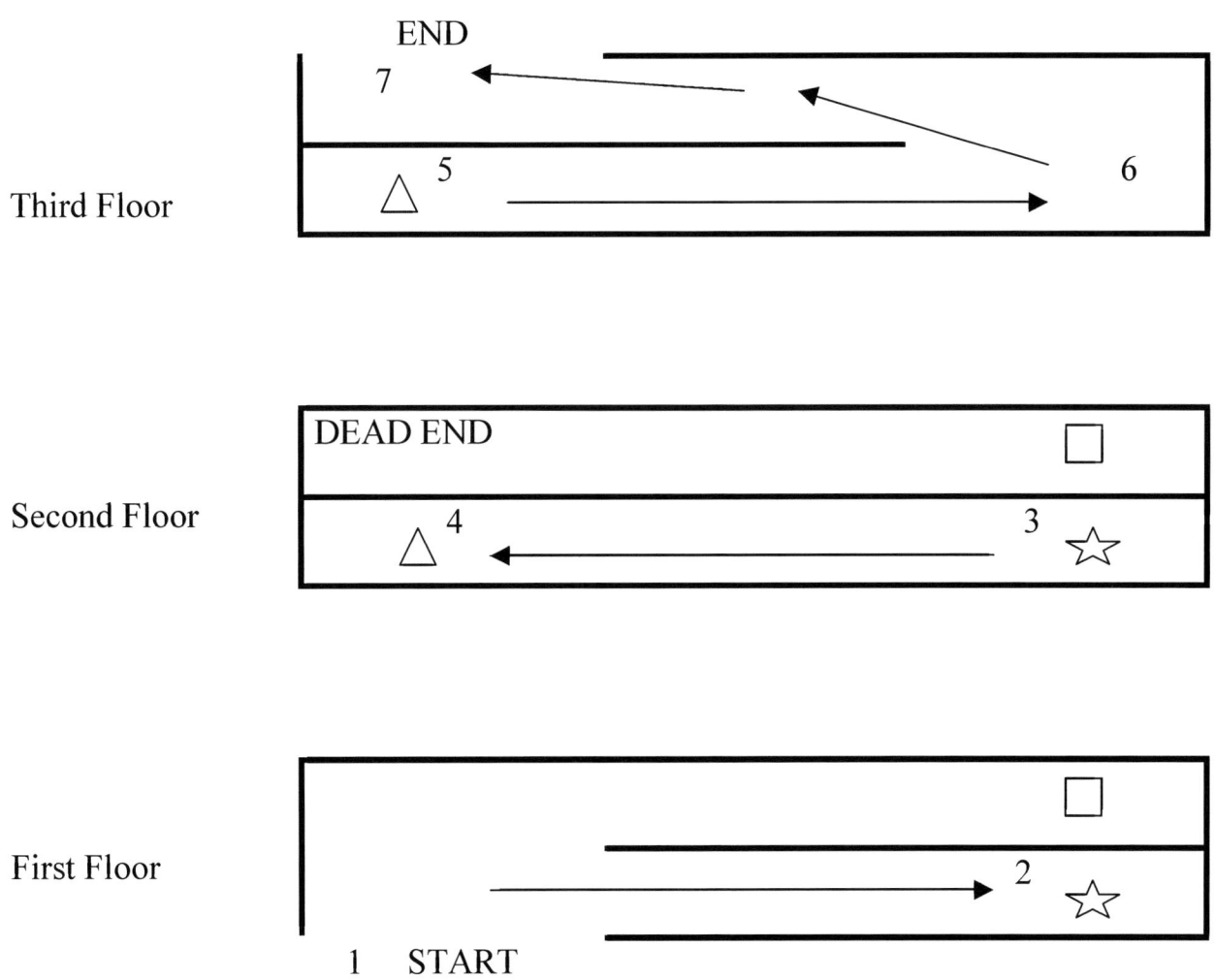

Sometimes you have to go 3 Floors out of your way before you reach a Dead End.

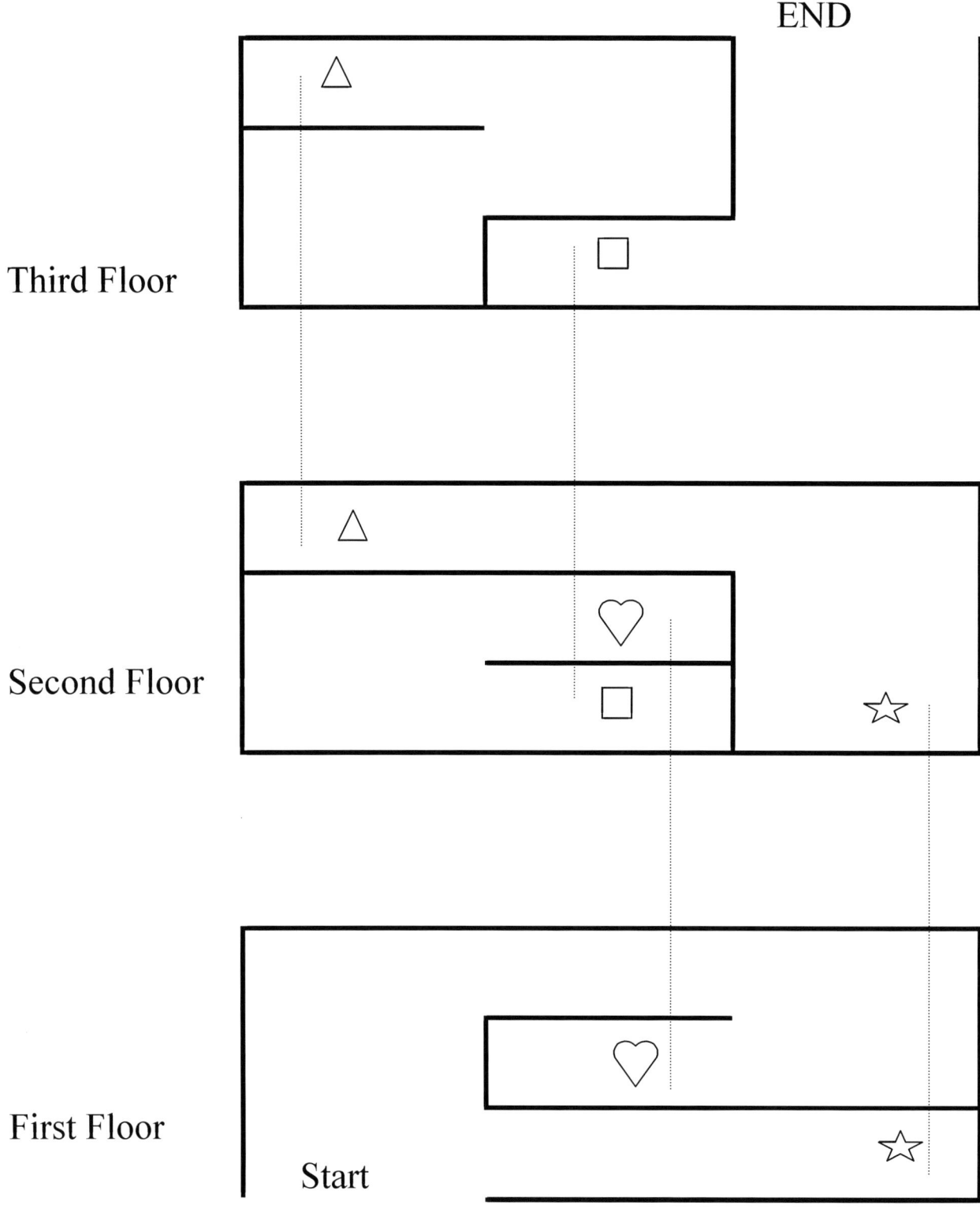

Follow the Numbers for the solution. Following the path with the ☆ and △ takes you to the Dead End.

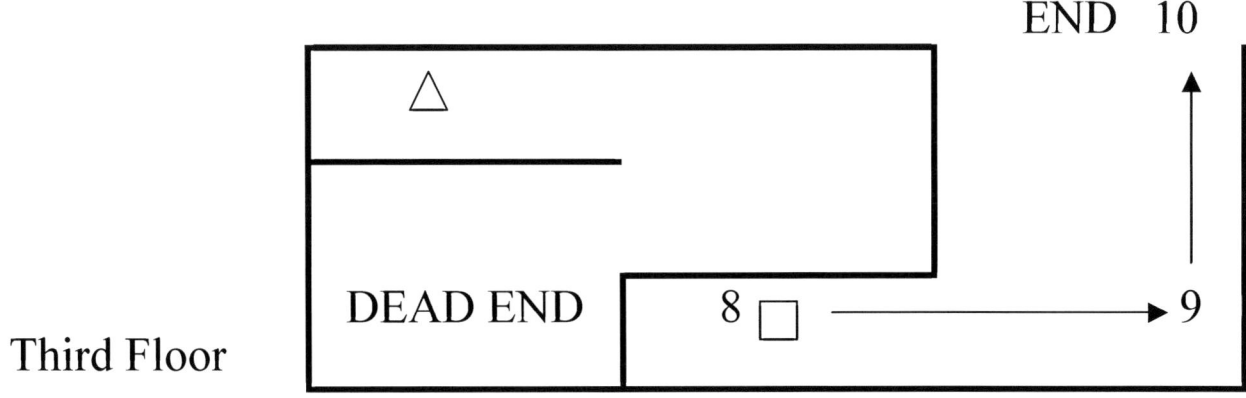

Third Floor

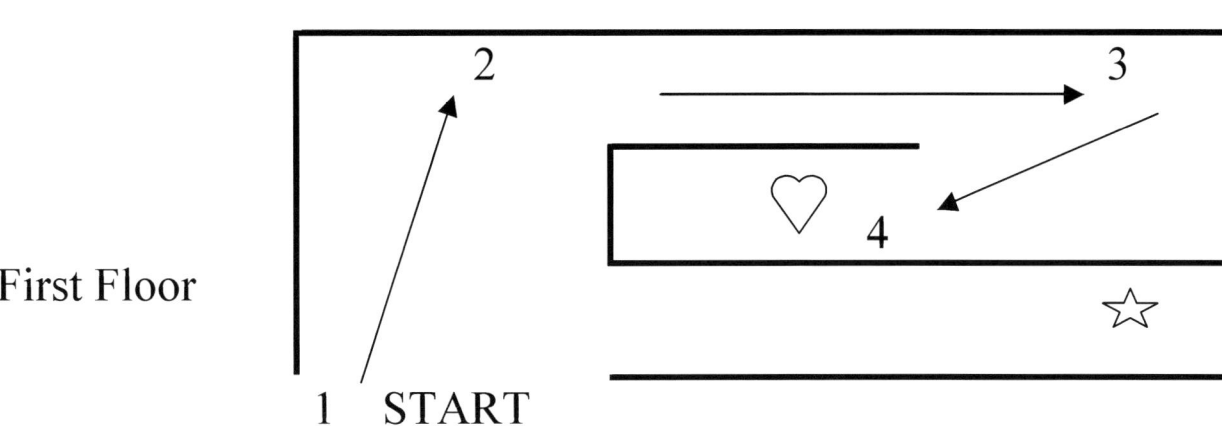

Second Floor

First Floor

Try this 3 dimensional maze with 2 floors. Do not look at the solution on the next page until you try to solve this maze yourself.

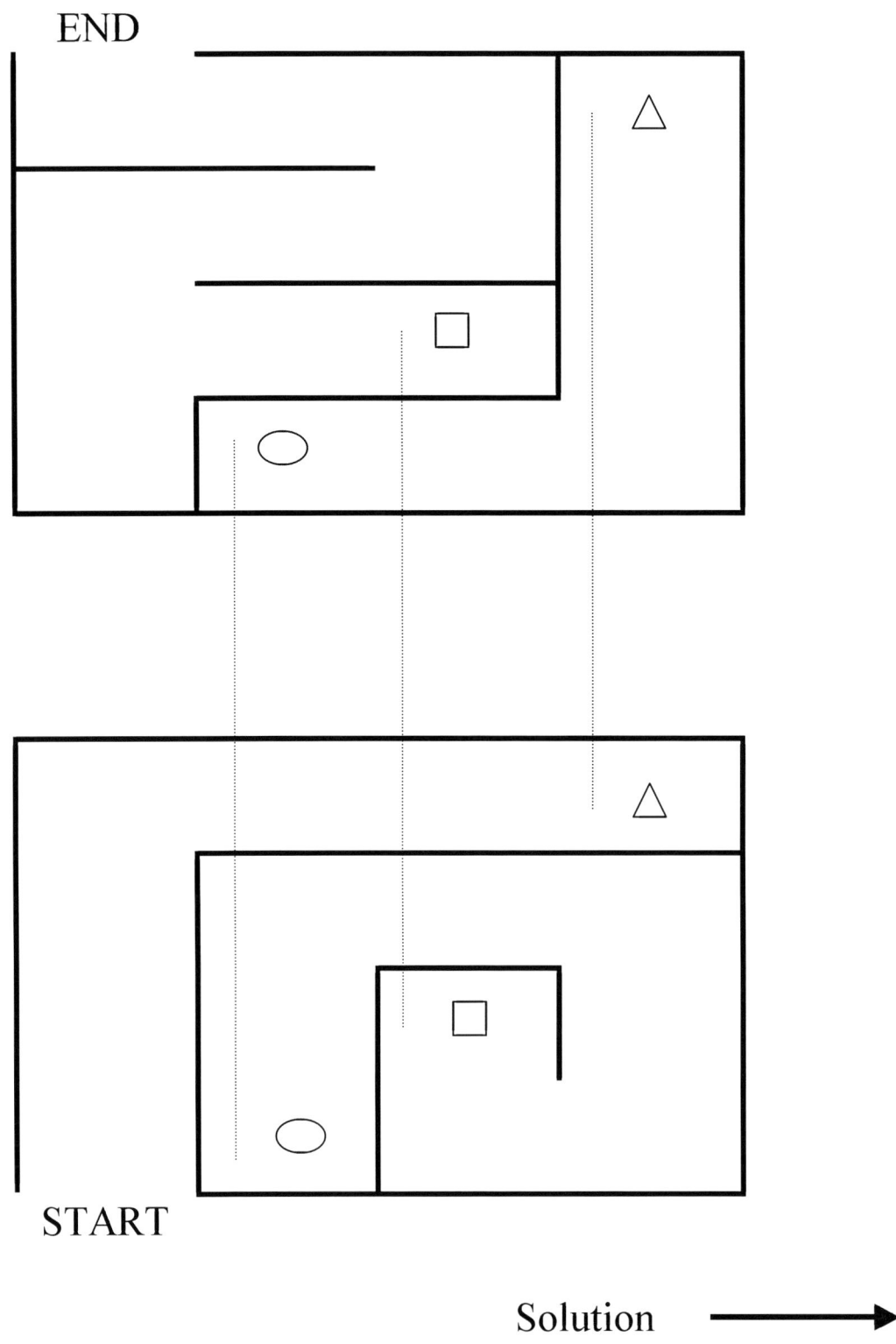

Solution ⟶

Here is the solution. Follow the Numbers.

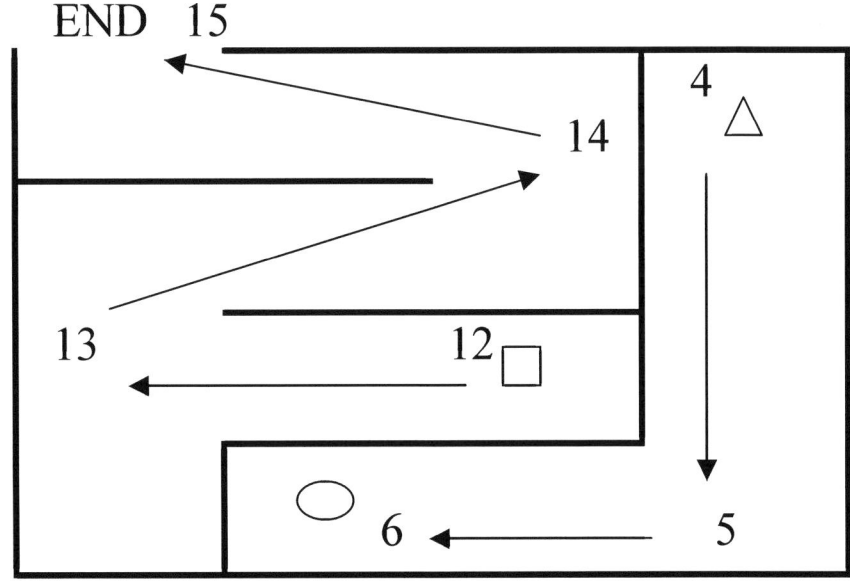

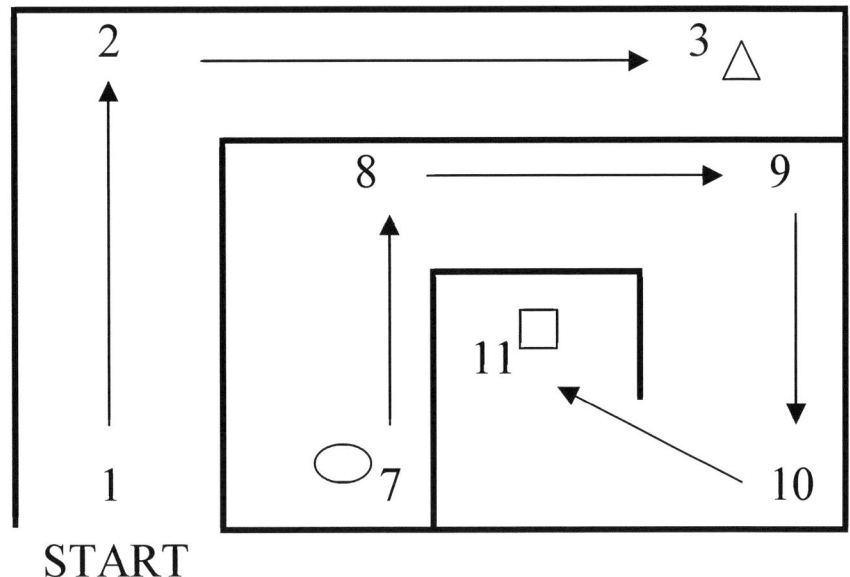

Try this maze with a Dead End. If your path takes you to a Dead End, retrace you steps.

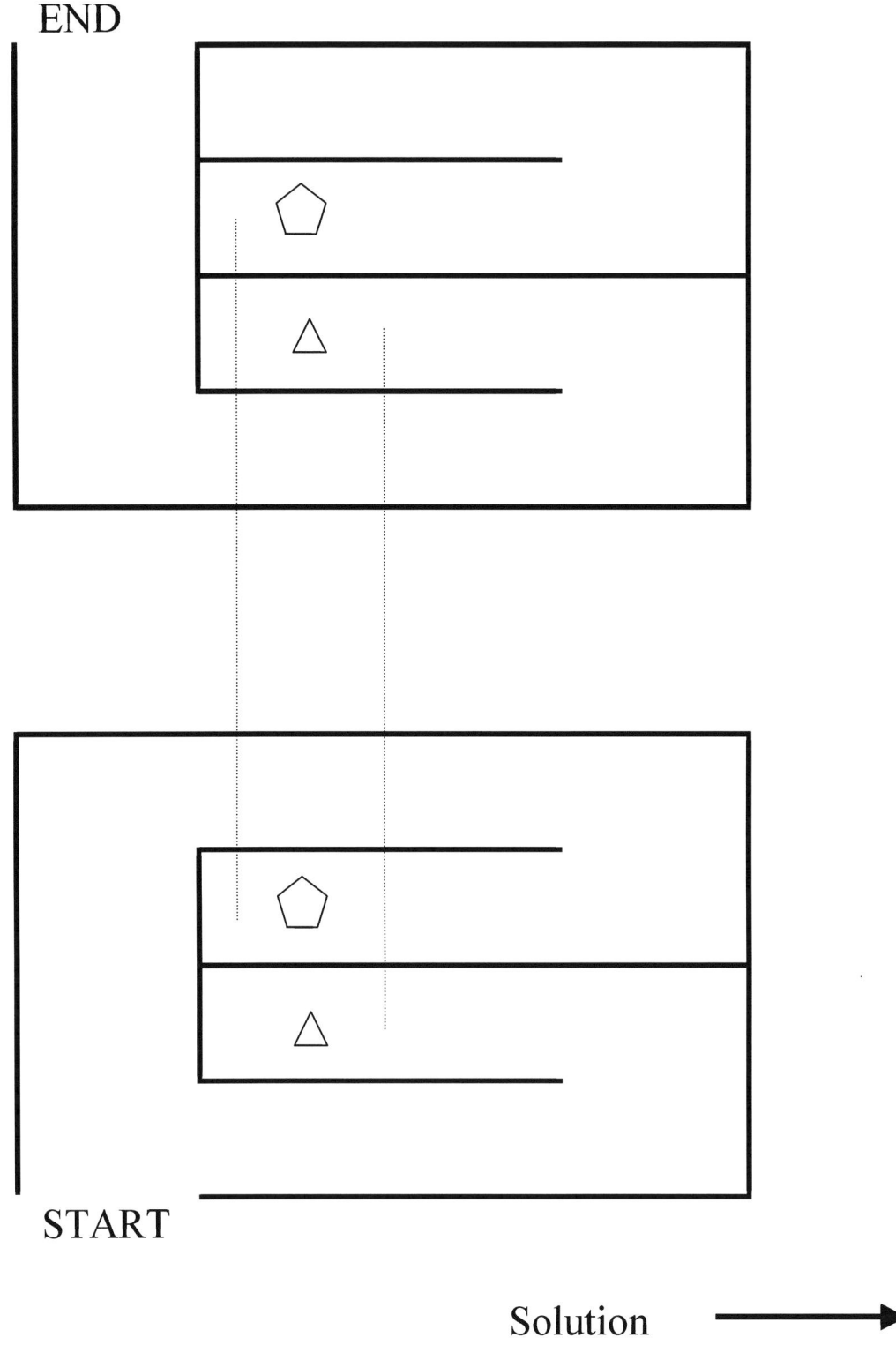

Solution ➝

Here is the solution. Follow the Numbers.

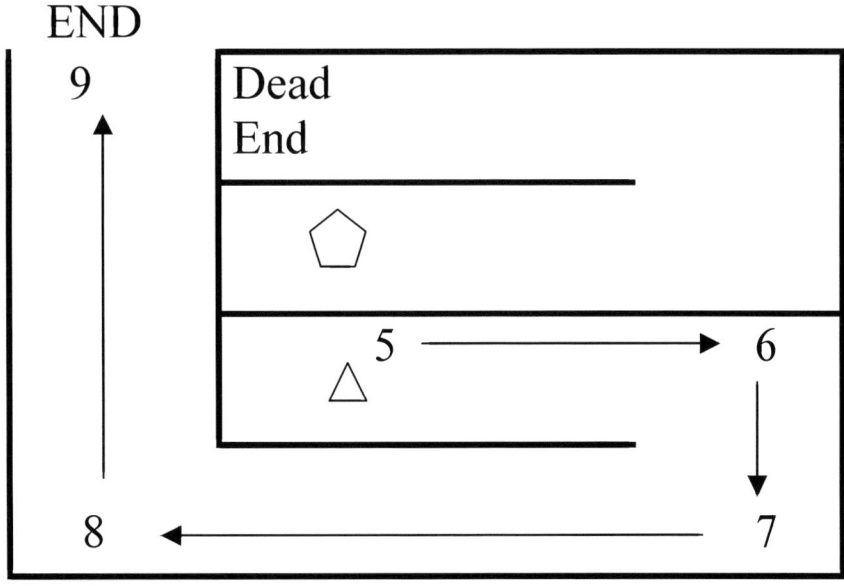

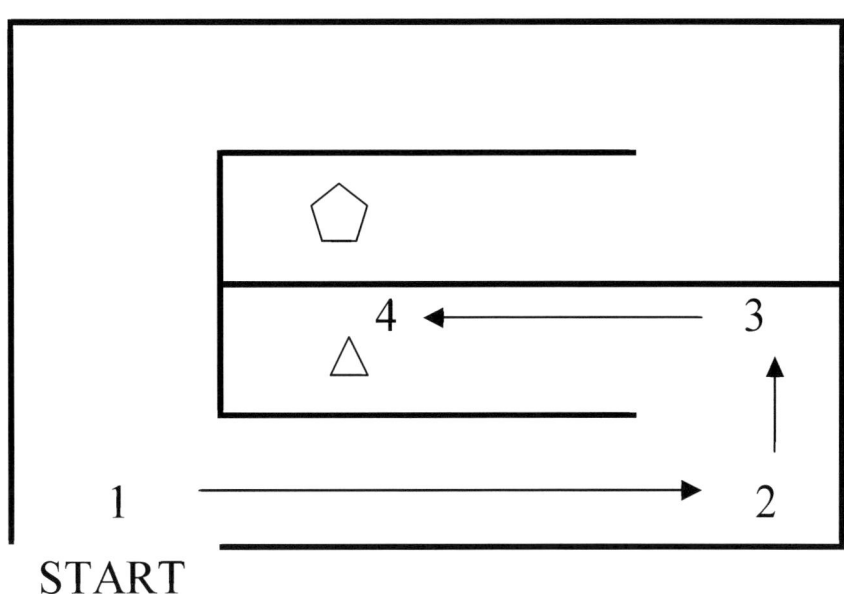

This maze has 2 paths and 5 imaginary ladders. Which path leads to the End?

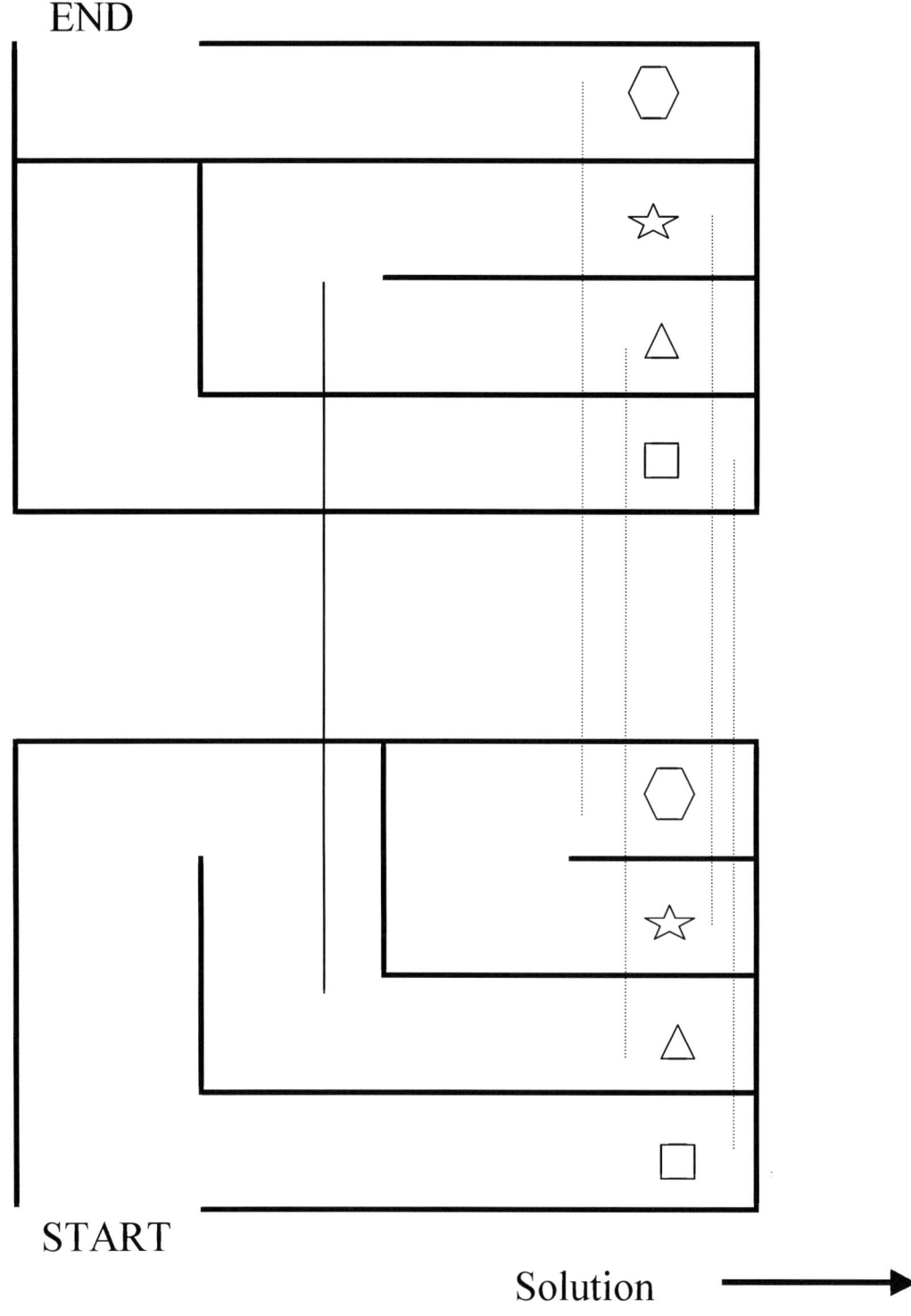

Solution →

This is the solution. Follow the Numbers.

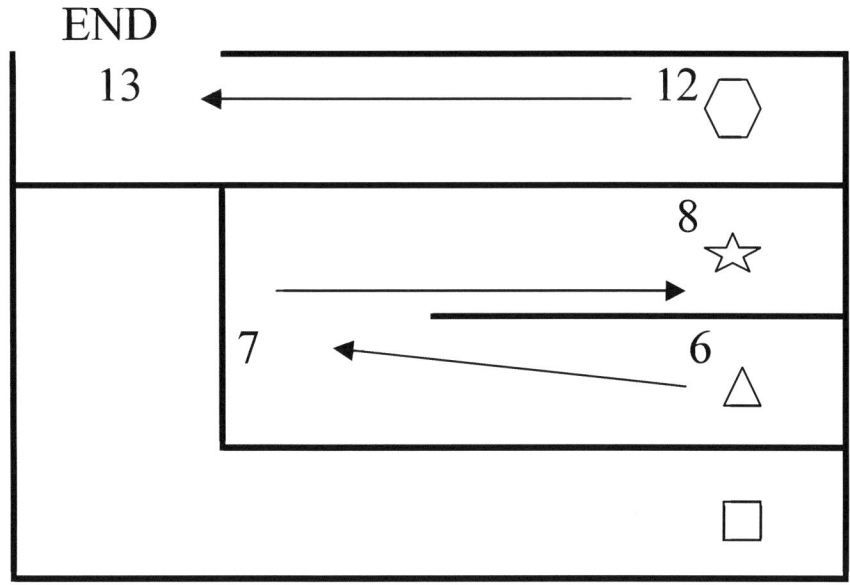

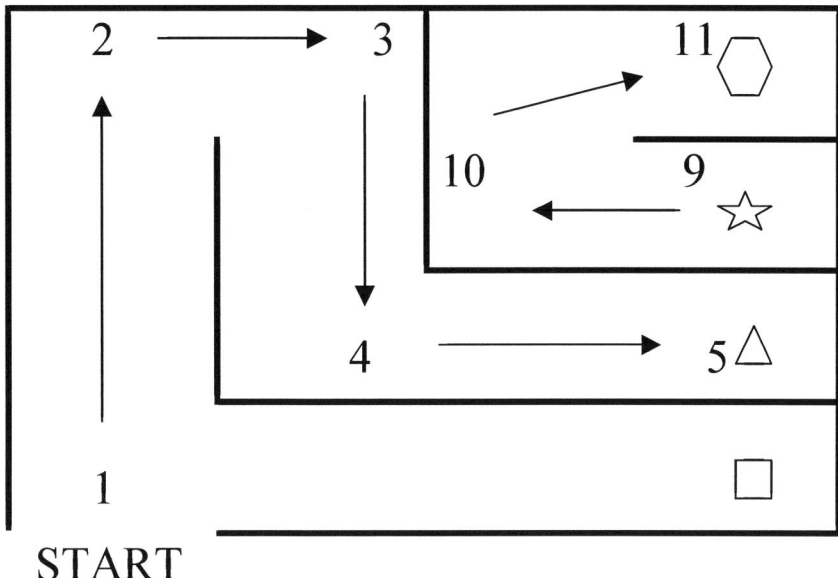

Here is a 3 dimensional maze with one long path and no Dead Ends.

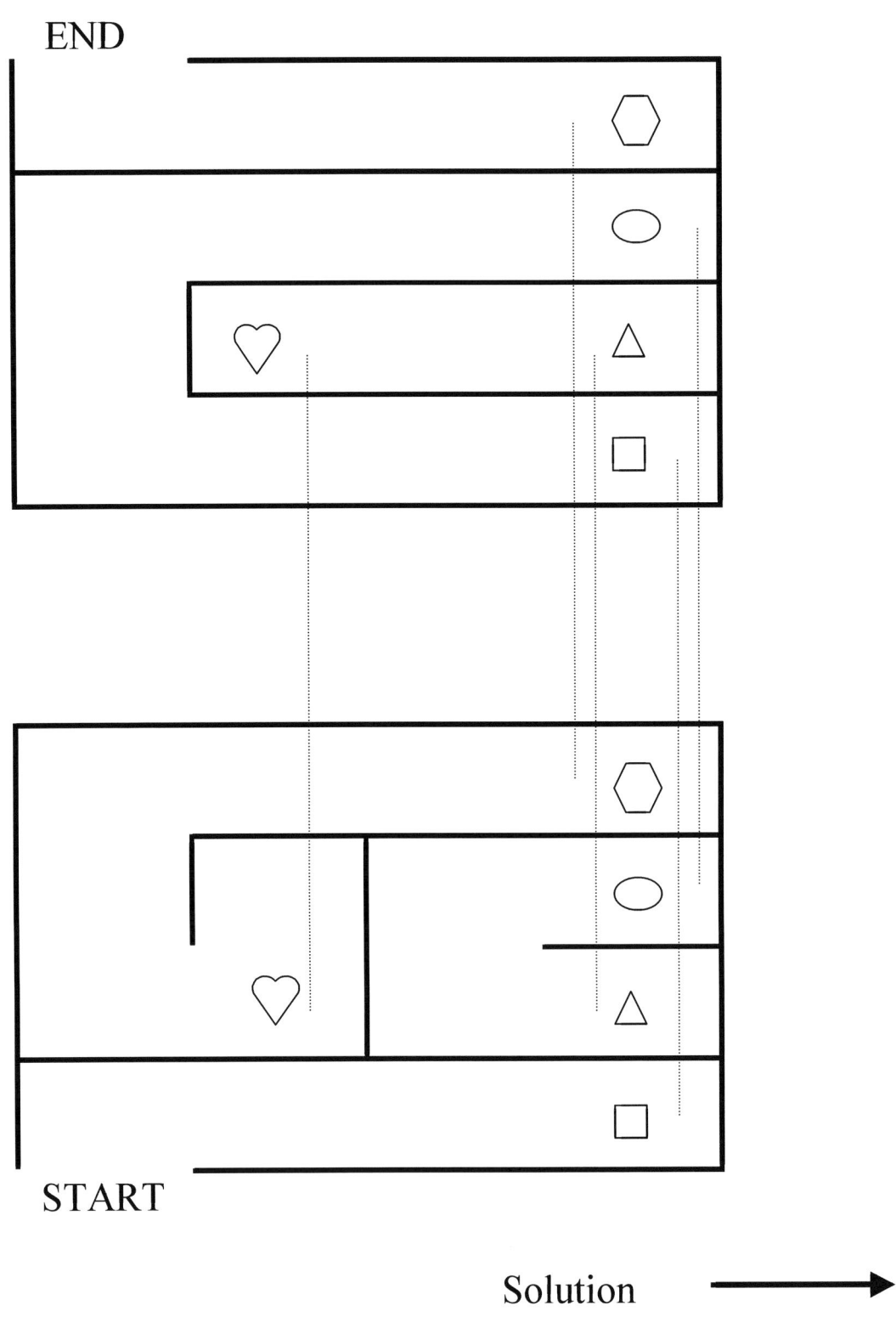

Solution ➡

Follow the Numbers to the Solution.

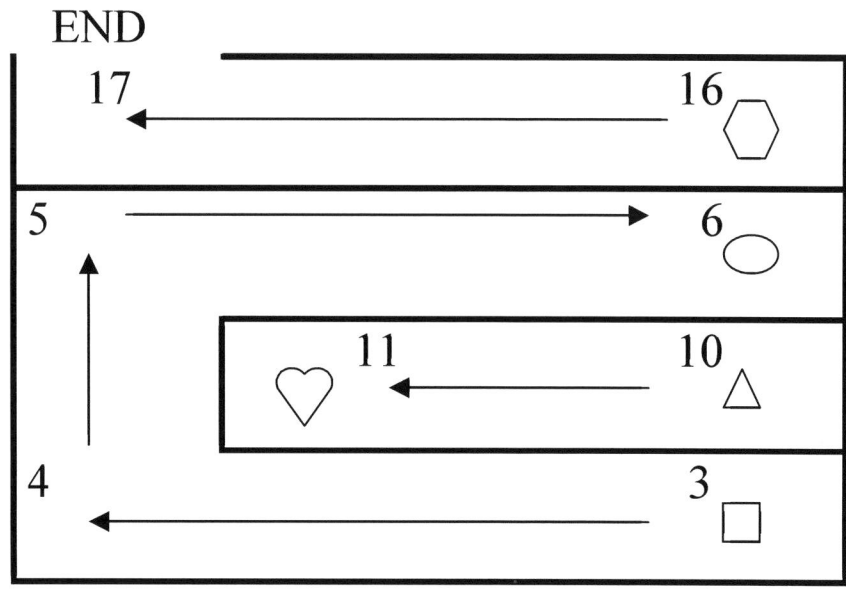

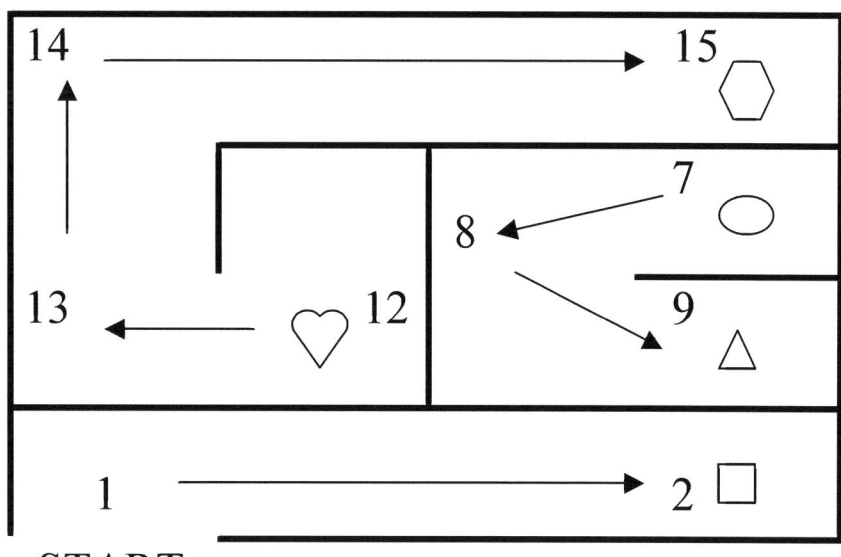

Now that you understand how to move through a 3 dimensional maze, when you read the next chapter, you will not need to follow dotted lines in order to connect the matching shapes.

Chapter 3   Mazes Without Helping Ladders
(3 by 3 by 3 Mazes)

How do you go from Start to End?

Third Floor

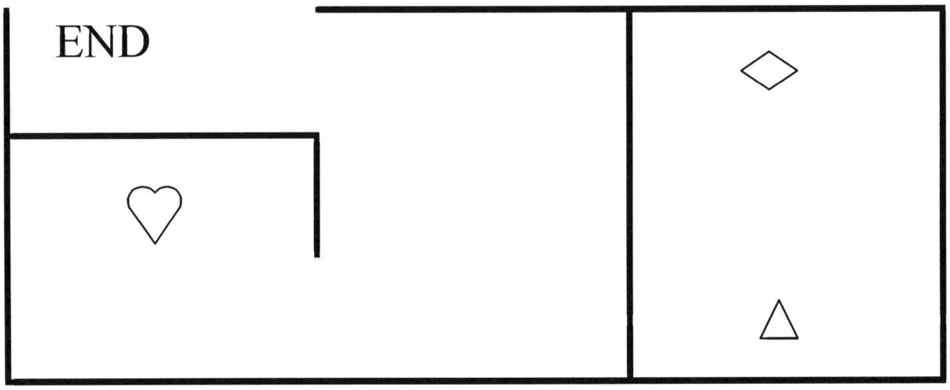

Second Floor

First Floor

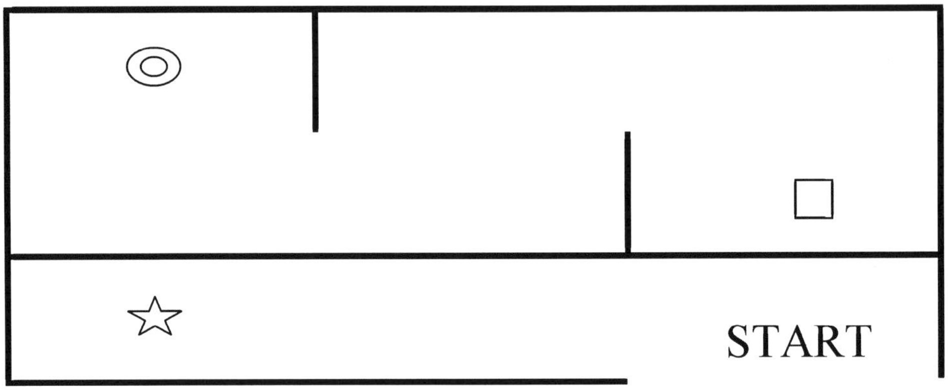

Solution →

Solution = Follow the Numbers

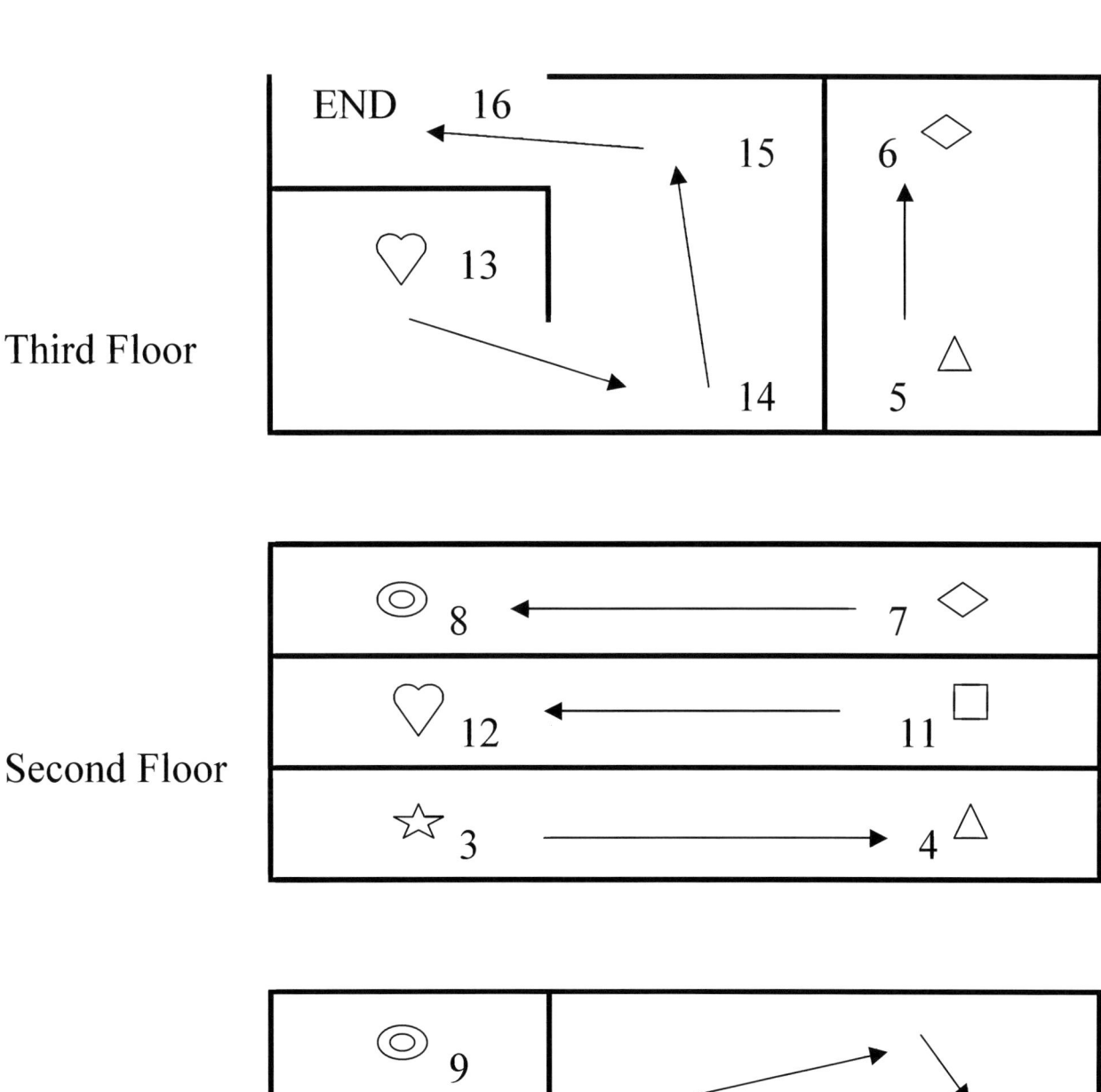

As you solve this maze, remember that you may not cross a Wall. You may go from Floor to Floor on the imaginary Stairs between Shapes.

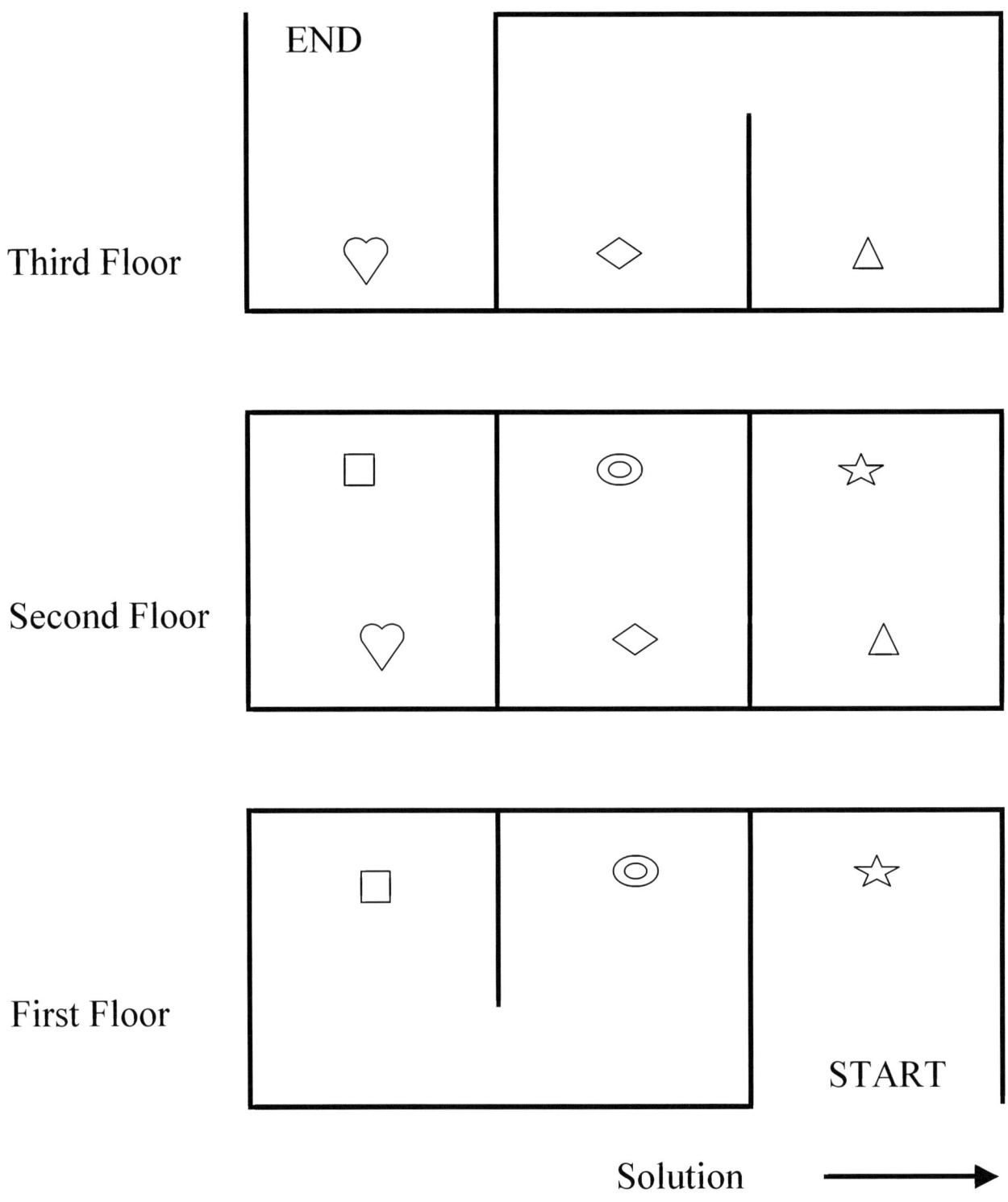

Solution = Follow the Numbers

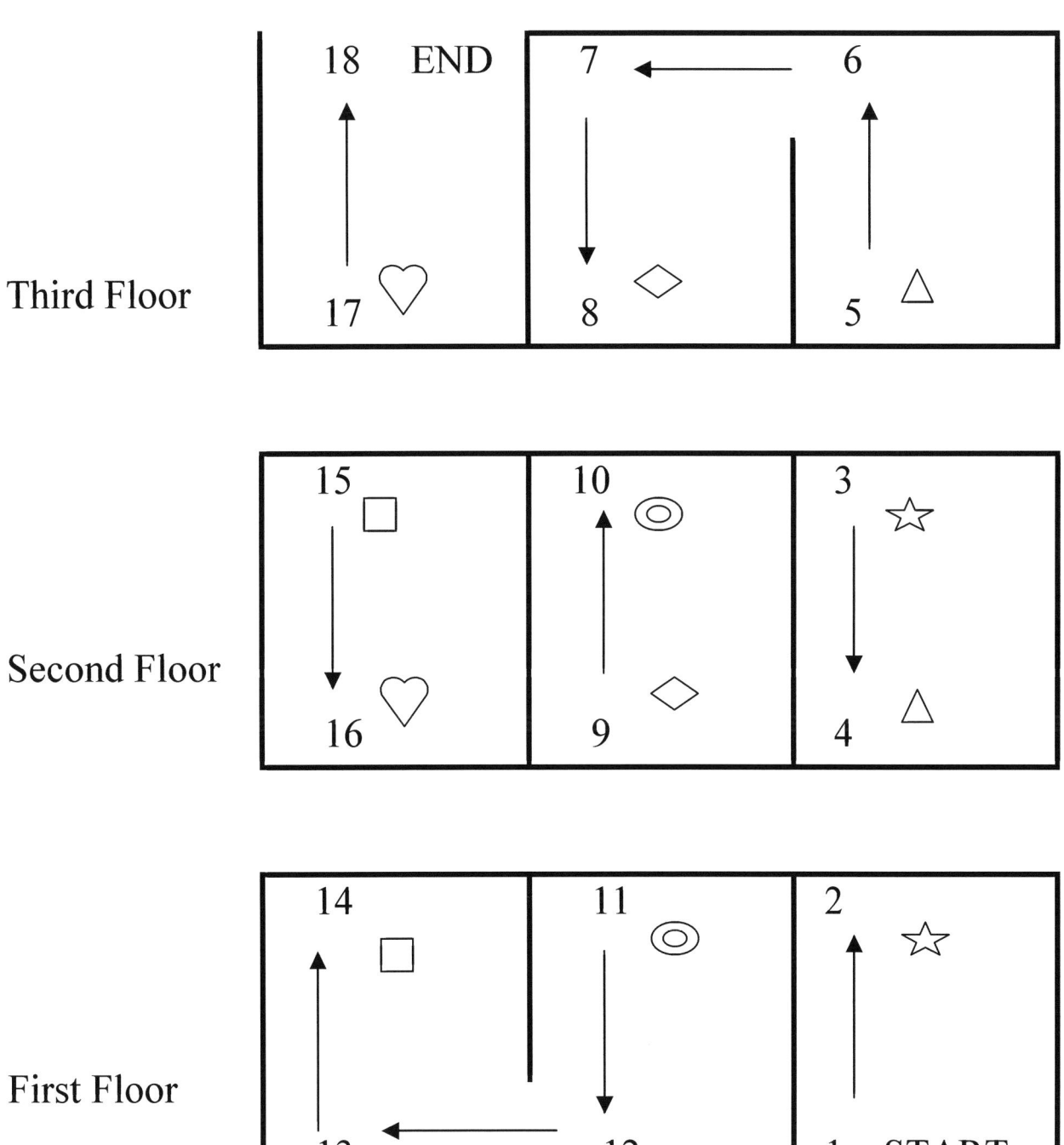

The pencil should leave the paper only when going from Floor to Floor on the Stairs.

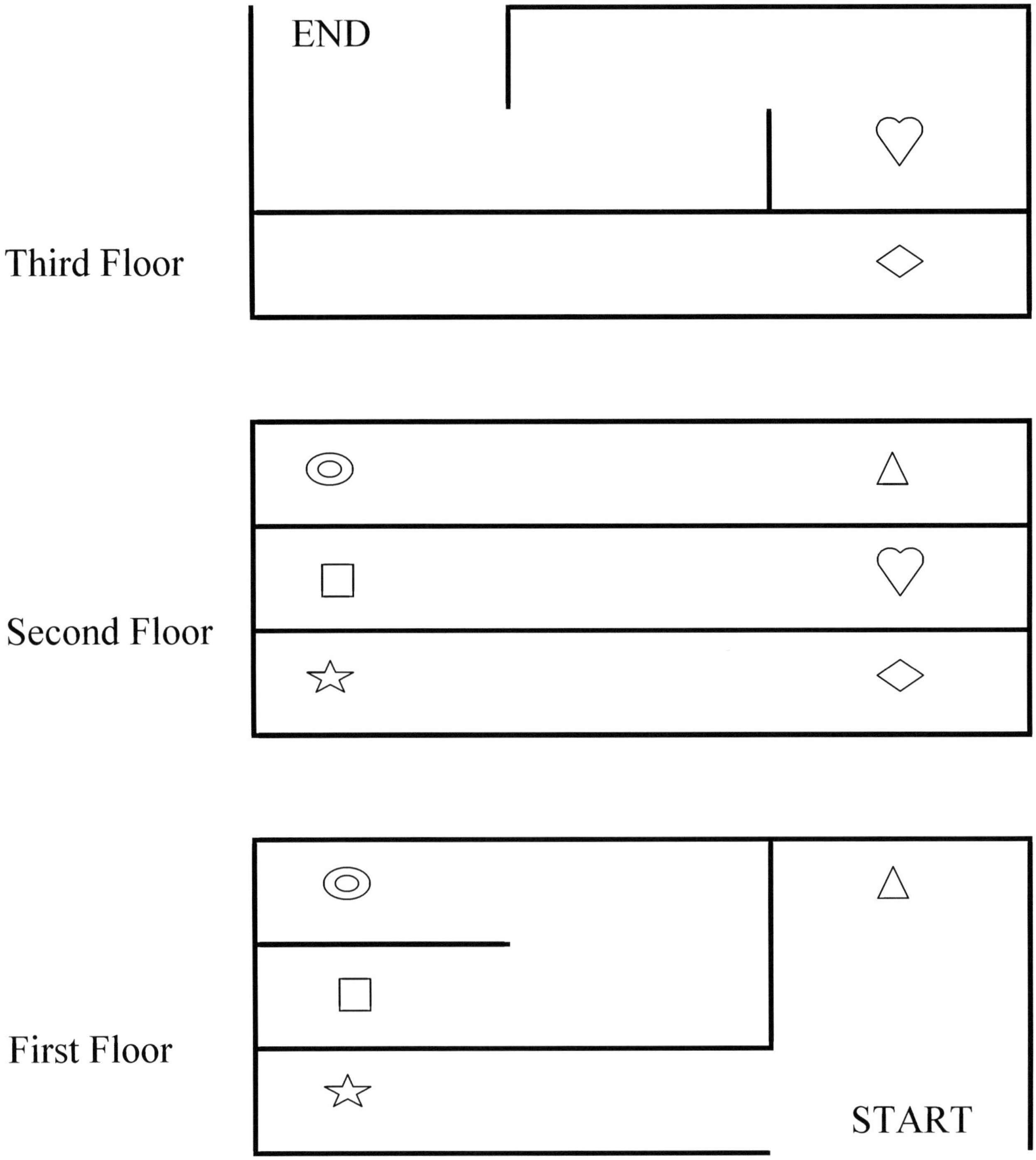

Third Floor

Second Floor

First Floor

START

END

There is one Dead End in this 3 by 3 by 3 Maze.

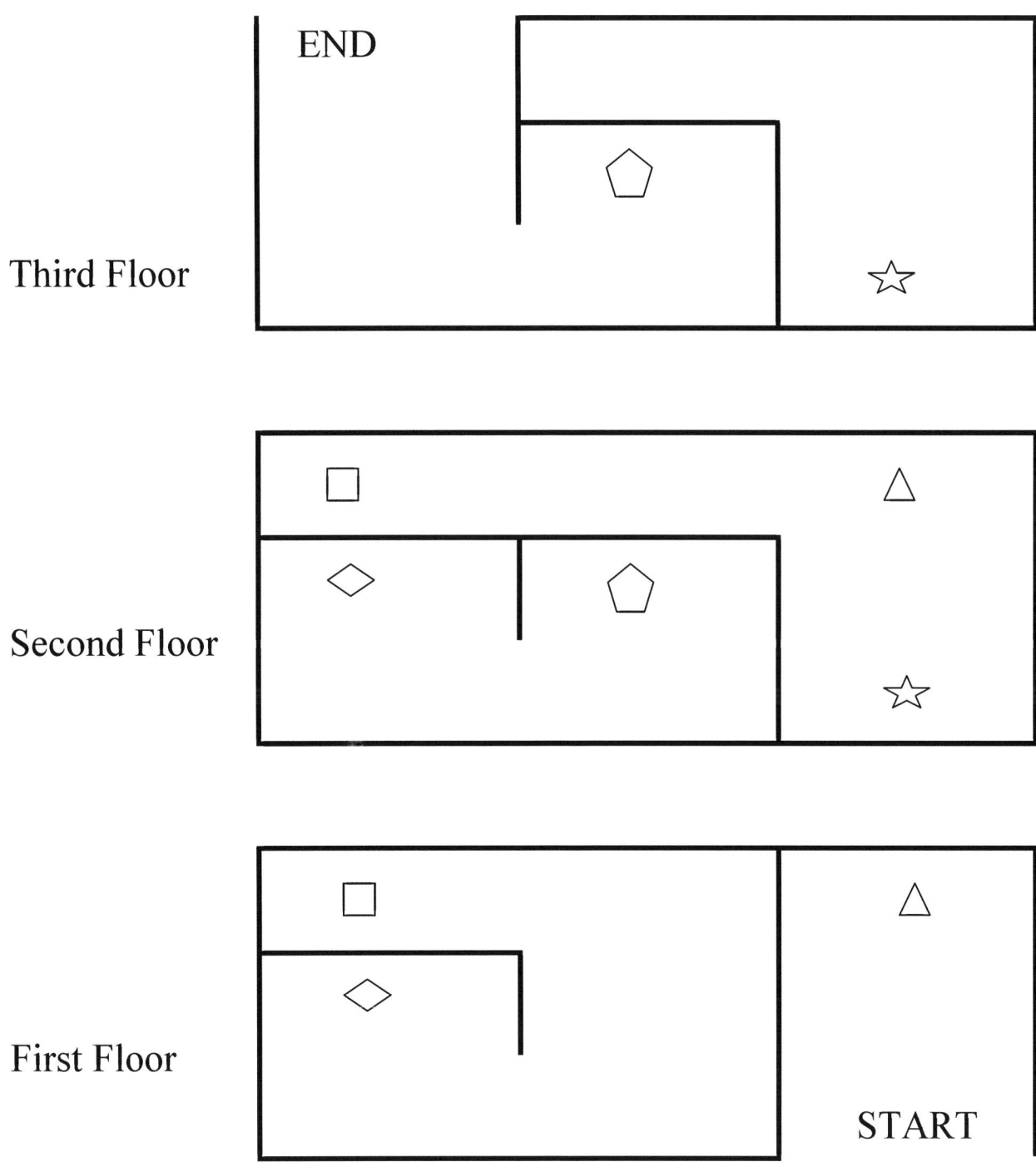

One Path takes you to the End: the other takes you to the Dead End.

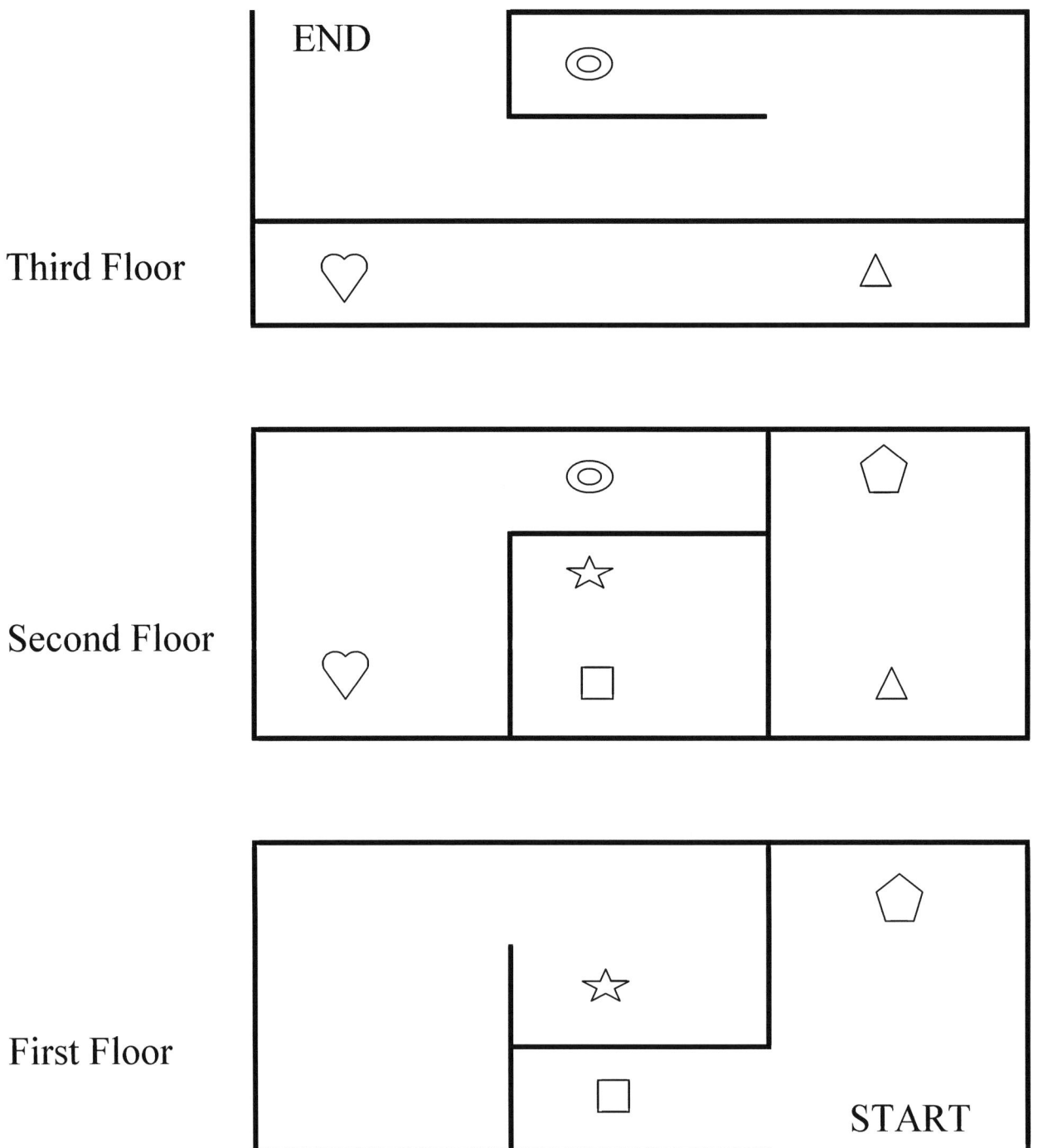

Chapter 4 The Size of a Maze
(length, width, height)

1. A Shape is 1 dimensional if it has only length, like the line below.

   ⎯⎯⎯⎯⎯⎯⎯⎯⎯⎯⎯⎯⎯⎯⎯⎯⎯

2. A Shape is 2 dimensional if it has only length and width, like a plane or the flat surfaces below.

   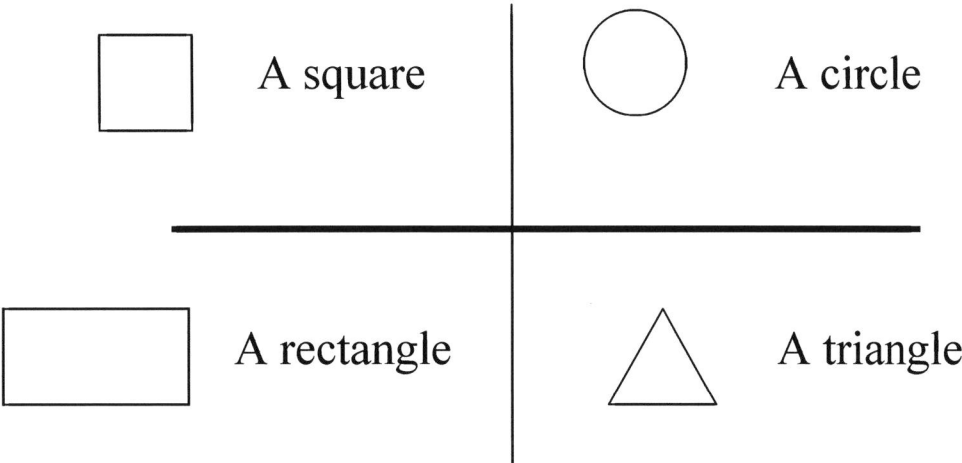

3. A shape is 3 dimensional if it has only length, width and height, like the cube or cylinder below.

   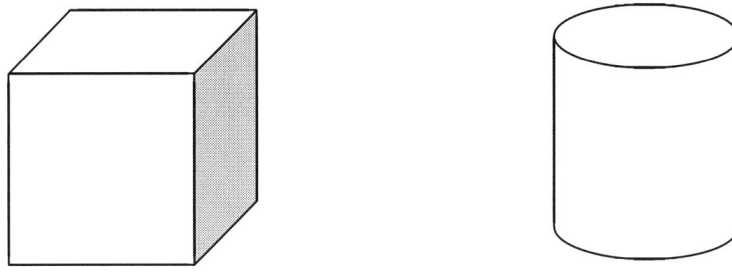

Each 1 dimensional line has a size that is its length. The size of a line is the number of spaces or intervals from its Beginning to its End. The line below has 4 spaces.

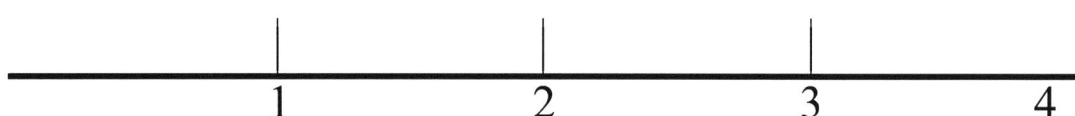

Therefore it has size or length 4.

What is the size of this 1 dimensional line?

The answer is that it has size 6.

What is the size of this 1 dimensional line?

The answer is at the bottom of the next page.

A 2 dimensional maze also has a size.
The size is measured by its length and width.

The size of the maze below is 6 long and 2 wide.
We say it is 6 by 2.

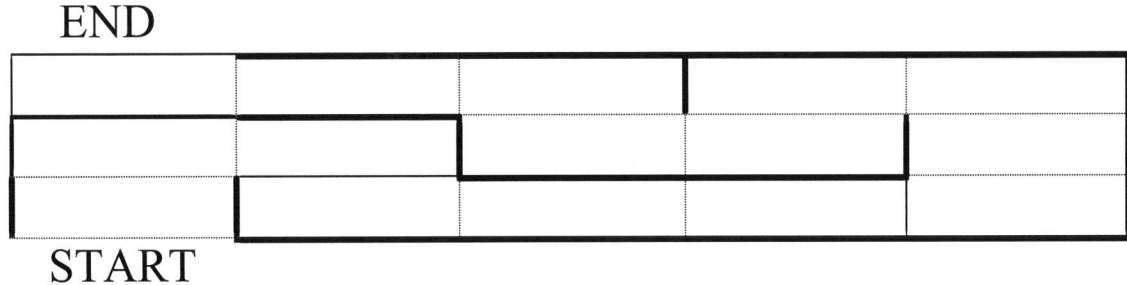

What is the size of this next maze?

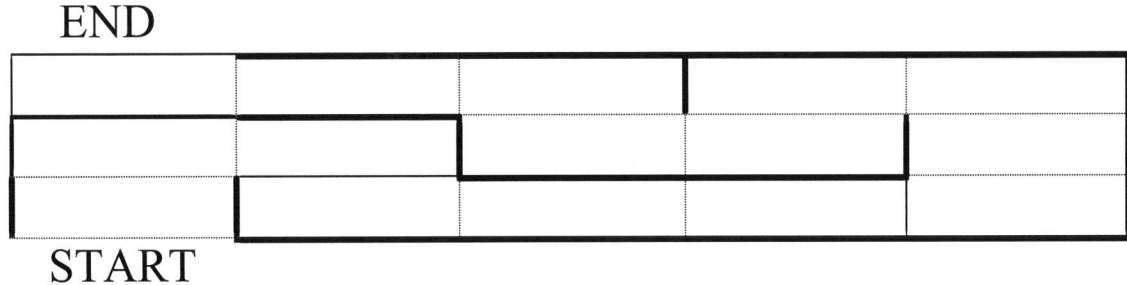

The length is 5 and the width is 3.

The size of this maze is 5 by 3.

The size of the 1 dimensional maze on the last page is 8.

What is the size of this next maze? Find your way through.

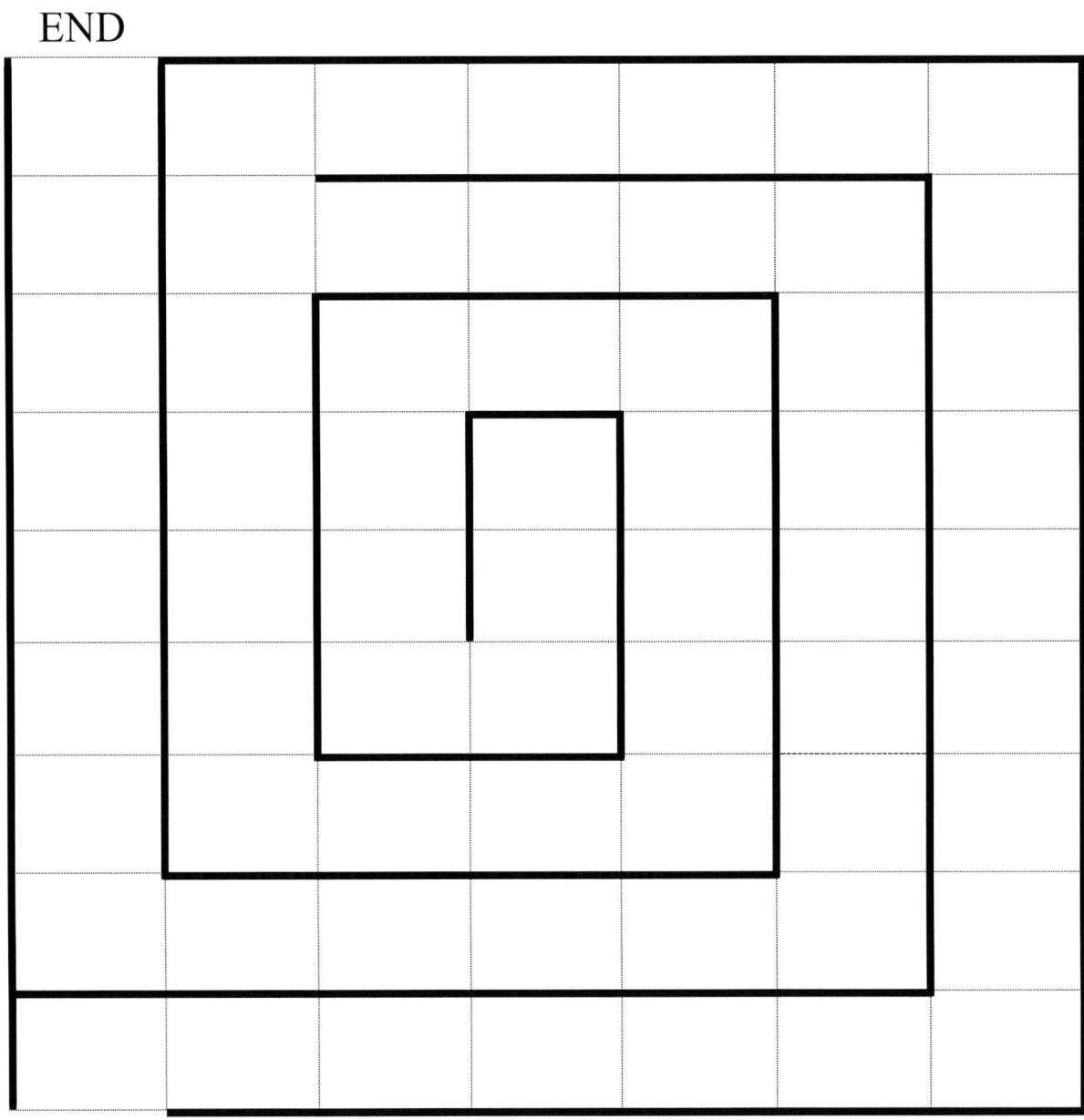

The answer is on the bottom of the next page.

A 3 dimensional maze also has a size.
The size is measured by the length, width and height.

Each Floor of the maze below is 5 long and 3 wide.
There are 2 Floors. Therefore, its height is 2.

So, the size of this next maze is 5 by 3 by 2.

END

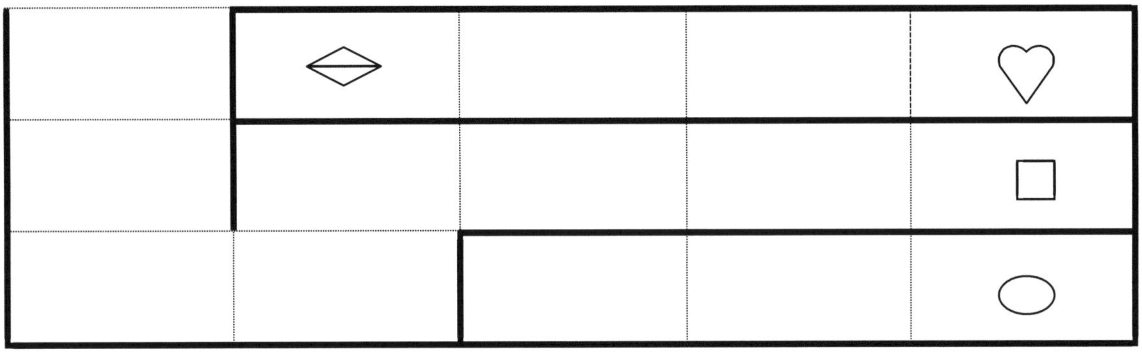

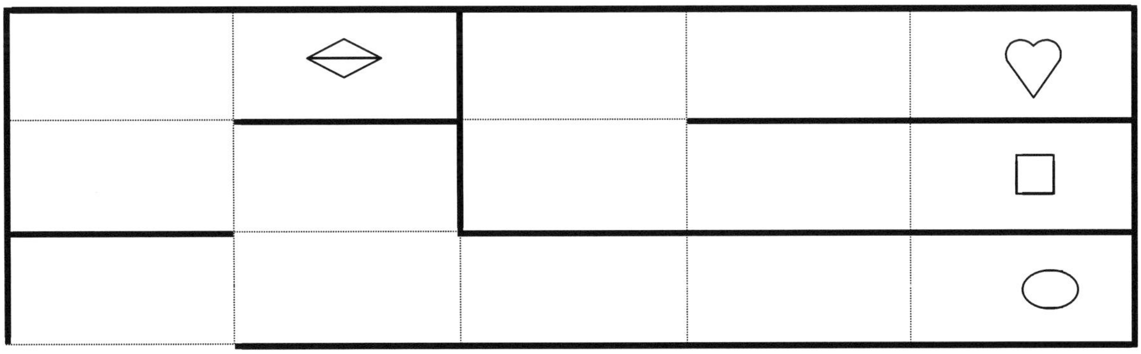

START

The 2 dimensional maze on the last page is 7 by 9.

What is the size of this 3 dimensional maze? The answer is on the bottom of the next page.

This size of this maze is on the top of the next page.
It zigzags a lot in 3 dimensions.   END

Third Floor

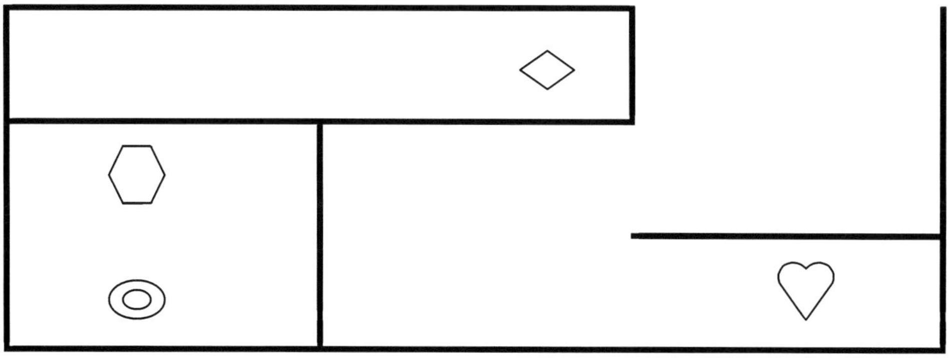

Second Floor

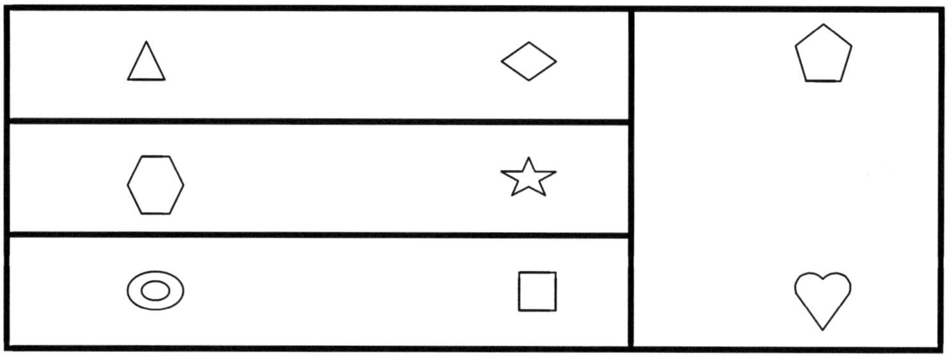

First Floor

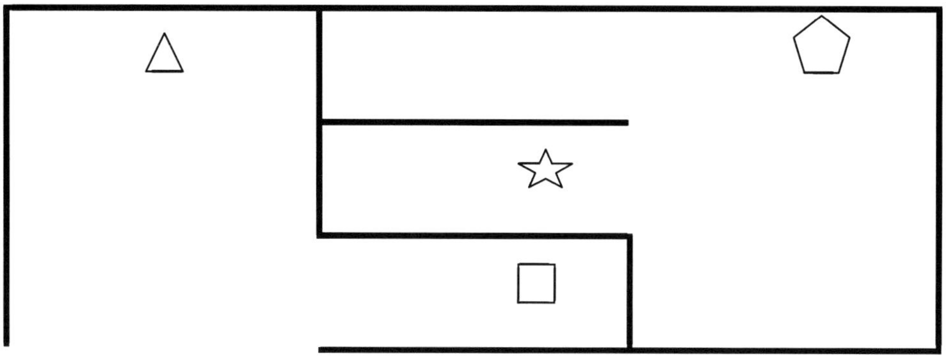

                    START
The size of the 3 dimensional maze on the last page is 6 by 4 by 2.

44

Solution: Follow the Numbers (The size is 3 by 3 by 3.)

Third Floor
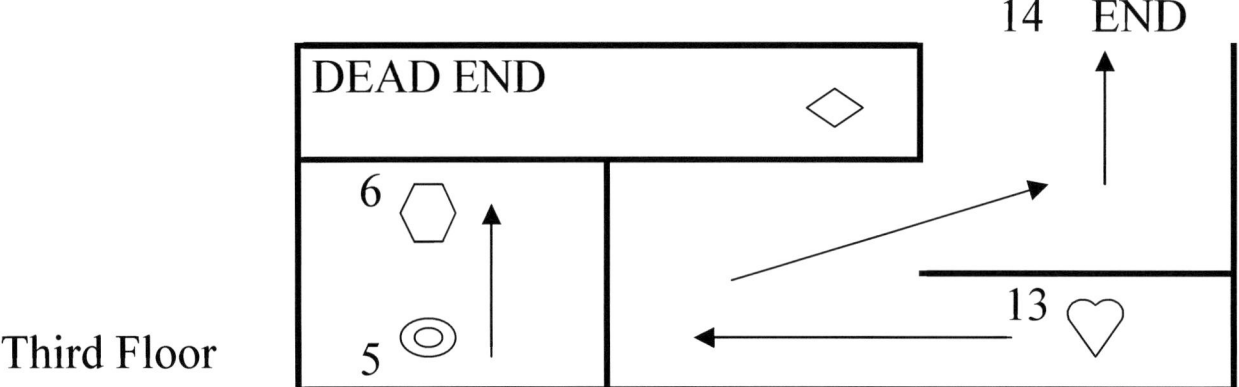

Second Floor
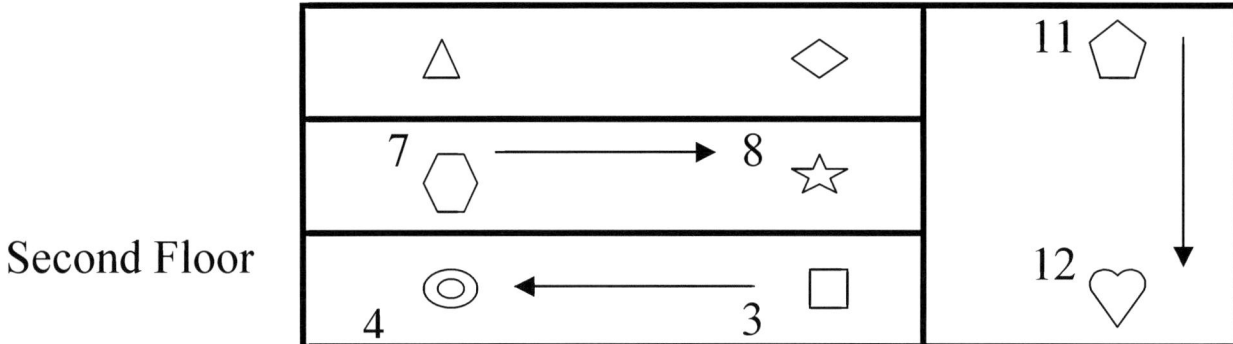

First Floor

The size of this next maze is 6 by 4 by 3.

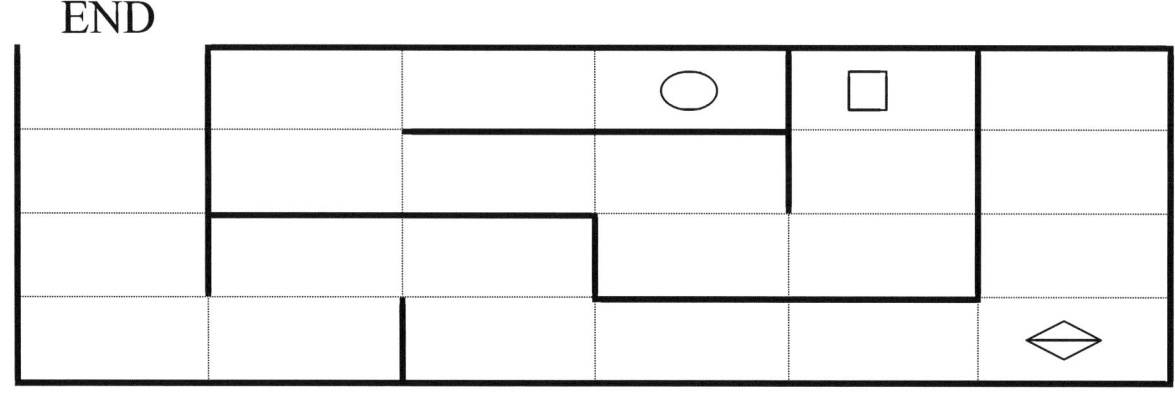

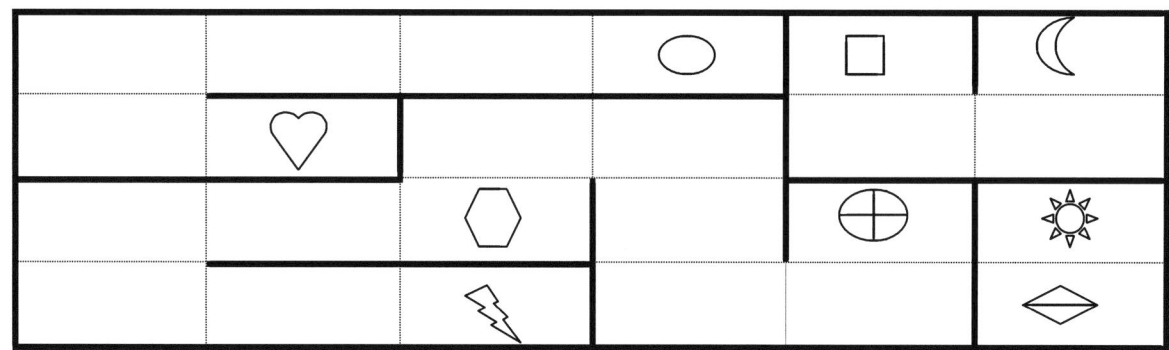

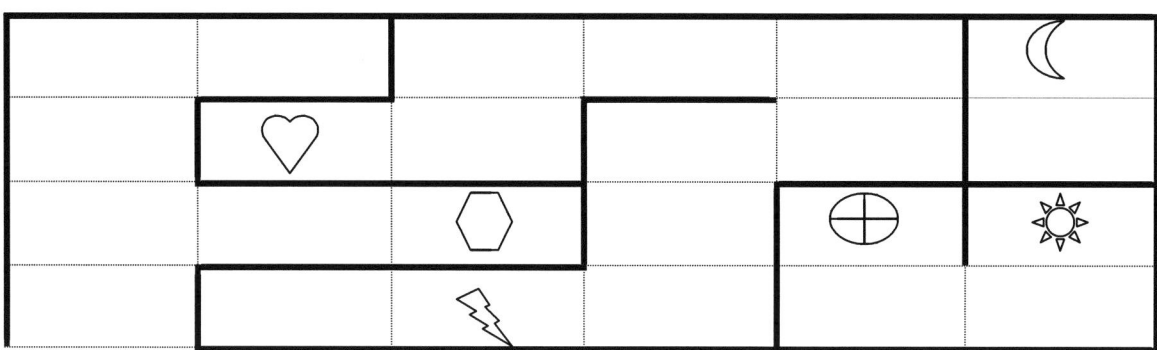

What is the size of this 3 dimensional maze? The answer is on the bottom of this page.

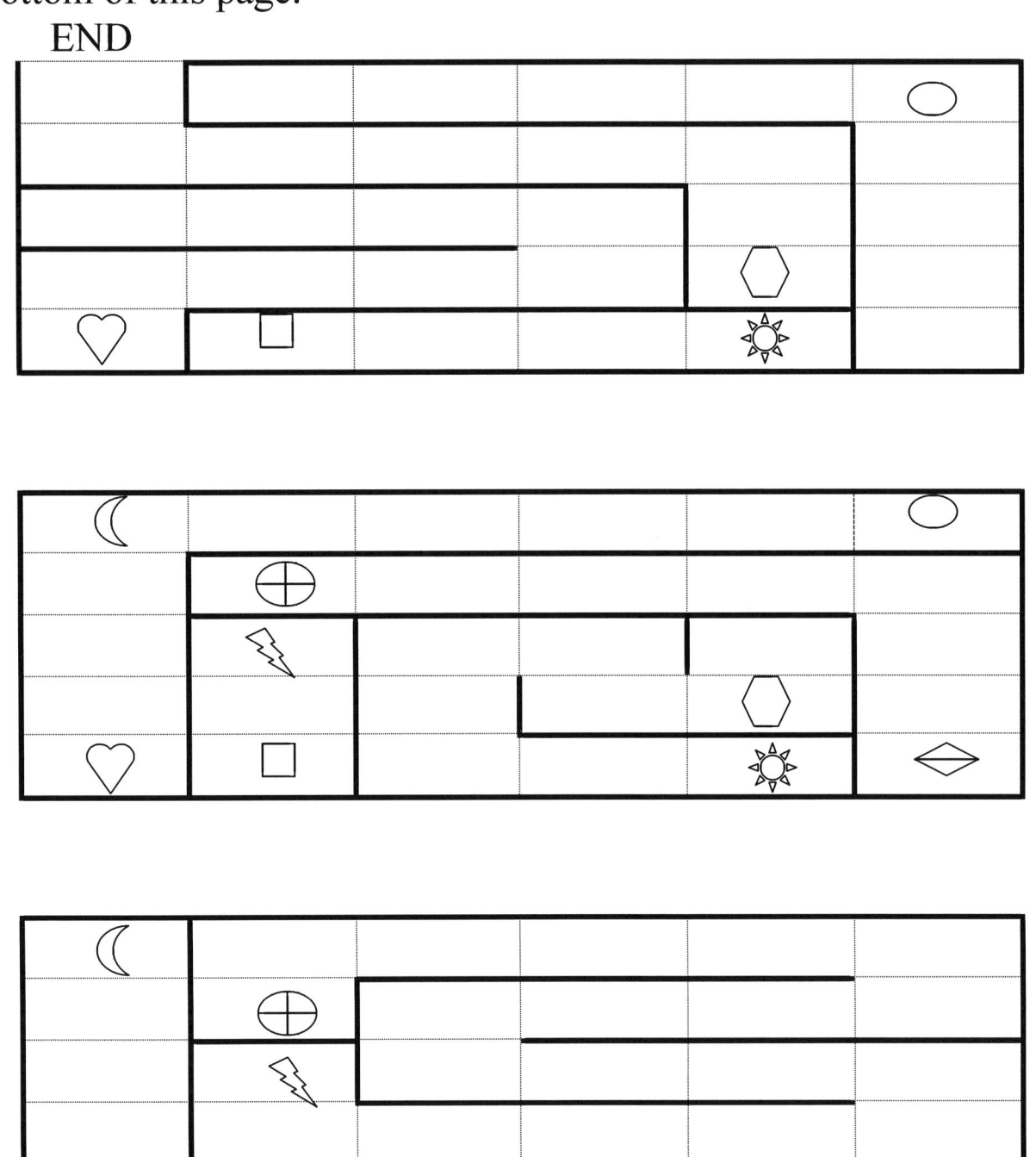

The size of the 3 dimensional maze on this page is 6 by 5 by 3.

Chapter 5   4 by 4 by 3 Mazes

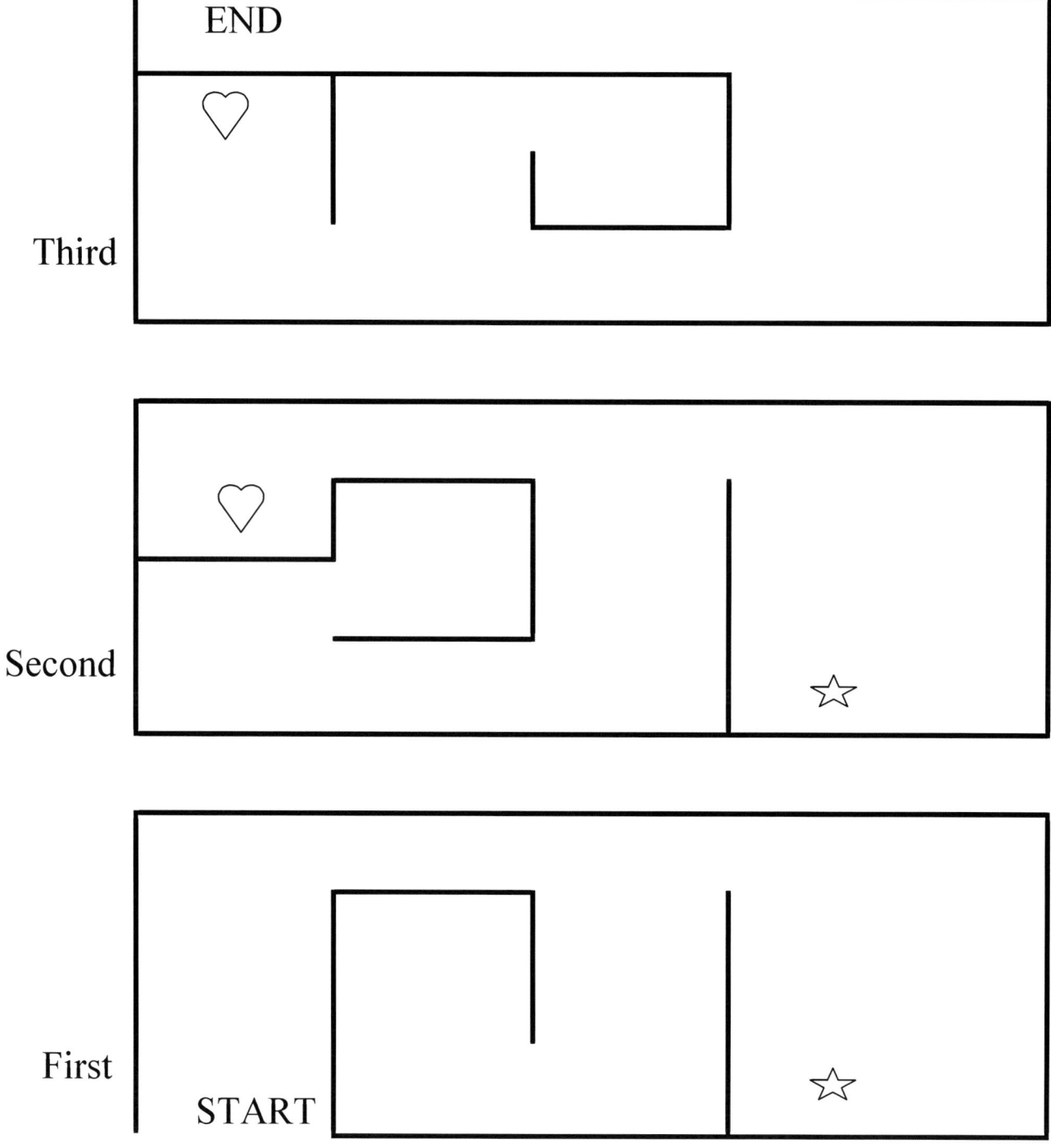

Not every Path leads to the End.

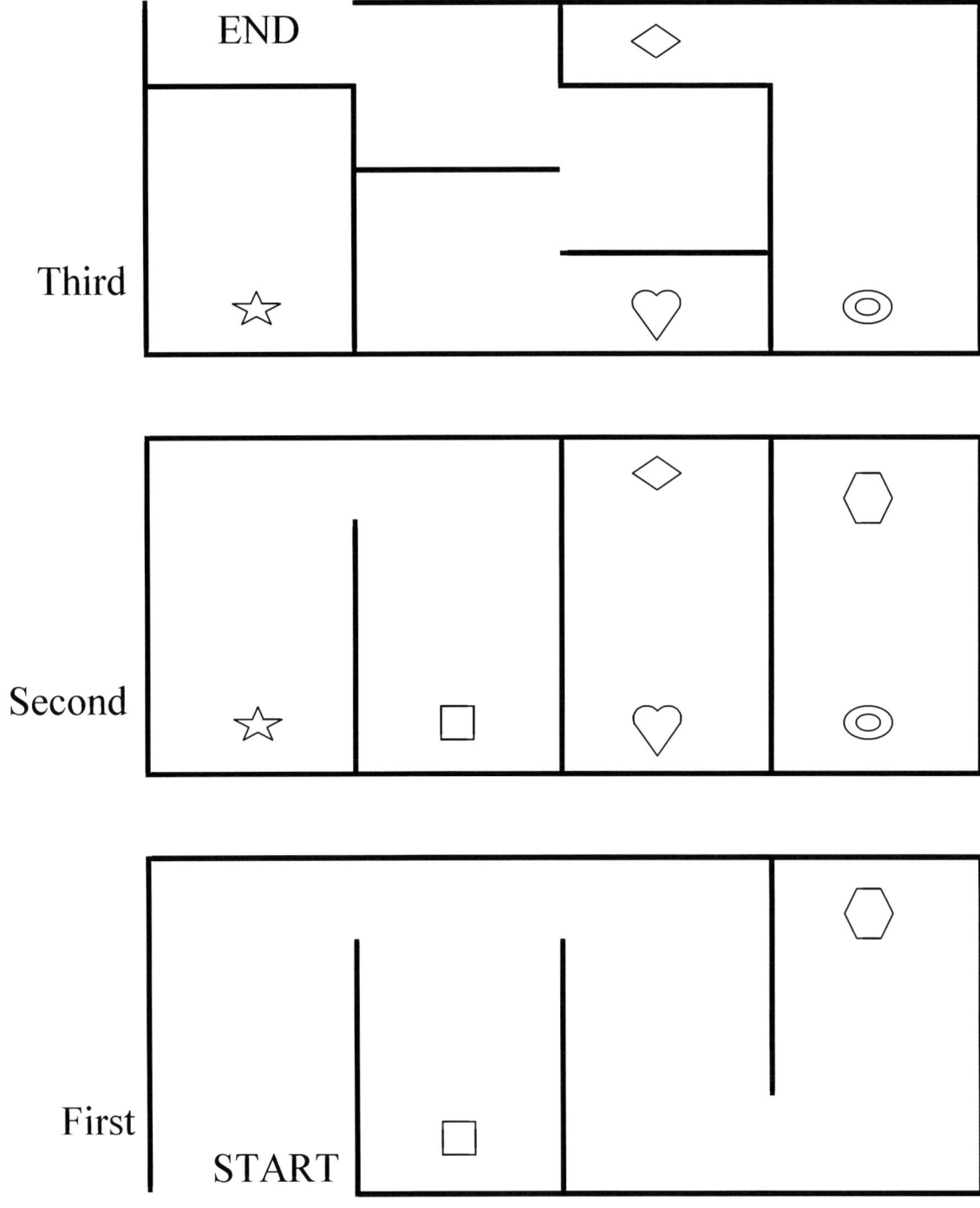

This Maze is too easy. Give it to your little sister or brother.

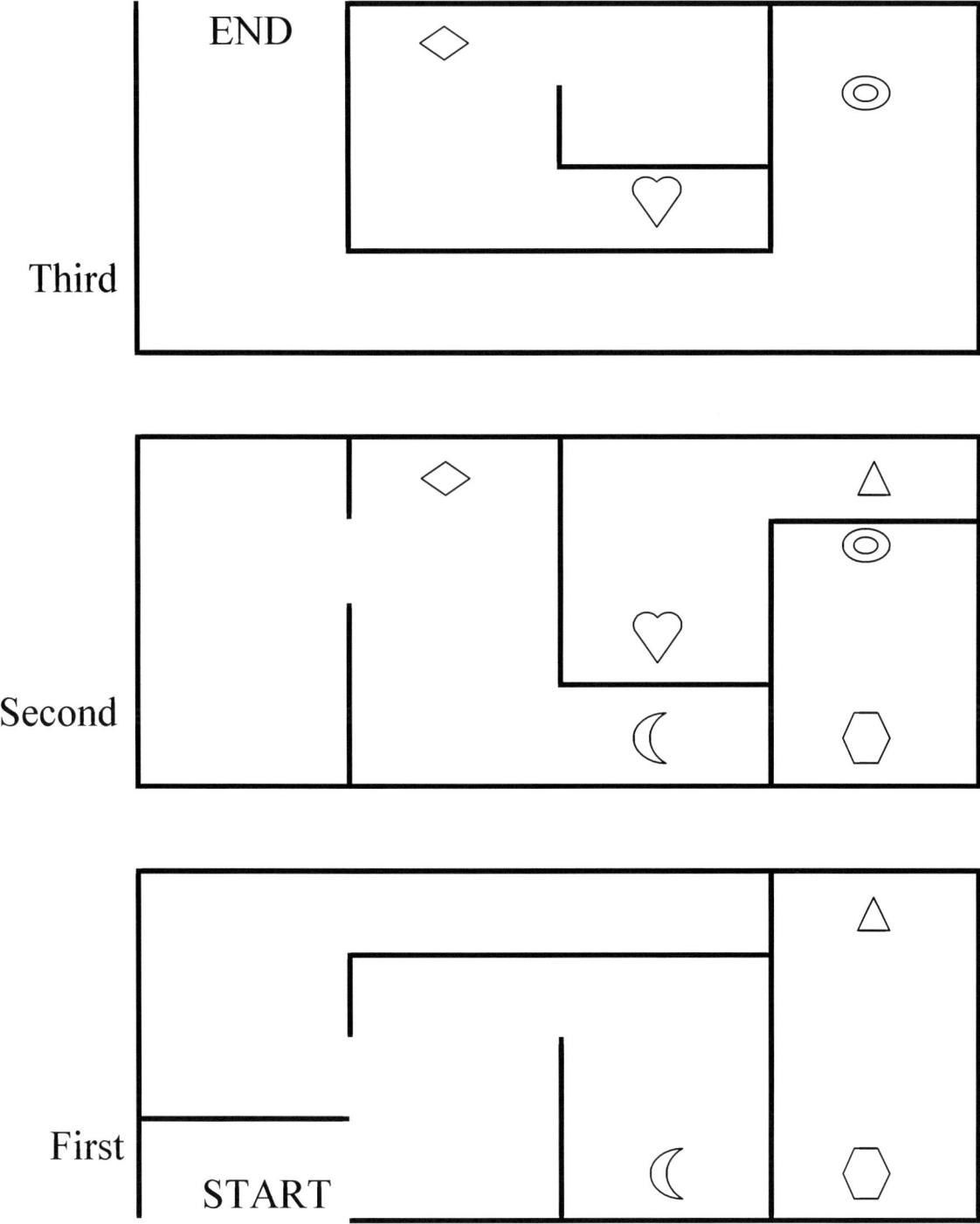

Where is the Fork in the Maze?

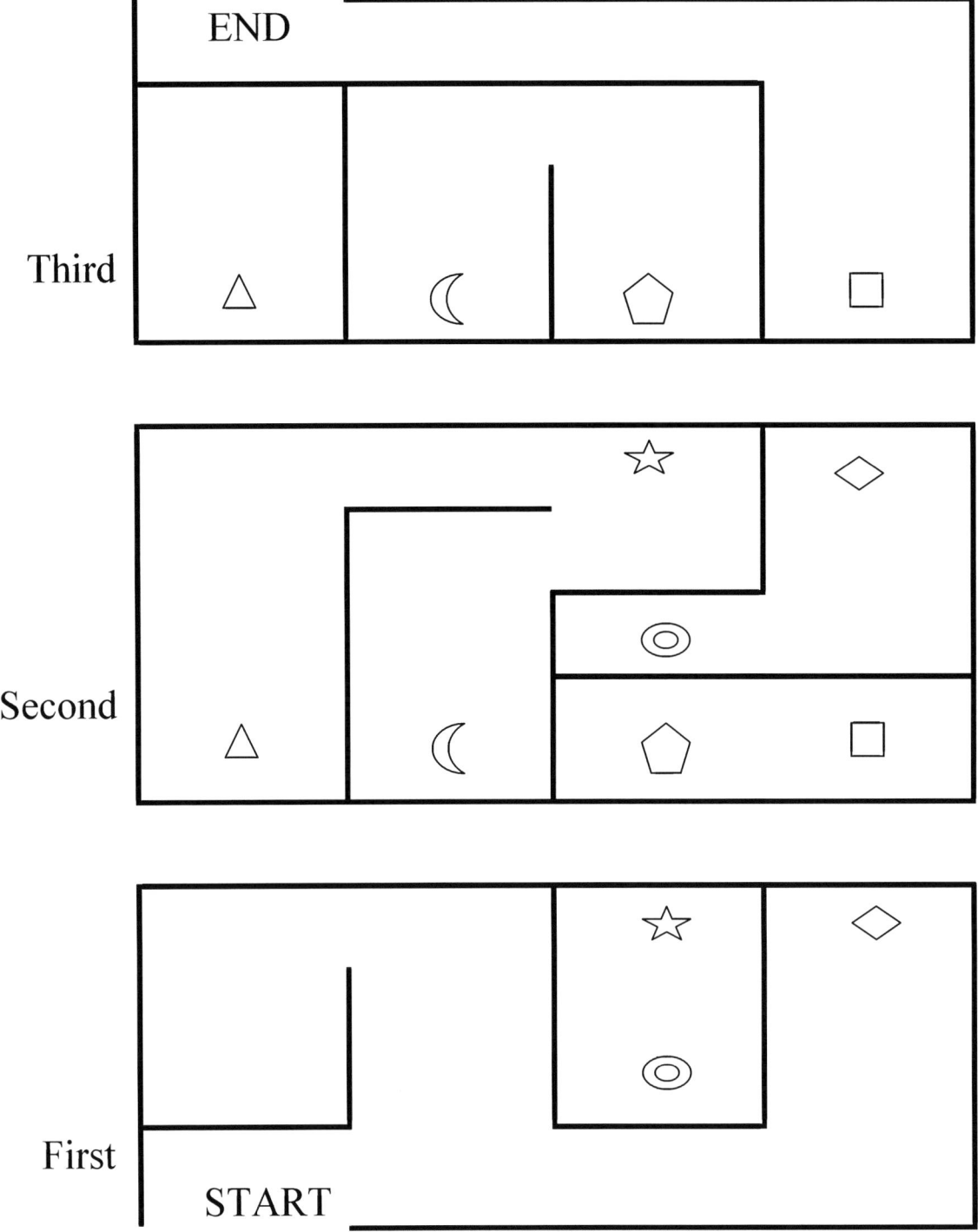

Slow down. Not too fast.

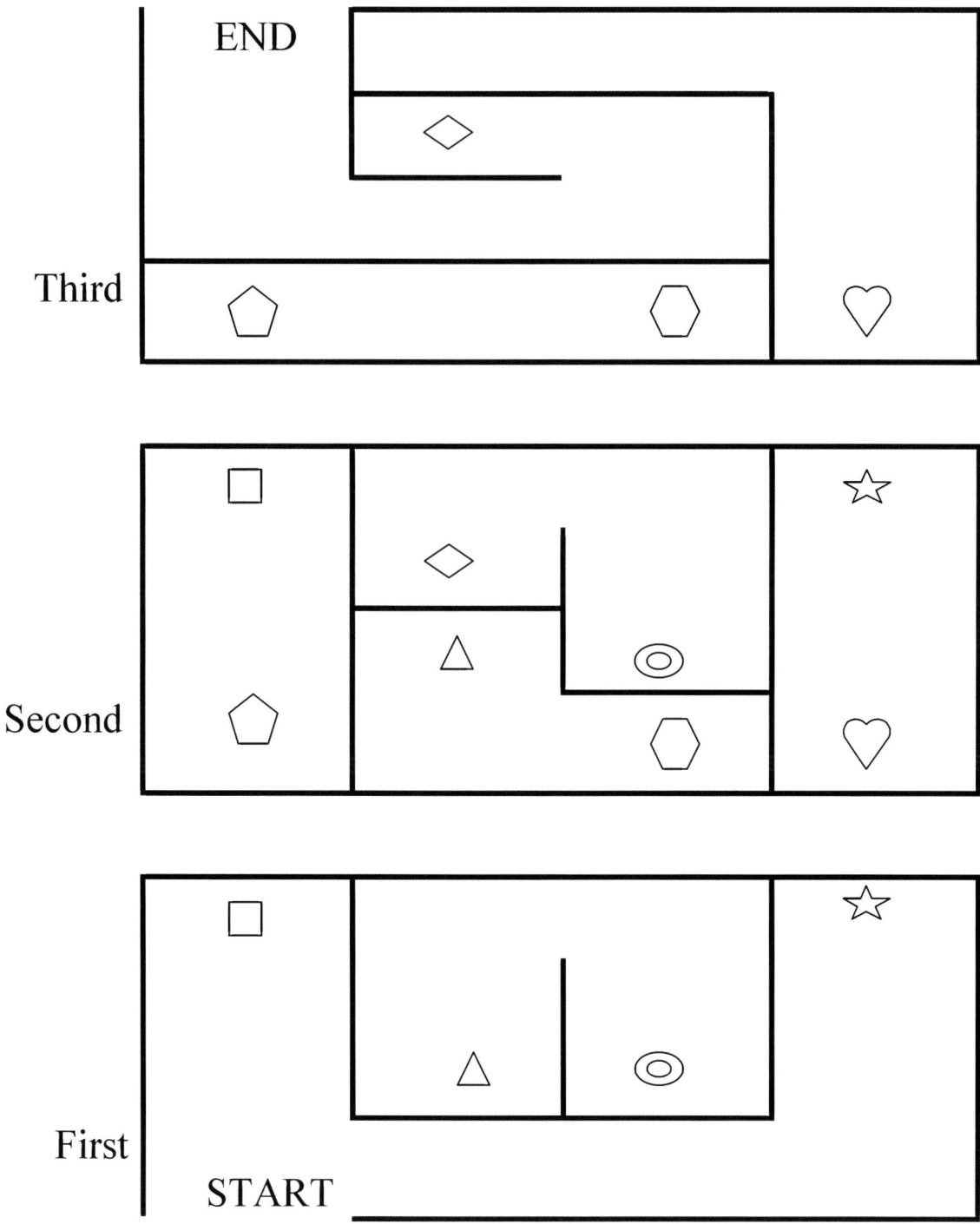

Be careful. Get it right.

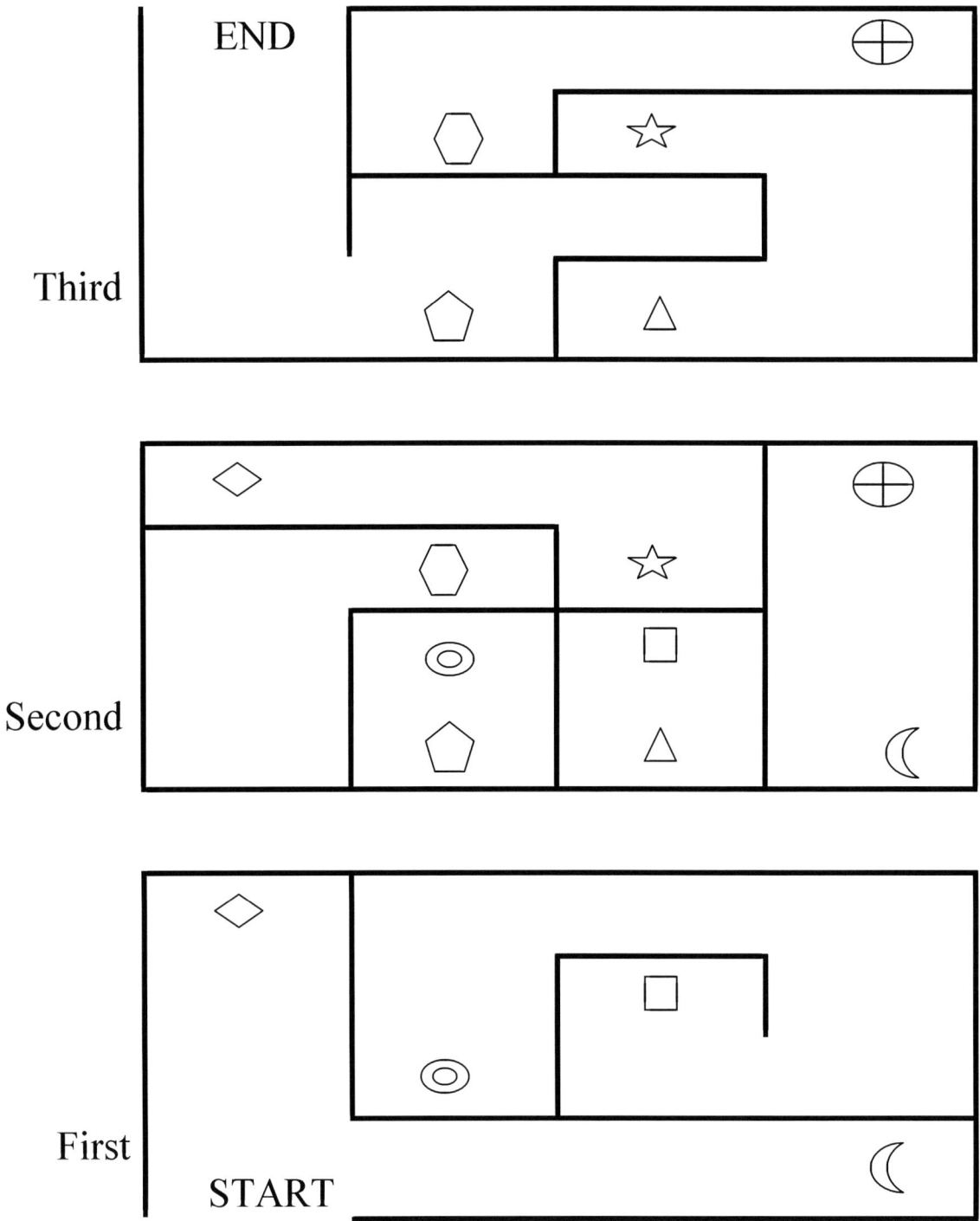

10 invisible imaginary Ladders are in this 3 dimensional Maze.

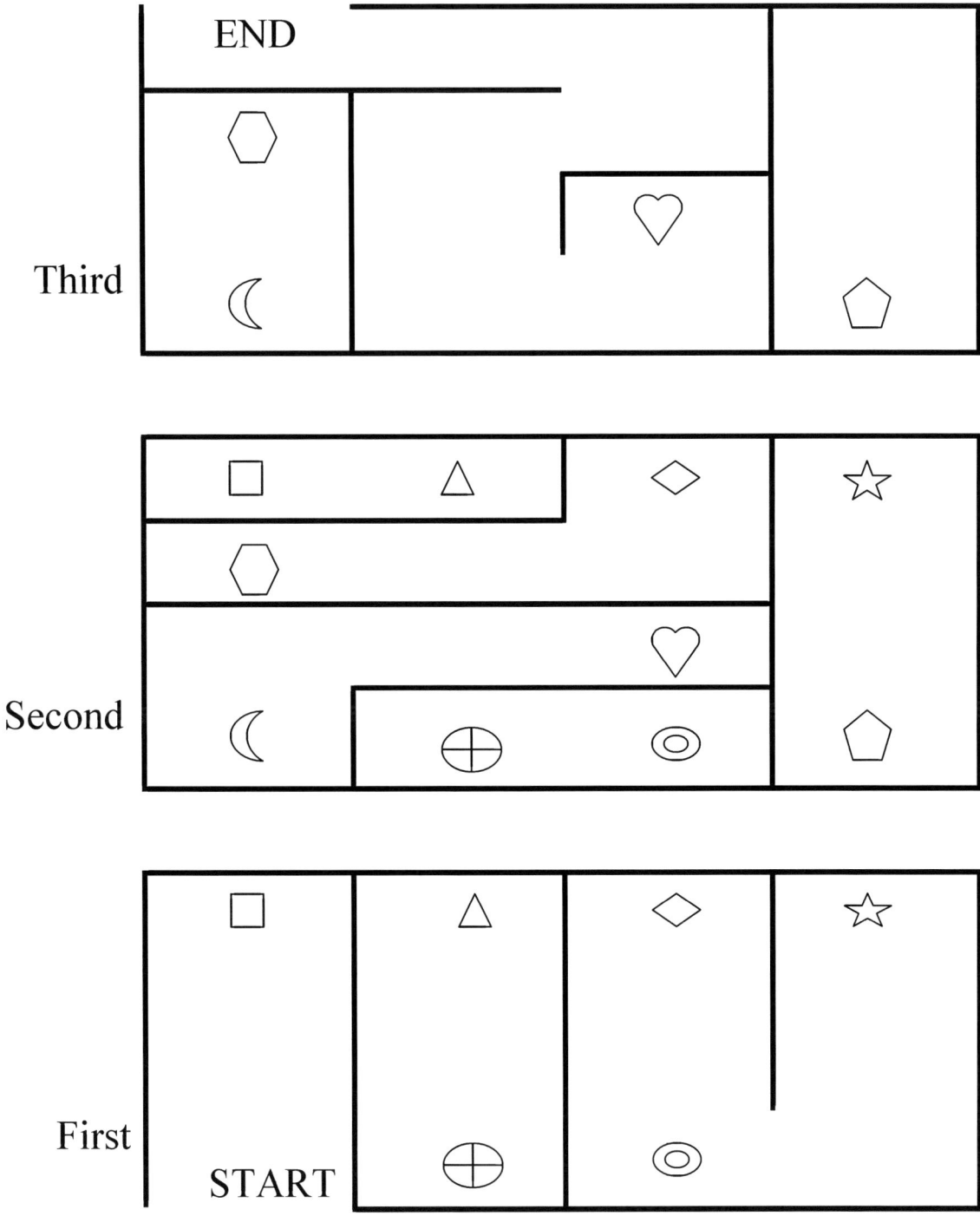

If you can do this, you deserve a rest before you advance to the next chapter to do the Number Mazes.

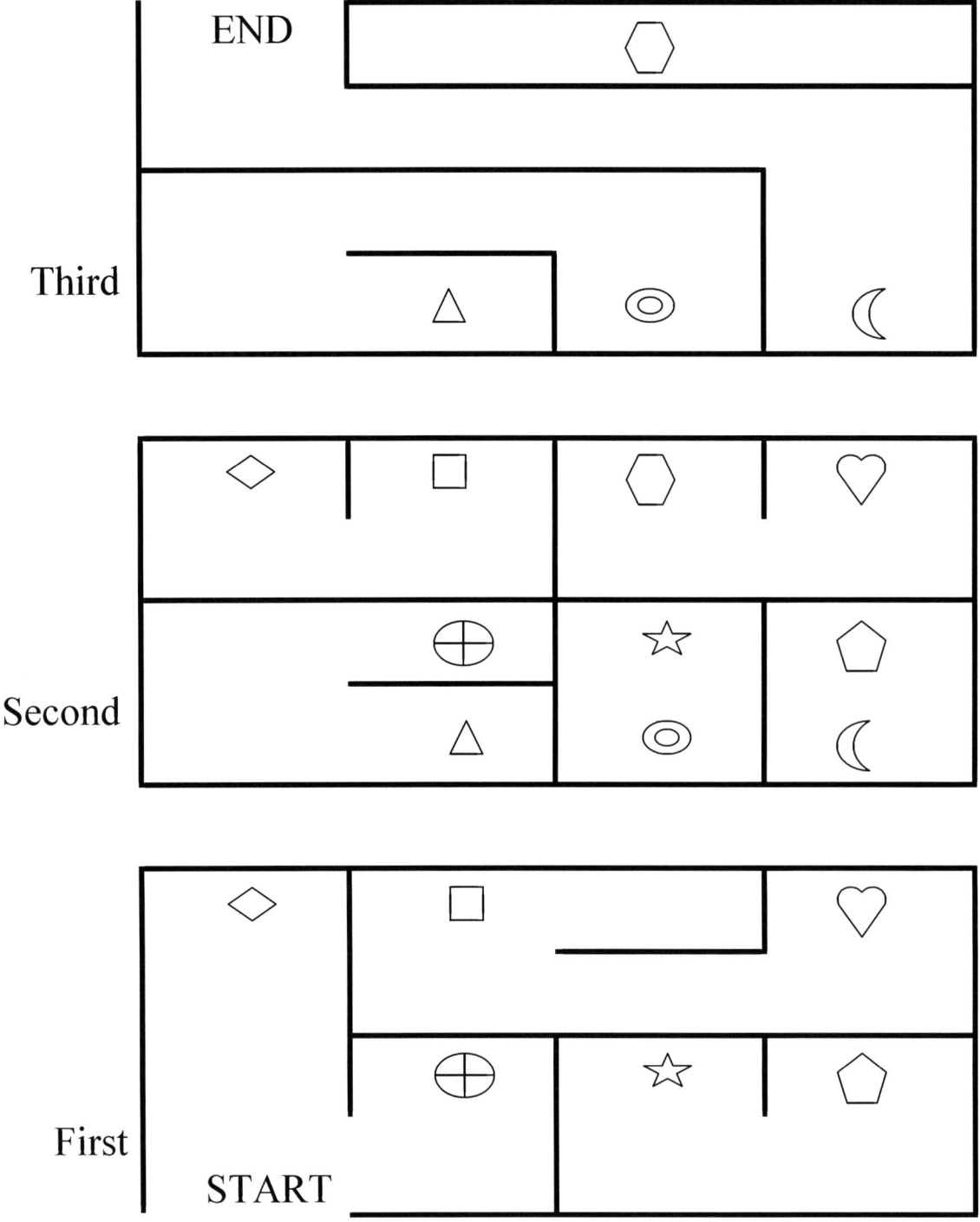

Chapter 6   Number Mazes

The Number Line is a line that has all the counting numbers.

```
_____
  1  2  3  4  5  6  7  8  9  10  11  12  13  14… and so on.
```

Each number is a point on the line as shown below by a vertical mark above the number. See the marks on this line.

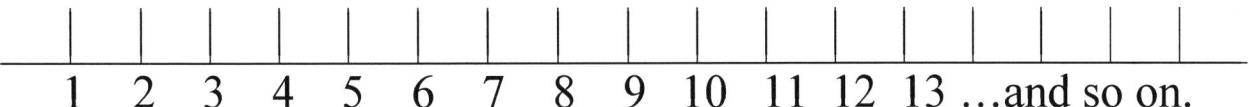

There are other points on the Number Line. The point 0 (called zero) is shown below. Other numbers on this line will be described in Chapter 10.

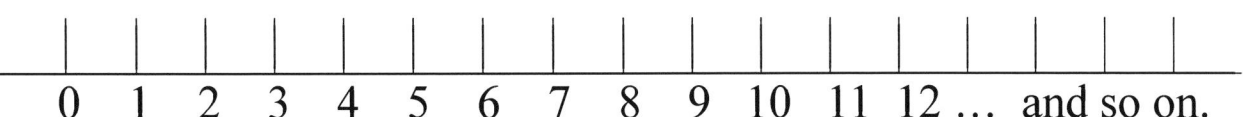

How do you add 2 + 3 on the Number Line?
First, starting at 0, you count up 2 spaces from 0 to 2 (think of stepping up stairs). Second, from where you are at 2, count up 3 spaces from 2 to 5.
So 2 + 3 = 5. See the picture below.

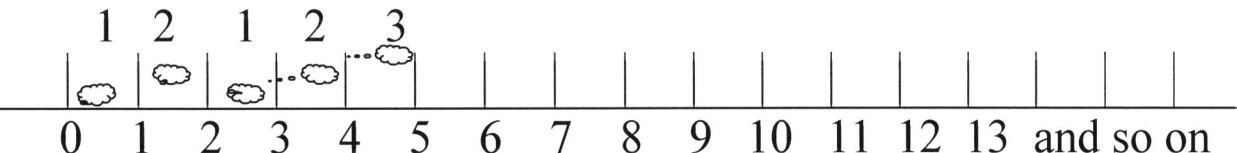

Can you add 4 + 5 using the Number Line?
First, starting at 0, you count up 4 spaces from 0 to 4 (think of stepping up stairs). Second, from where you are at 4, count up 5 spaces from 4 to 9.

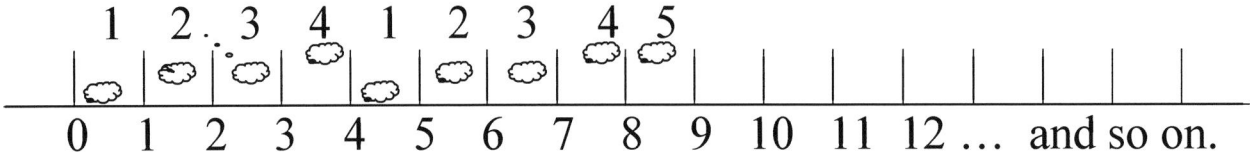

You step up to 9. So 4+5=9

Add 5 and 4 using the Number Line.
First, starting at 0, you count up 5 spaces from 0 to 5 (think of stepping up stairs). Second, from where you are at 5, count up 4 spaces from 5 to 9.

You step up to 9. So 5+4=9.

It does not matter if you add 4 to 5 or 5 to 4.
Both times you count up to 9, the same number.

This is a Number Maze:

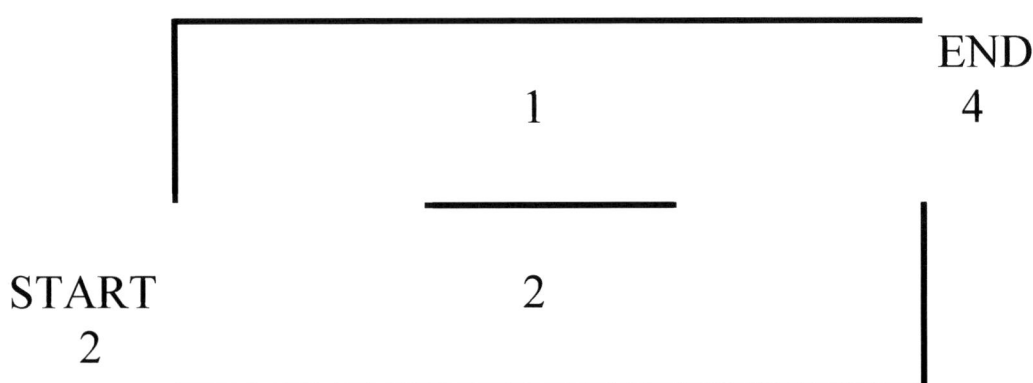

The aim of the Number Maze is to go through the maze from Start to End and finish with the correct number. Start with the number (2), and finish with the number (4). Every time you pass a number (like 1 or 2) in the Number Maze you must add it to the number you already have.

If you take the bottom path, you have chosen the right way!

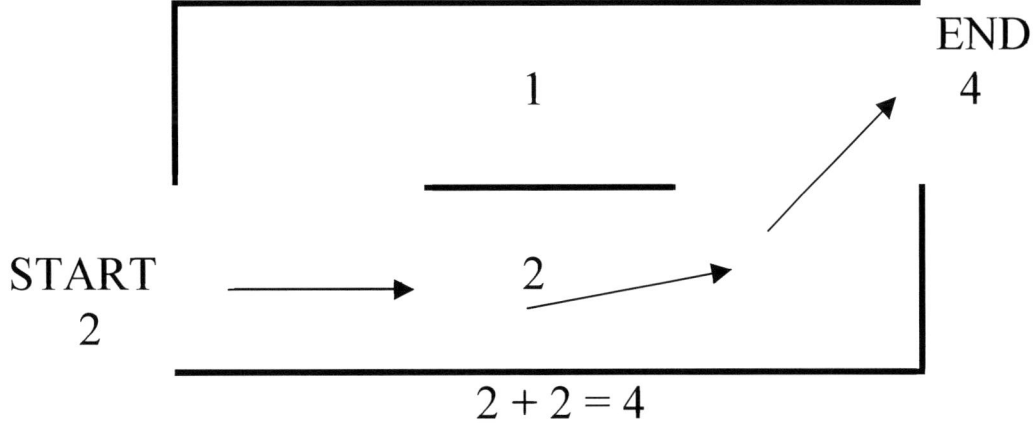

Start with 2 and pass by 2.
Add 2 + 2 = 4, and reach the End with the number 4.
Therefore this is the correct path and is called the solution to the Number Maze.

If you take the top path, you have chosen the wrong way.

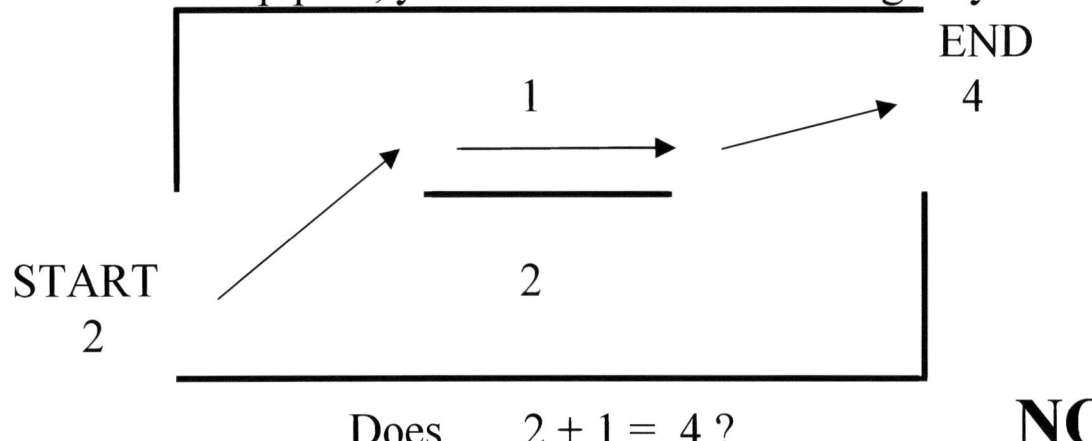

Does 2 + 1 = 4 ? **NO.**

Why? If you Start with 2 and pass by 1, you must add 2 + 1 = 3. But since 3 is not the number at the End of the maze, the upper path is the not the correct solution to the Number Maze.

You may not pass a number twice.

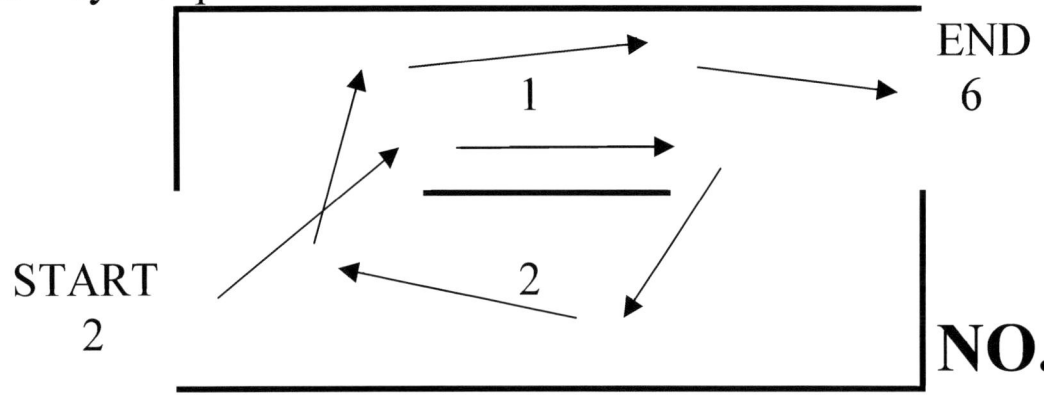

NO.

And you may not touch and then reverse direction

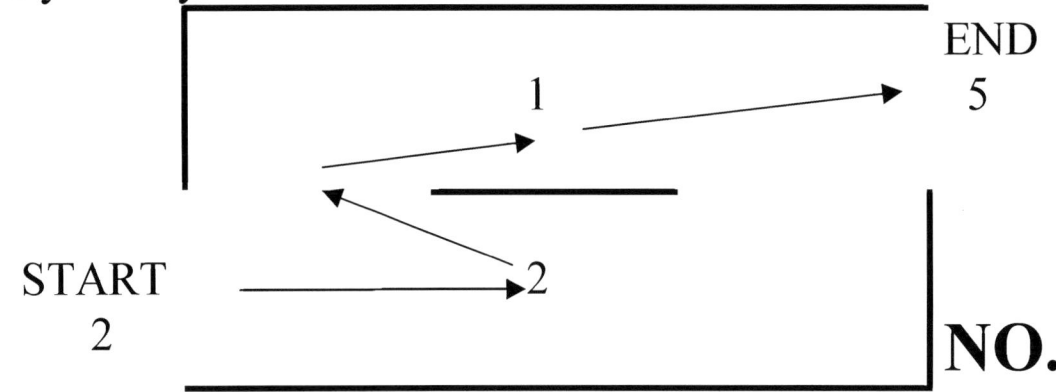

NO.

How do you do the Number Maze below?
You draw a line from START to END.
Each time you pass a number you add it to what you had.
The only way through the maze is the path beginning with the number 2 at START, passing by 1, and finishing with the number 3 at the END.

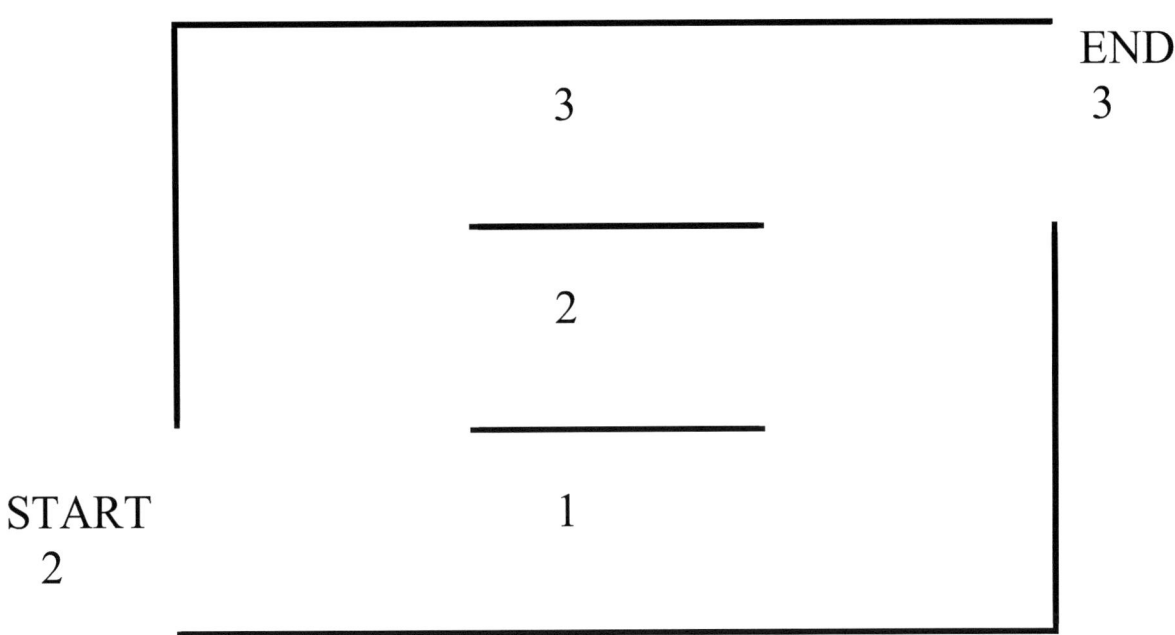

The solution is along a path on the bottom. 2+1=3.

If the END number is changed to 4, what is the solution?
The path must cross the 2. 2+2=4. Yes.
If the END number is changed to 5, what is the solution?
The path must cross the 3. 2+3=5. Yes.

If the END number is changed to 6, can you go though the maze?
No. The path is not allowed to pass through the same section of the maze twice.

Below is almost the same number maze as on the last page. What is different? The END number is now 8.

There is a solution to this!!

```
                         3                    END
                                              8



                         2



                         1
START
  2
```

The path that is the solution to this problem must snake around to all 3 numbers in the middle of the maze. 2+1+2+3=8. Good work.

The solution path starts where? At 2 it starts and goes past 1 to 2 and then to 3 and ends at 8. See the next page for the solution.

Solution:

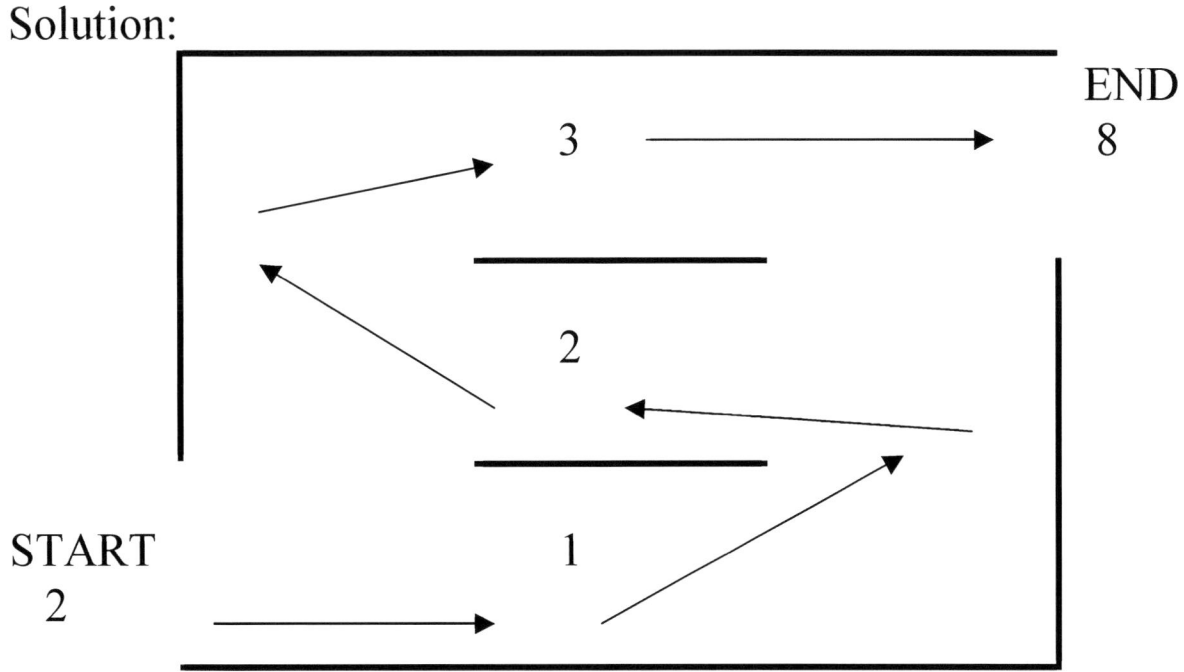

The solution below is <u>not</u> correct because the path passes twice over the same section of the maze.

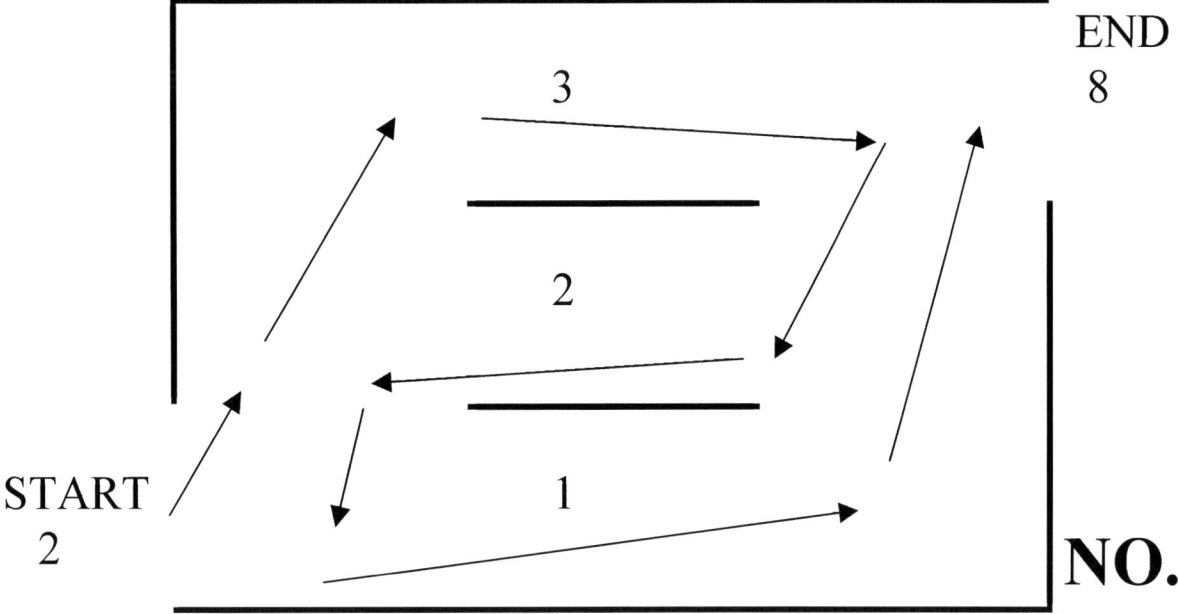

Here is a Number Maze with more possible paths.

```
          ┌─────────────────────────────────┐
          │                                 │  END
          │      1              1           │   3
          │    ─────          ─────         │
START            2              3           │
  1                                         │
          └─────────────────────────────────┘
```

The solution is to take the path across the top. Using the Number Line add 1+1+1 to get the solution of 3.

What is different in the Number Maze below?
What is the new path through the Maze?

```
          ┌─────────────────────────────────┐
          │                                 │  END
          │      1              1           │   4
          │    ─────          ─────         │
START            2              3           │
  1                                         │
          └─────────────────────────────────┘
```

See the bottom of the next page for the solution.

Solve this Number Maze.

```
          ┌─────────────────────────────┐
          │                             │ END
          │     1           1           │  5
          │   ─────       ─────         │
START     │                             │
  1             2             3
          └─────────────────────────────┘
```

See the bottom of the next page for the solution.

How many different ways can you go through this Number Maze?
1, 2, 3, 4, 5, or 6 ways?

Solution to the Number Maze on the last page (62).

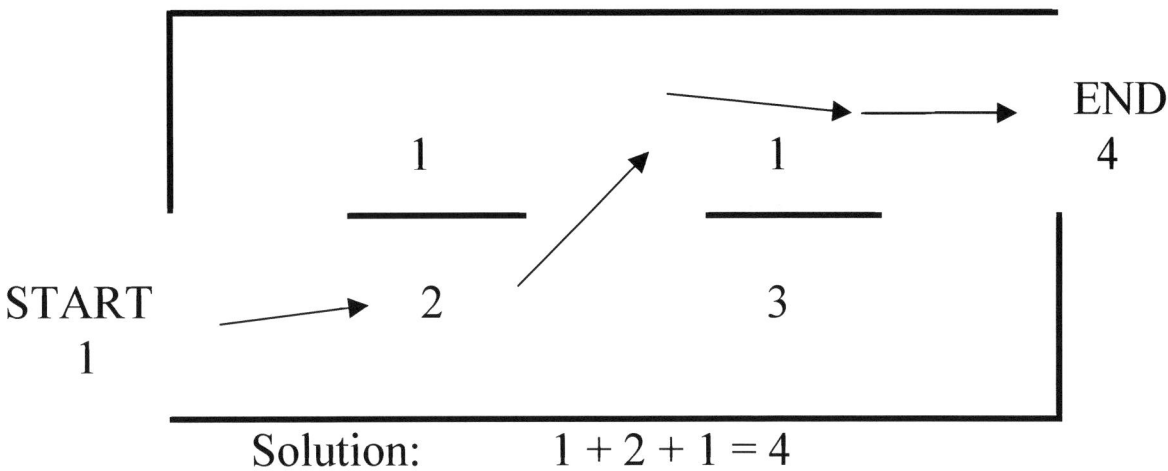

Solution: 1 + 2 + 1 = 4

There is one more way through the Number Maze. Solve:

```
        ┌─────────────────────────────────┐
        │                                 │  END
        │      1              1           │   6
        │    ─────          ─────         │
START   │                                 │
  1     │      2              3           │
        └─────────────────────────────────┘
```

The solution to this is to take the bottom path through 2 and 3. So 1+2+3 =6.

There are 4 ways from the START to the END.

Solution to the Number Maze on the last page. (63)

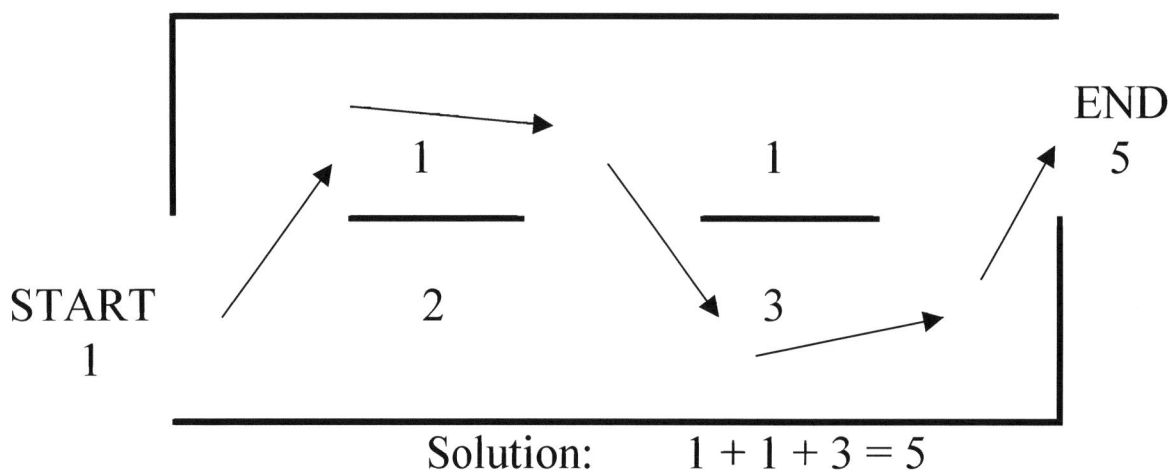

Solution: 1 + 1 + 3 = 5

Try this Number Maze.

```
         ┌─────────────────────────────────────┐
         │   1         3         5       END   │
         │                               10    │
         │  ───       ───       ───            │
START    │                                     │
  1      │   2         4         6             │
         └─────────────────────────────────────┘
```

There is only one way through this maze so that the numbers add up to 10.
START at 1, go to 1, then 3, then 5.
1+1+3+5=10.

This Number Maze has different numbers in the same diagram.

```
         ┌─────────────────────────────────────┐
         │   1         1         1       END   │
         │                                8    │
         │  ───       ───       ───            │
START    │                                     │
  1      │   2         3         5             │
         └─────────────────────────────────────┘
```

There is only one solution of this Number Maze.
START at 1, go to 1, then 1, then 5.
1+1+1+5=8.
If you change the End number to 7, how do you solve it?
See the next page.

```
         ┌─────────────────────────────────┐
         │    1        1        1     END
         │   ___      ___      ___     7
START    │
  1           2        3        5
         └─────────────────────────────────┘
```

Now, change the End number to 6. Solve it if you can.

```
         ┌─────────────────────────────────┐
         │    1        1        1     END
         │   ___      ___      ___     6
START    │
  1           2        3        5
         └─────────────────────────────────┘
```

If you change the End number to 5, you get a different solution path.

```
         ┌─────────────────────────────────┐
         │    1        1        1     END
         │   ___      ___      ___     5
START    │
  1           2        3        5
         └─────────────────────────────────┘
```

If the END number is 2 or 20, can you solve the maze?

This number maze is larger. Zigzag.

```
                    5              END
                                    11
            ┌──────────┐
                  4
            ──────────
                  3
        ──────────────
                  2
```

START
1

The solution is on the bottom of the next page.

Try this.

```
        ┌────────────────────────┐
           4        6        1     END
                                    11
          ───      ───      ───
           2        3        5
        └────────────────────────┘
```

START
3

$3 + 4 + 3 + 1 = 11$

Here is another shape.

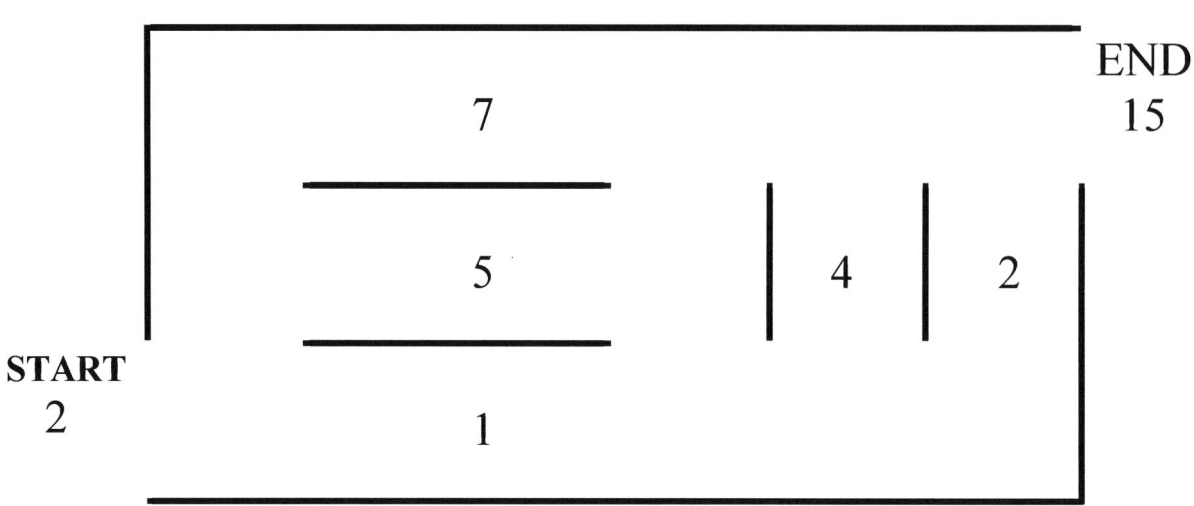

The Solution is to START at 2, go to 7, then go 4, then to 2 and END at 15. 2+7+4+2=15.

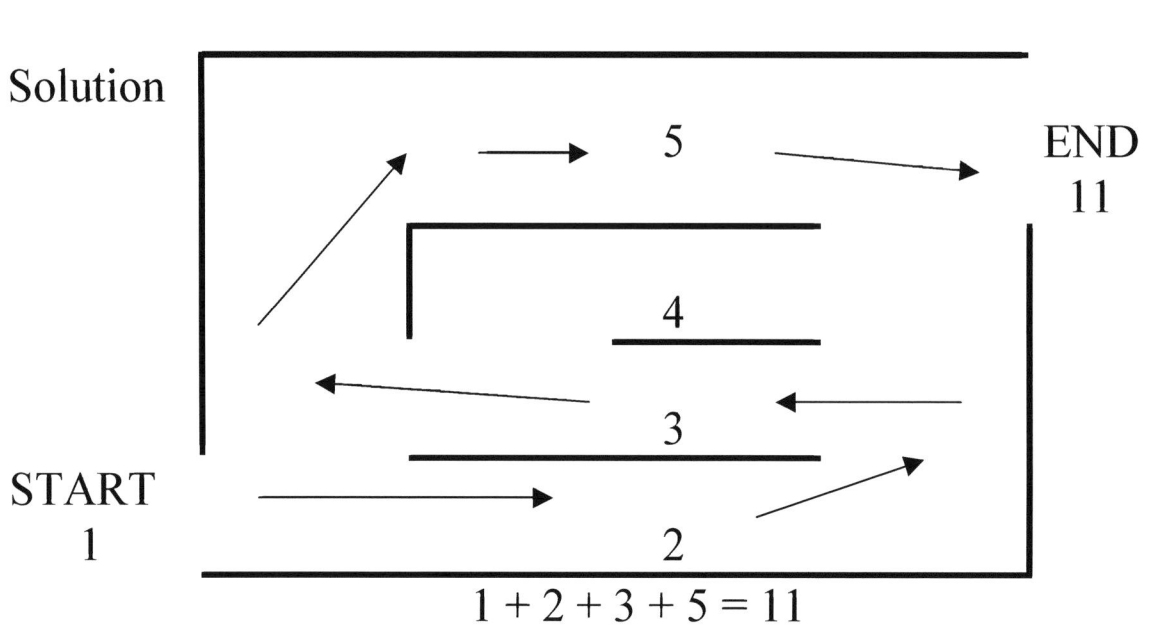

In these Number Mazes you do not have to use every number or go along every path.

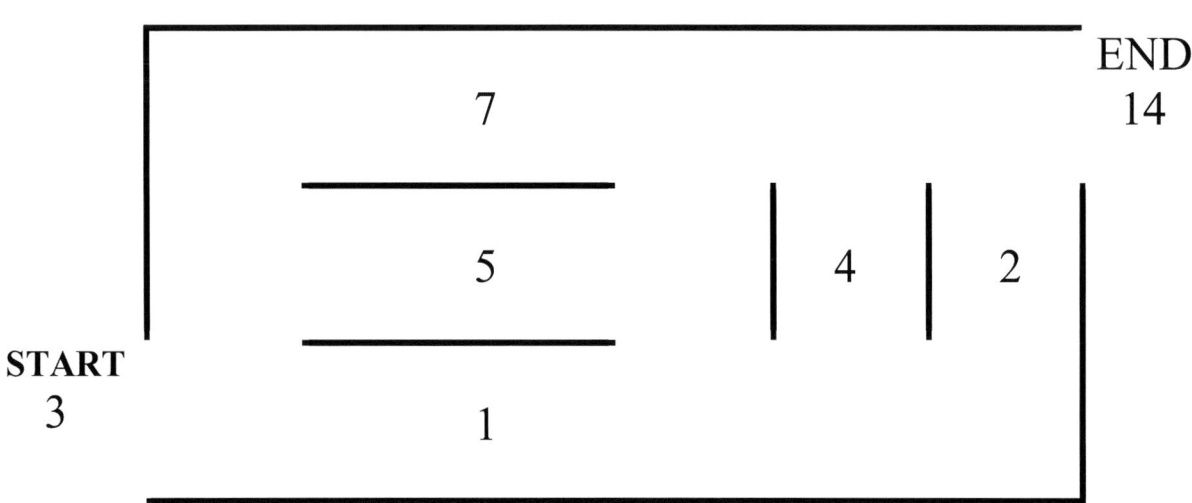

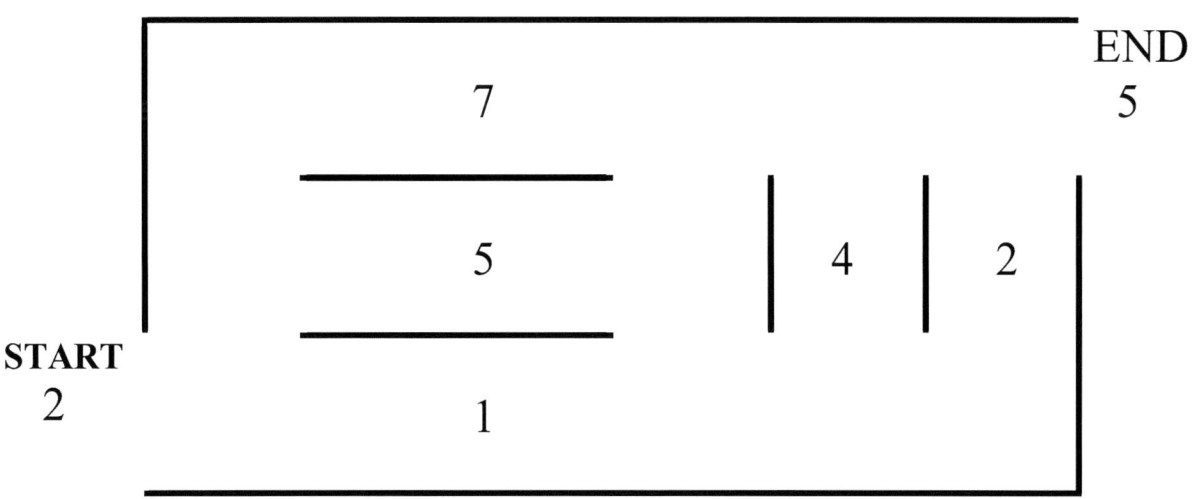

Draw your own Number Maze on a piece of paper.

Do not get lost.

```
                            7                    END
                                                  27
                    ┌─────────────┐
                          4        │ 5 │ 6
                    └─────────────┘
START
  2                       3
```

Add along your way.

```
                    1              4             END
                                                  12
                ┌─────────┐    ┌─────────┐
                    4              5
                └─────────┘    └─────────┘
START
  2                 3              6
```

There are 2 paths through this Number Maze.

	1		4		END
					11
	4		5		
START					
2	3		6		

This one is harder.

	1		4		END
					14
	4		5		
START					
2	3		6		

In this Number Maze there are 2 paths to the End. Only one path's numbers add up correctly.

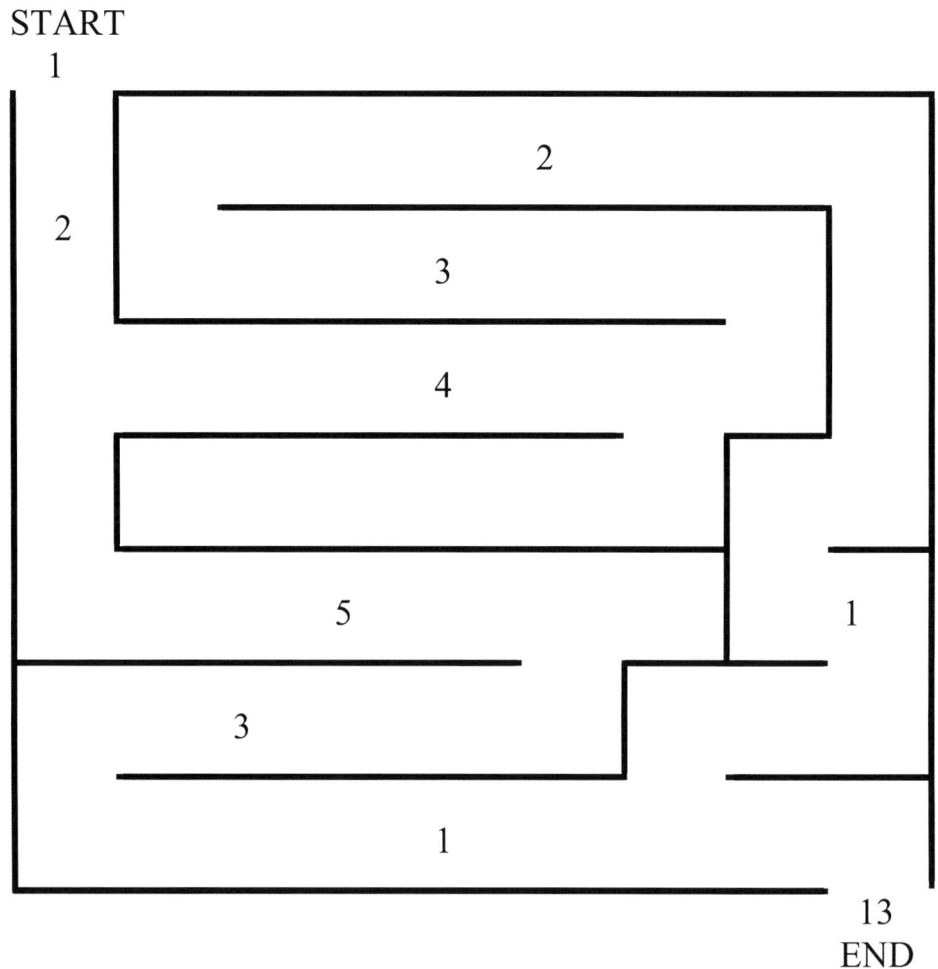

Make your own Number Maze. Fill in the numbers and Solve.

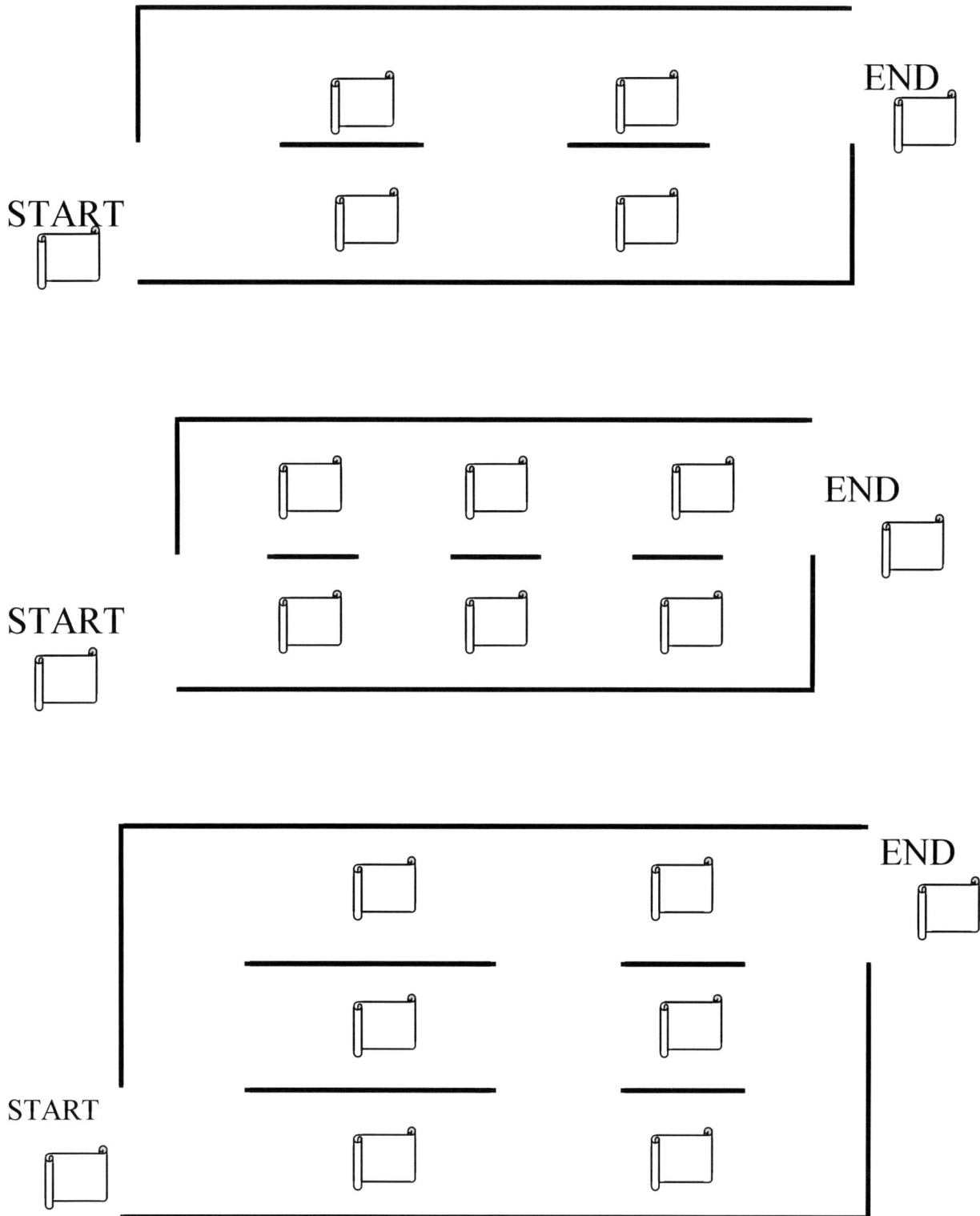

Chapter 7 6 by 4 by 3 Mazes

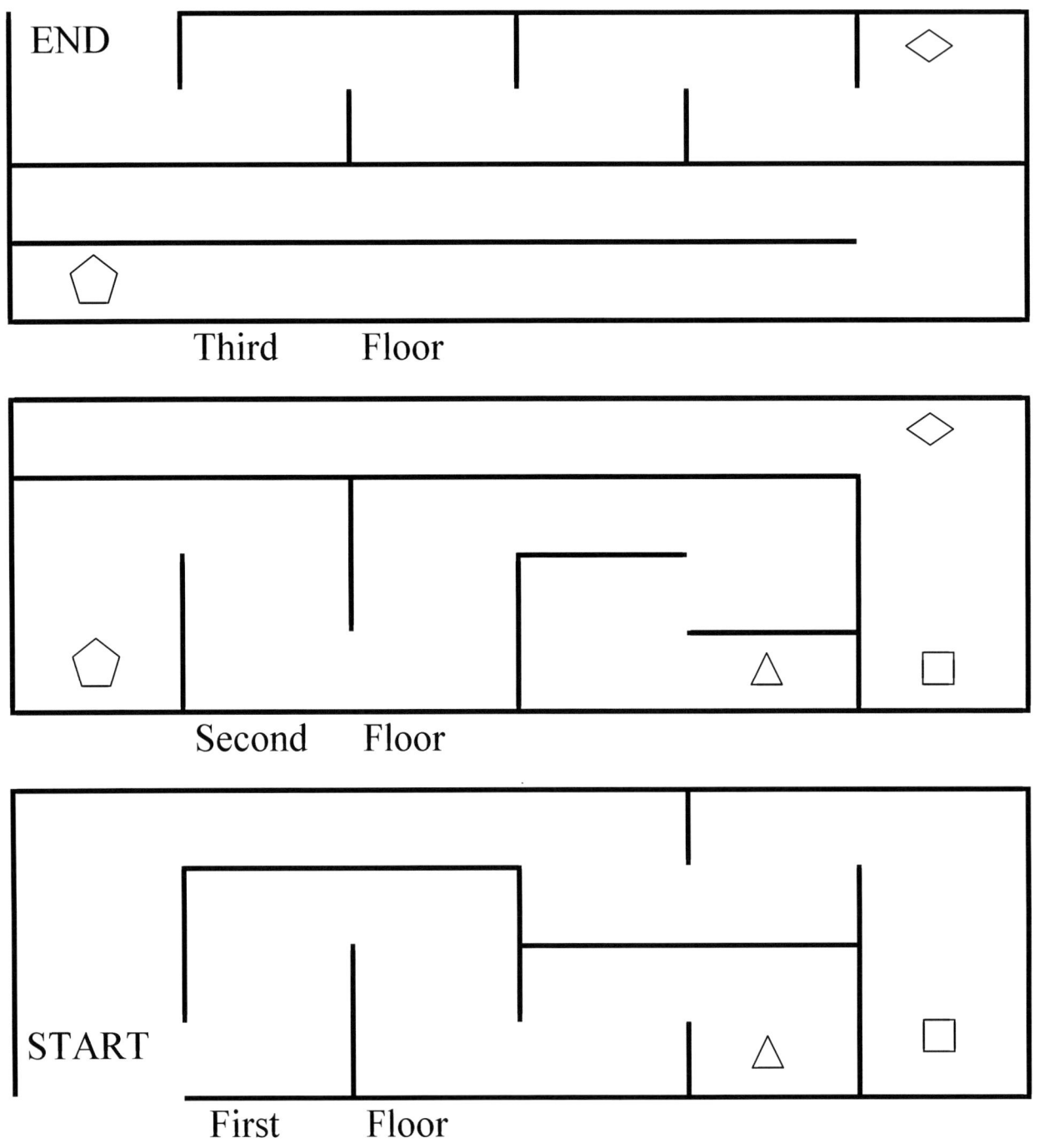

This is fun. Find the middle of the maze.

How many imaginary Stairs are there in this maze?

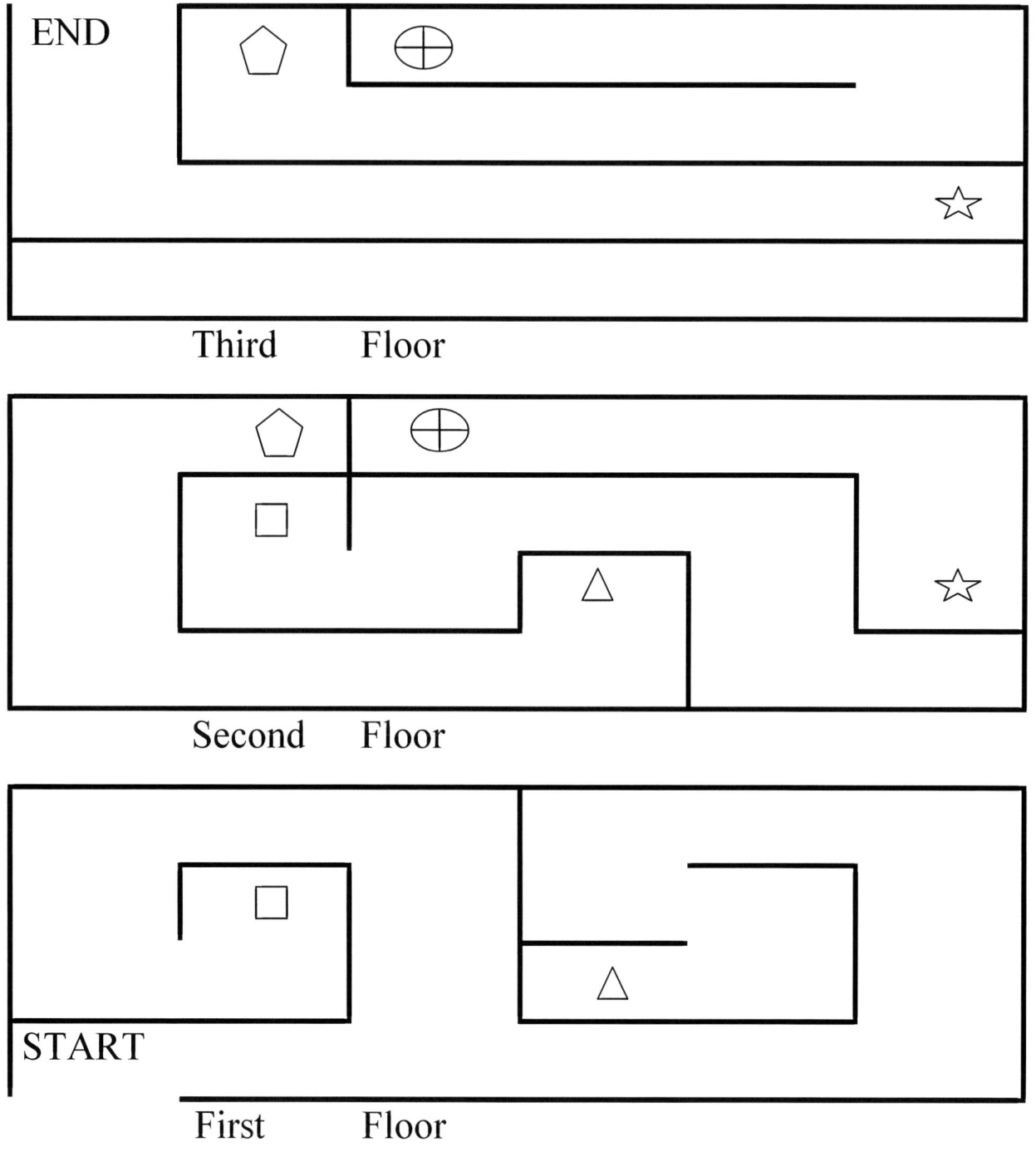

How many sides does a triangle △ have?
(The solution is on the bottom of the next page)

Did you come to the Dead End before you reached the End?

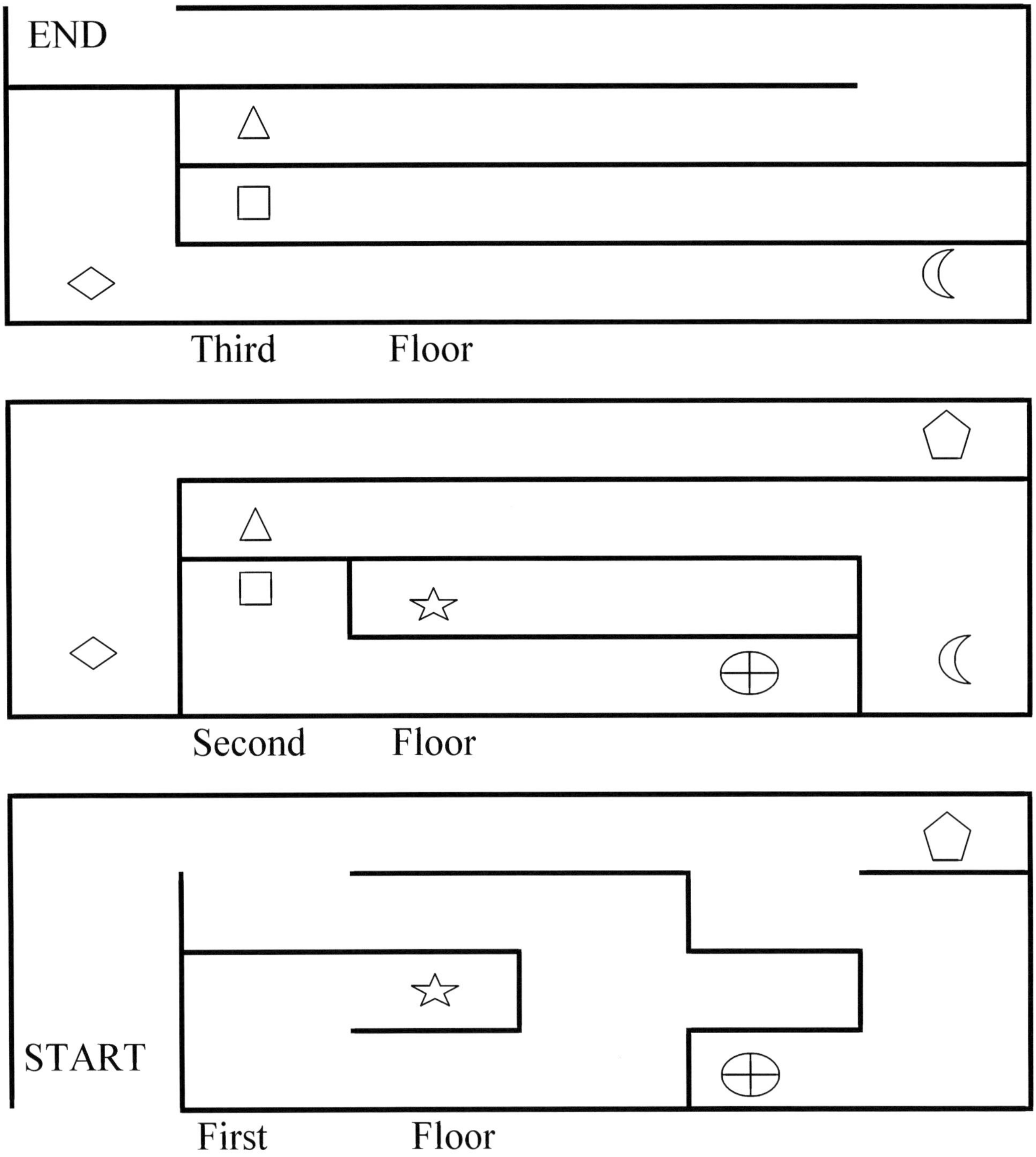

Third Floor

Second Floor

START

First Floor

(Answer 3) A vertex of a triangle is one of its points. How many vertexes does a triangle have? (The solution is on the bottom of the next page)

Is the star ☆ always on the correct Path to the End?

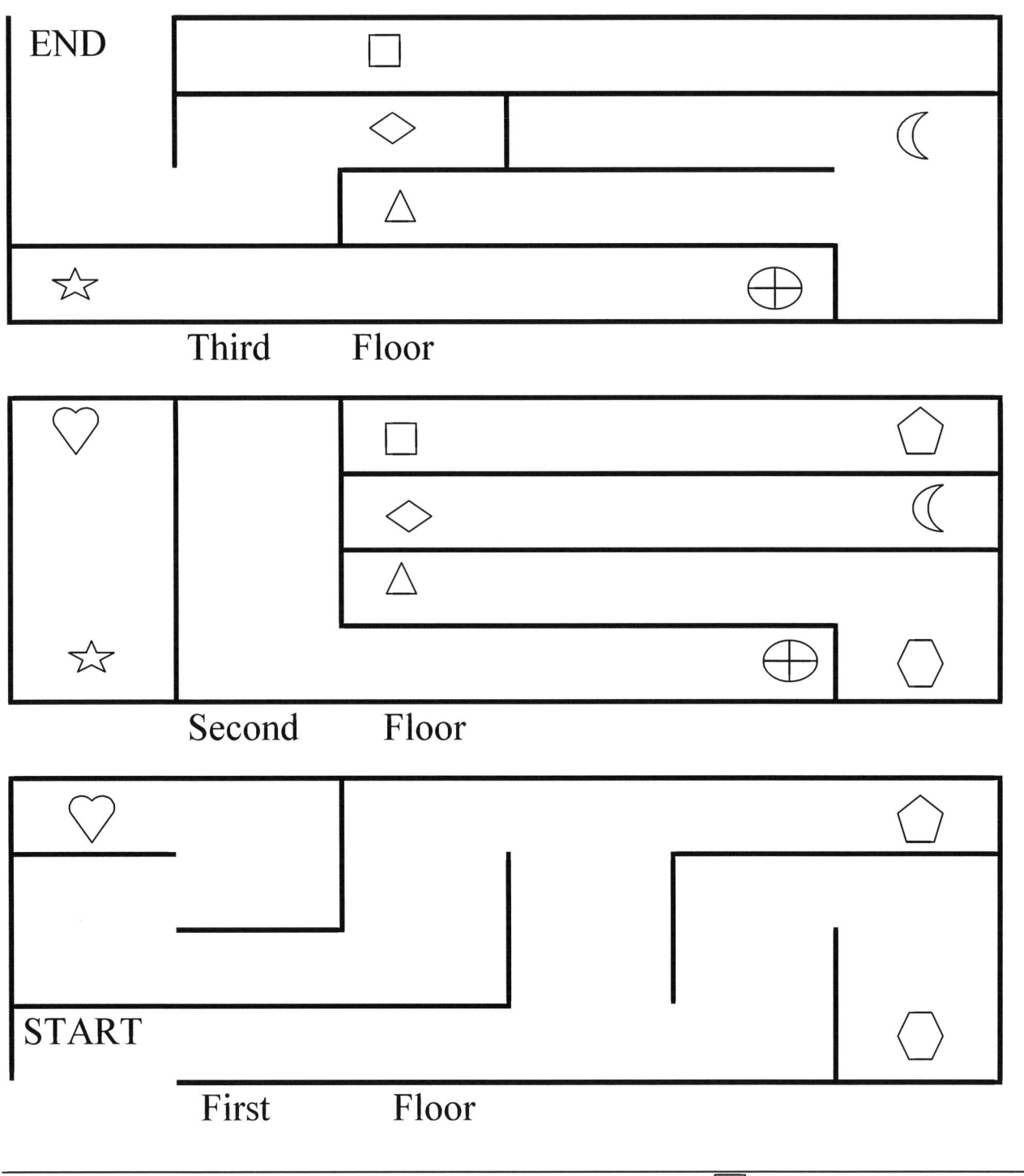

(Answer = 3) How many sides does a square ☐ have?
(The solution is on the bottom of the next page)

At the START, circle a number, either 1, 2, or 3, to see if you can guess the correct Path.

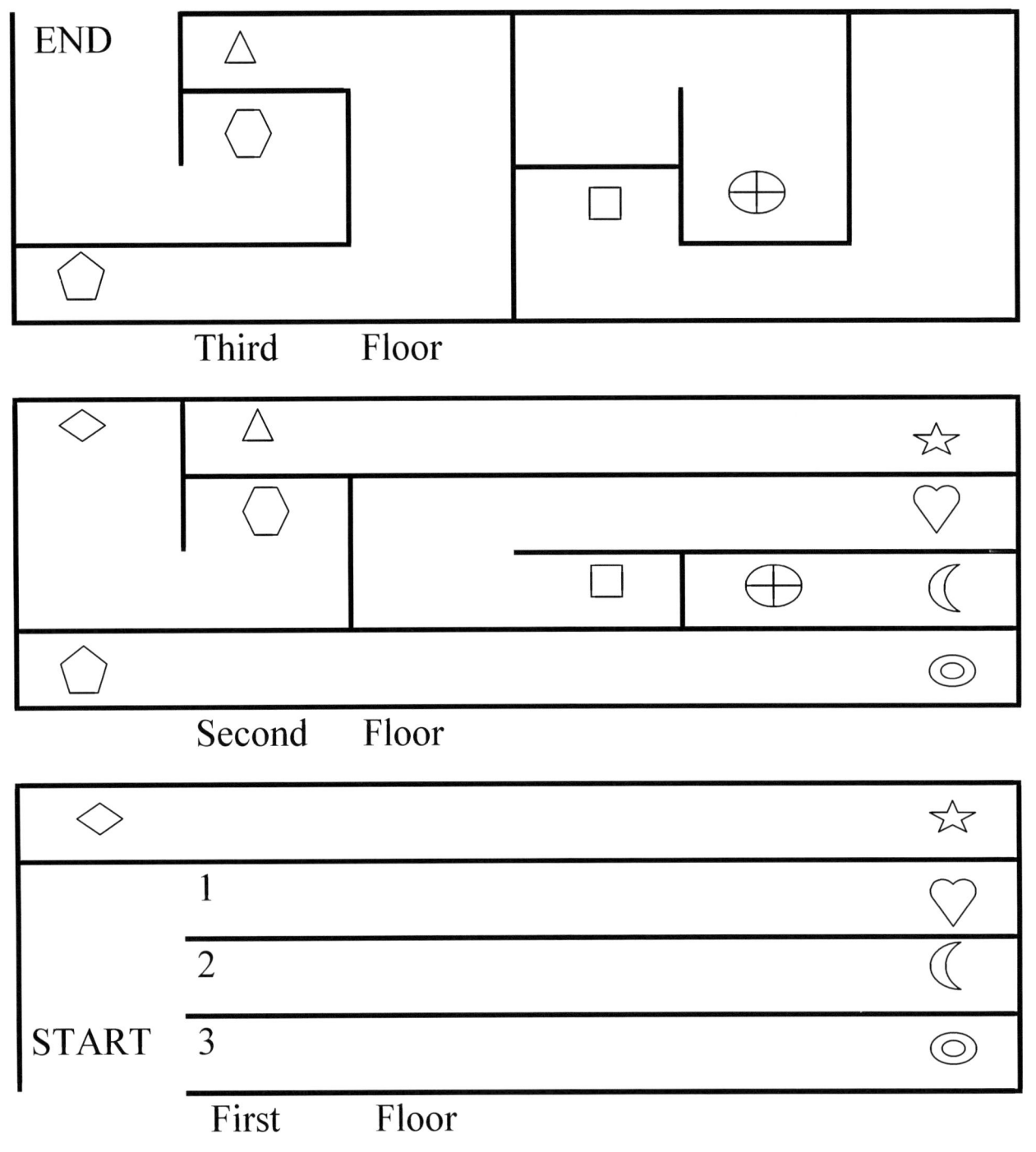

(Answer = 4) How many vertexes does a square have?

Is the moon ☾ always near the End?

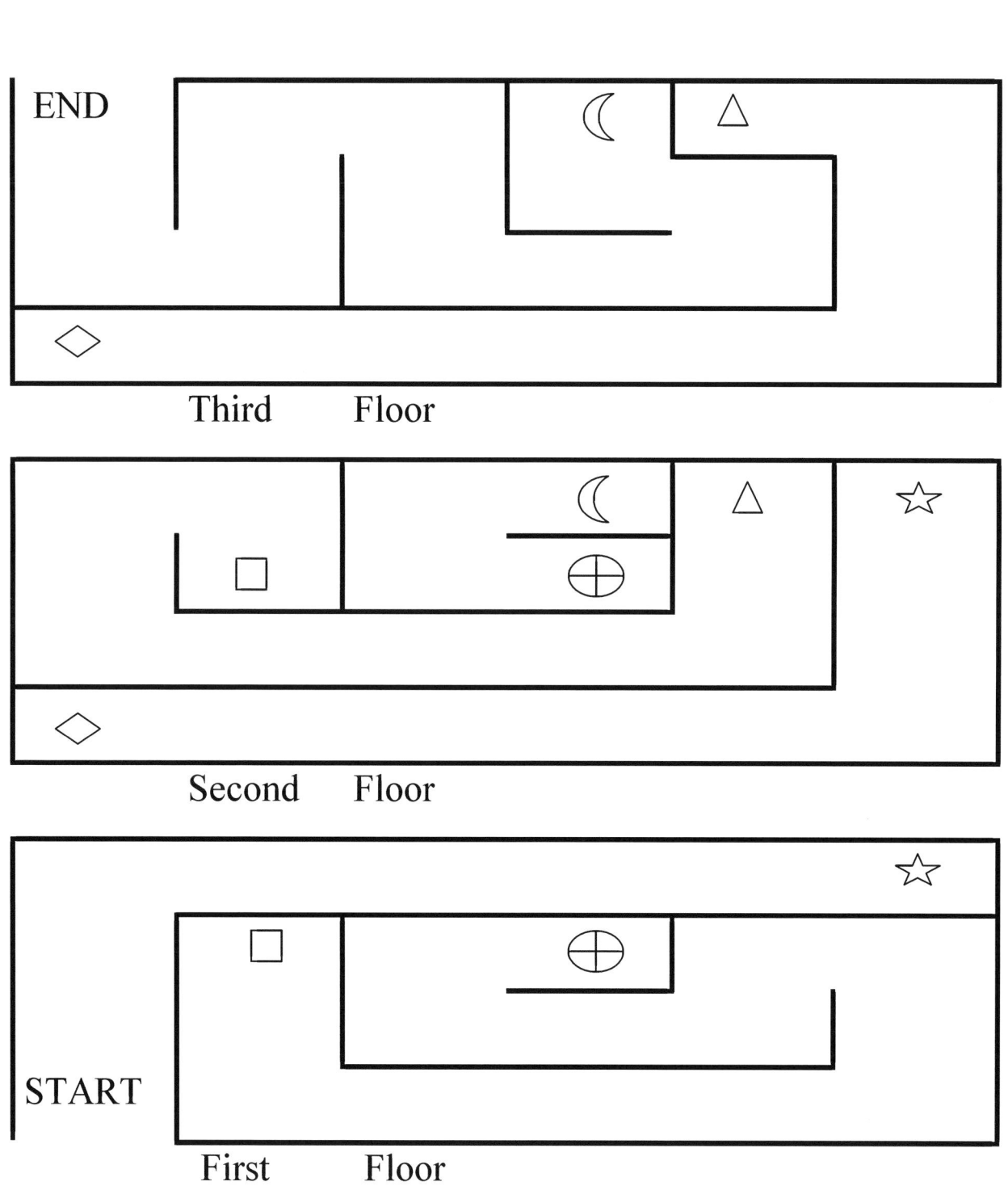

(Answer = 4) In a square ☐ all the sides have the same length.

When you pass the heart ♡ you will know that you love 3 dimensional mazes.

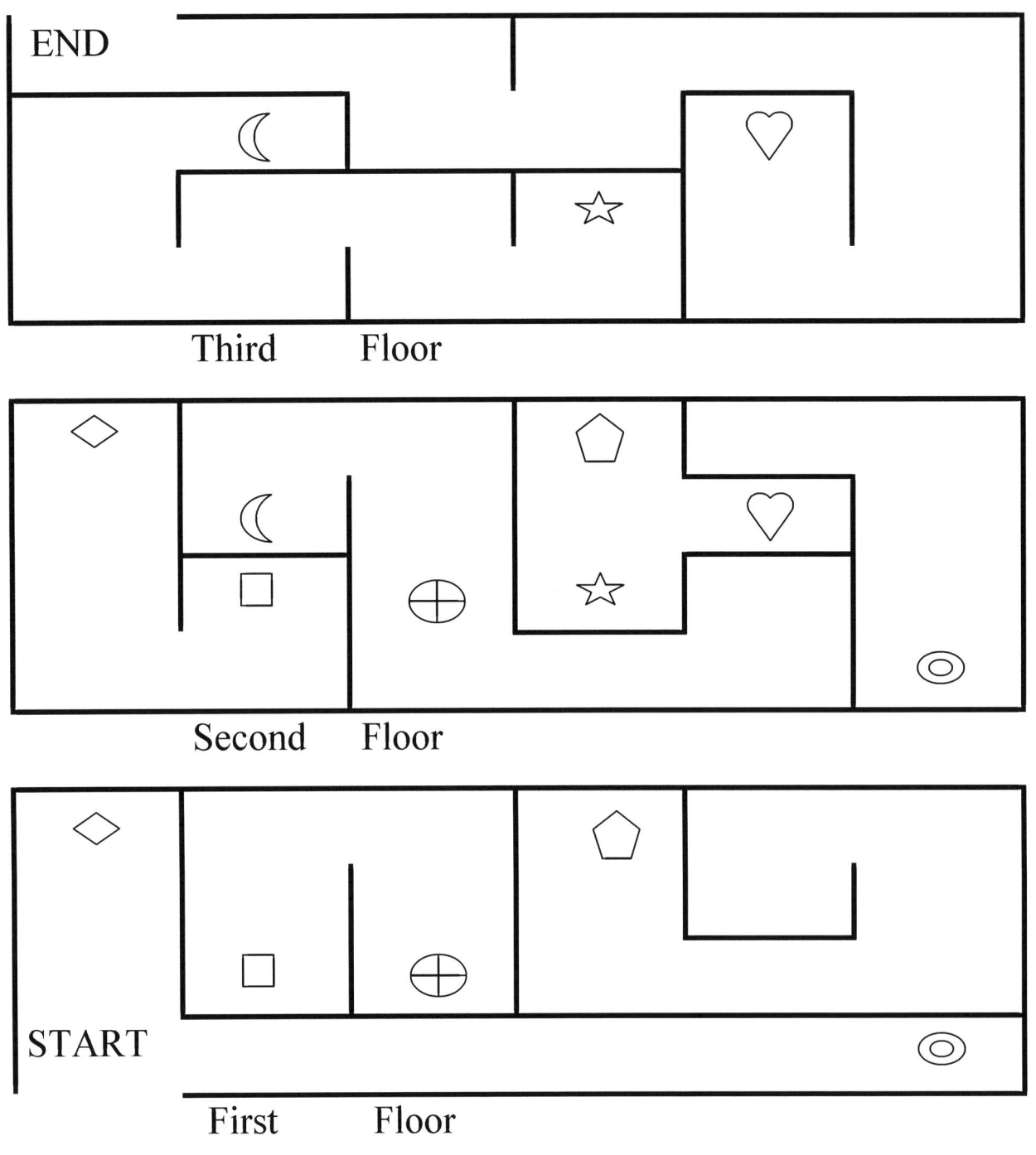

How many sides and vertexes does a diamond ◇ have?

Now are you an expert at 3 dimensional mazes?

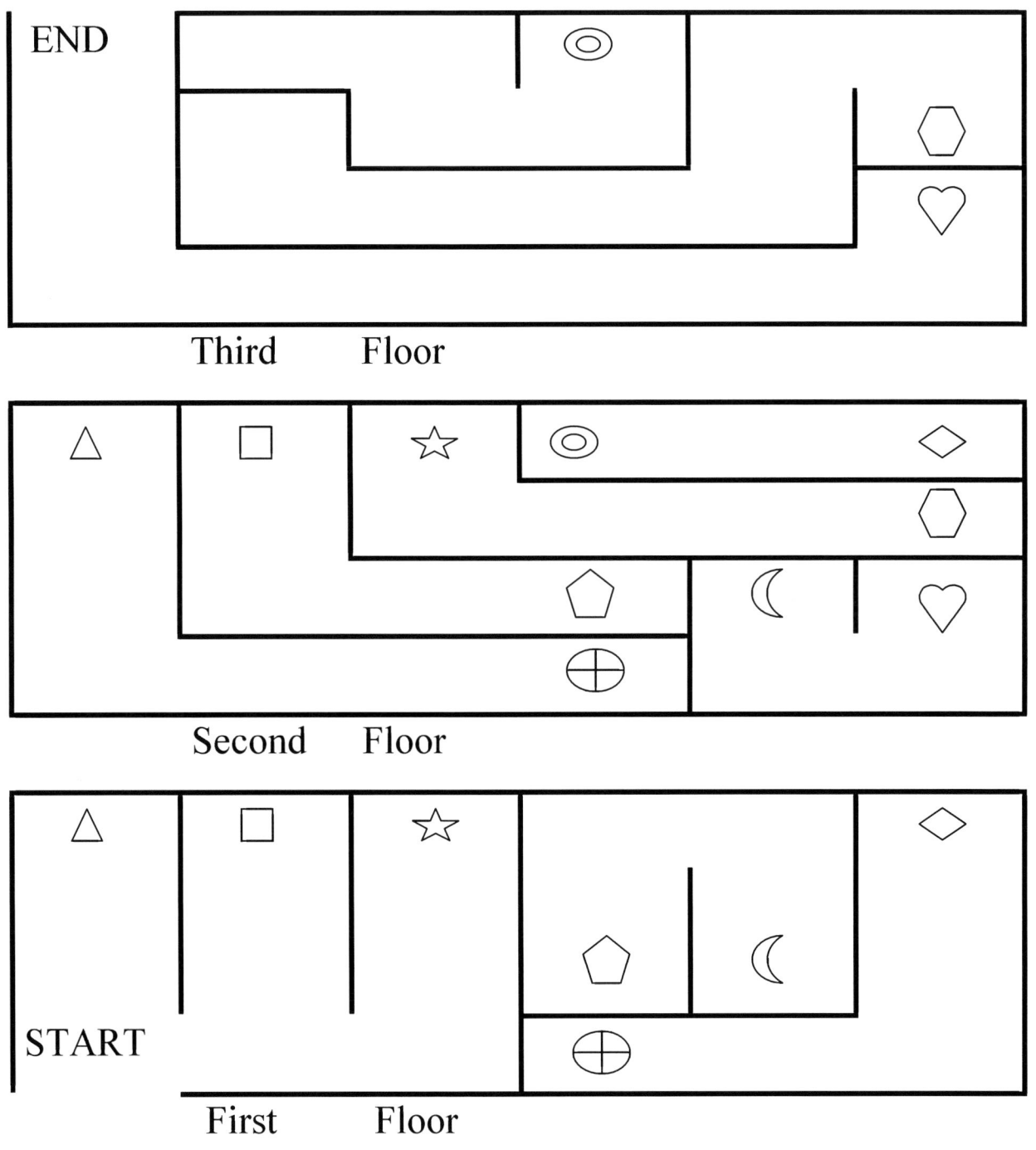

(Answer = 4 and 4) Do all the sides of the diamond ◇ have the same length?

How many times did you go through this maze before you came to the End?

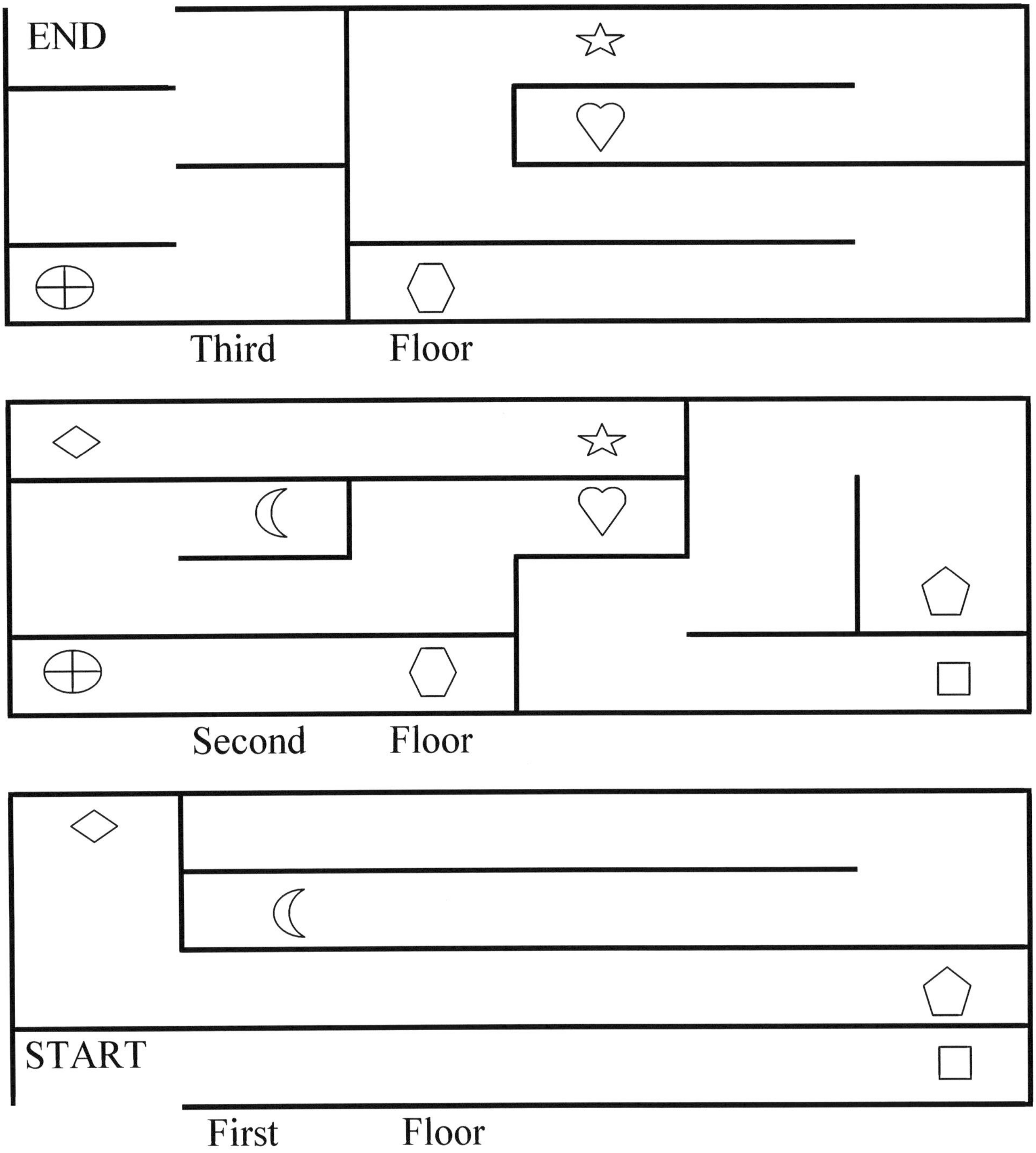

Third Floor

Second Floor

START

First Floor

(Answer = Yes.) A right angle is an angle with 90 degrees just like the corner of this page.

This maze has a Branch at the triangle △ on the second floor.
If you go down the wrong path, go back to this triangle.

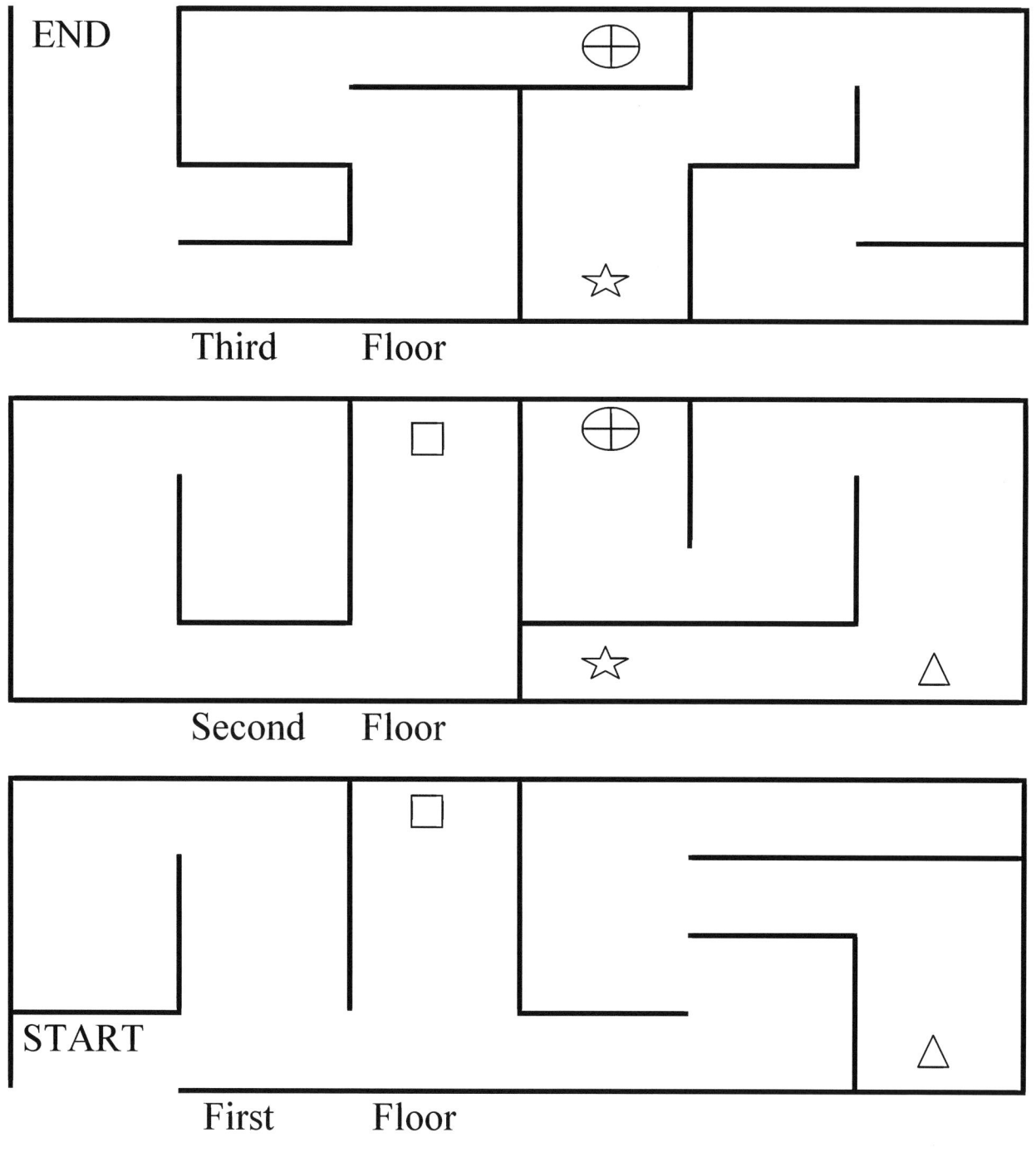

The angle at a vertex of a square is what type of angle?

This is harder. Can you do it?

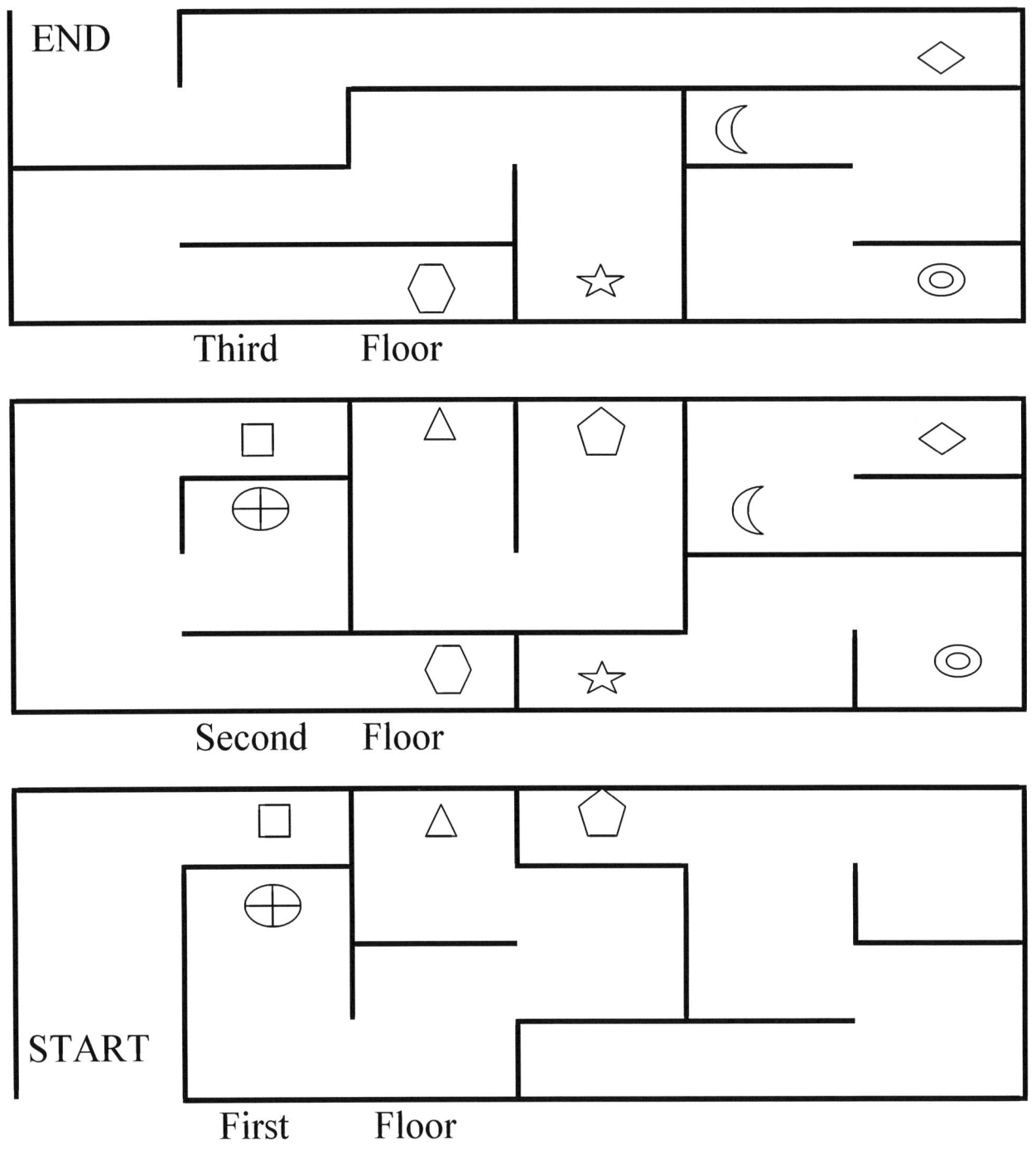

(Answer = a right angle) Are the angles of a diamond ◇ equal? Are they right angles?

Keep going from floor to floor, up and down the imaginary stairs.

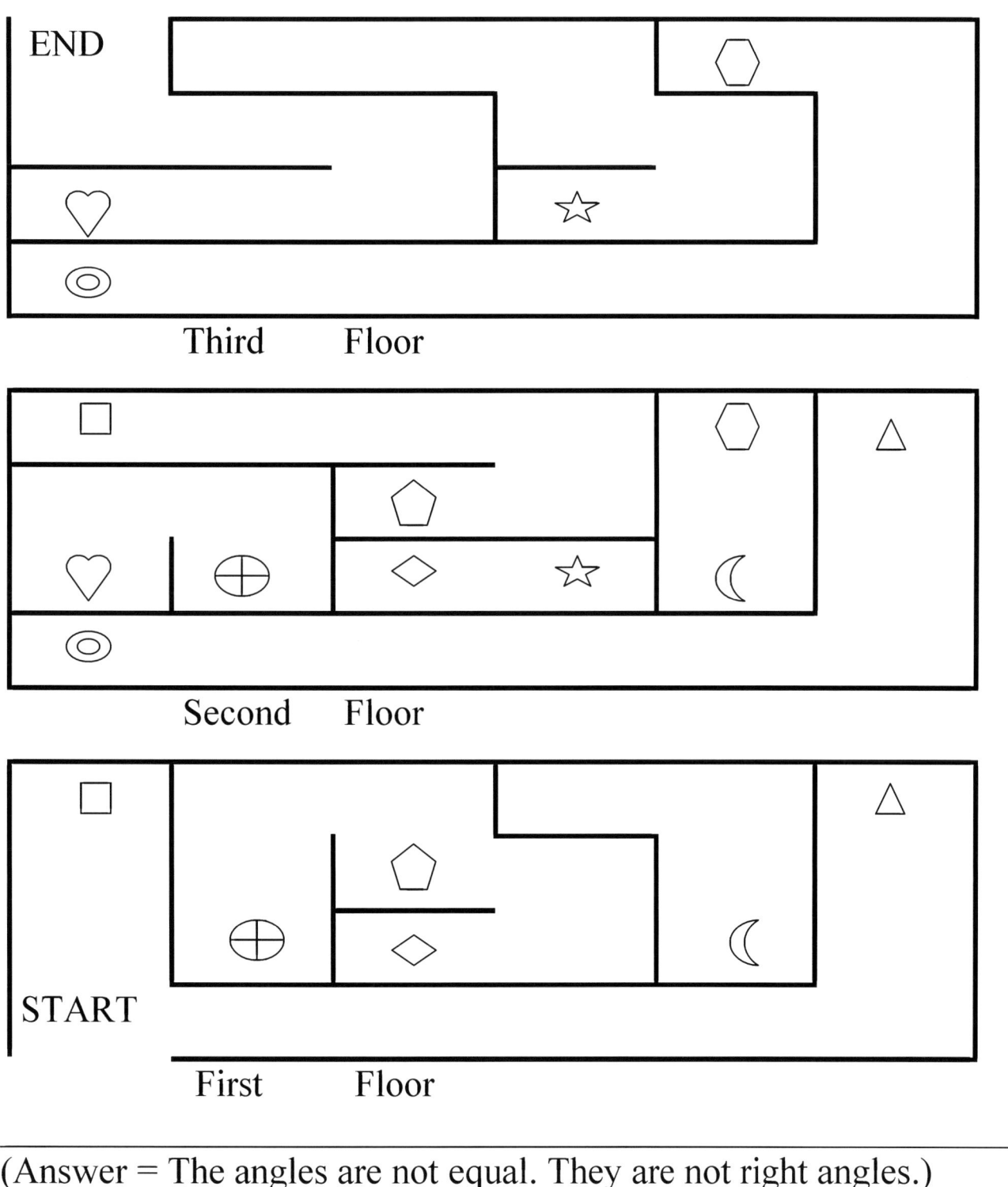

(Answer = The angles are not equal. They are not right angles.)
How many sides does a pentagon ⬠ have?

Can you draw your own 3 dimensional maze?

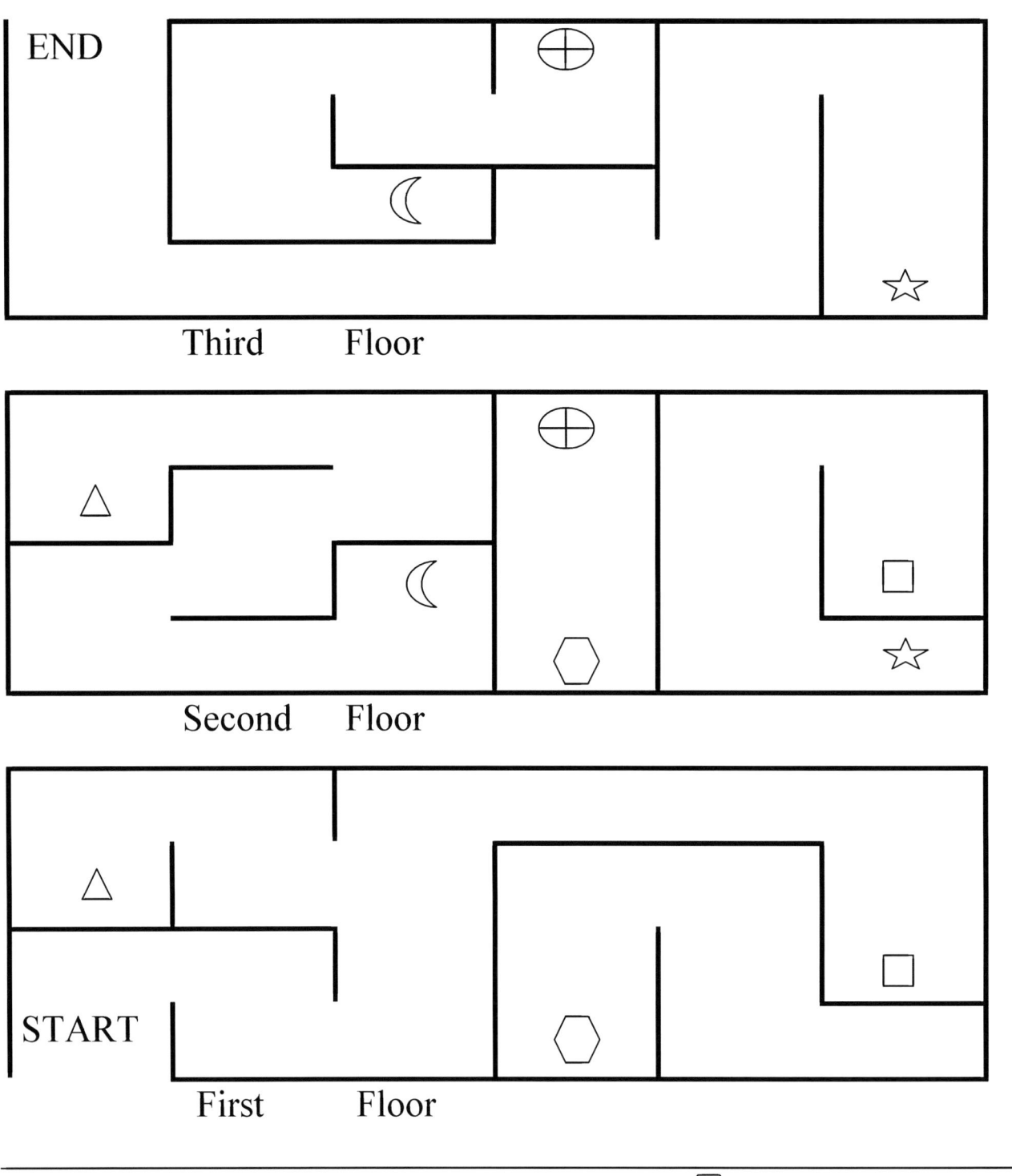

(Answer 5) How many sides does a hexagon ⬡ have?

Are you boxed ☐ in?

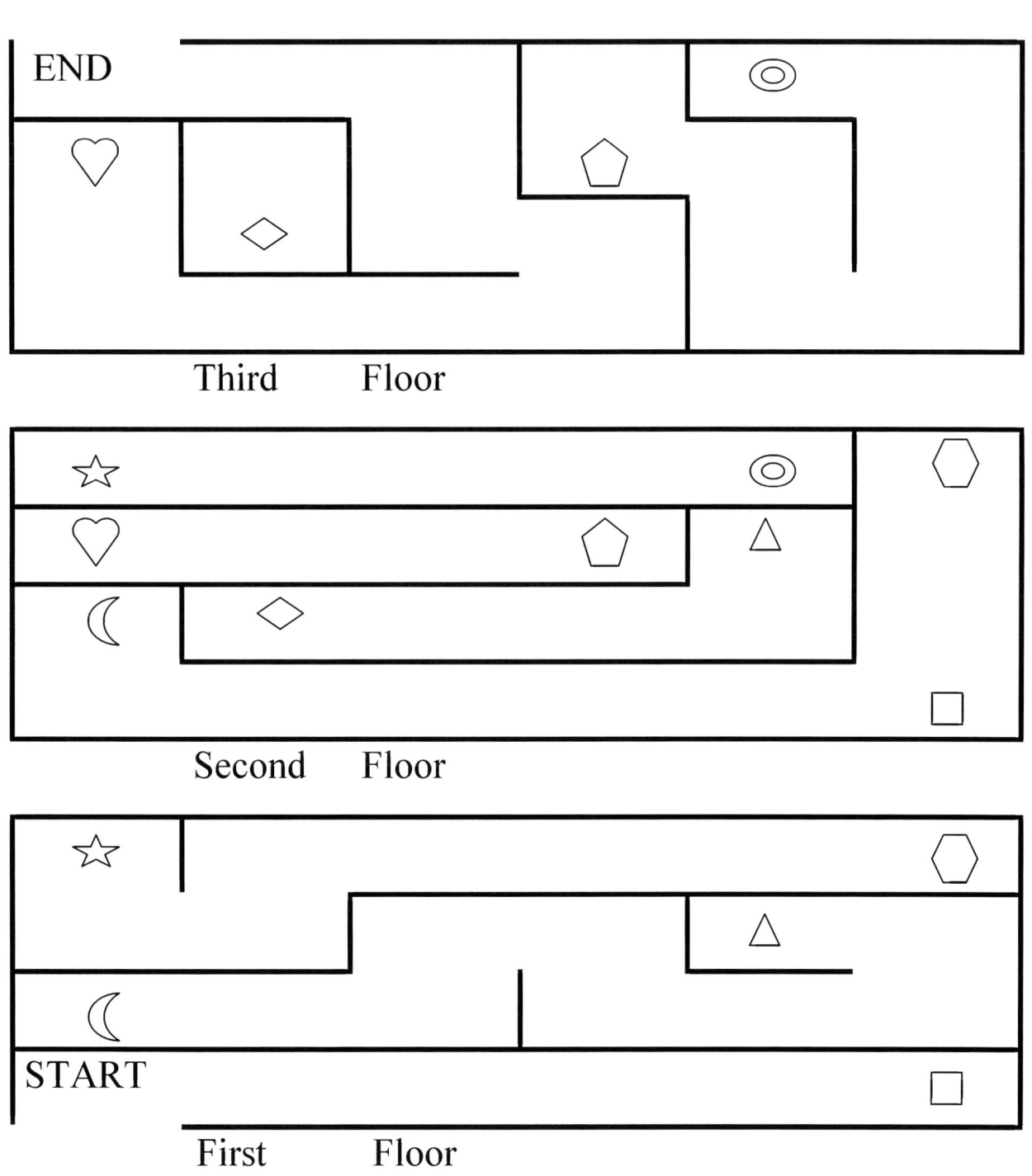

(Answer = 6) How many sides does a star ☆ have?
This is a decagon.

If you were a person walking in this maze which way would you go?

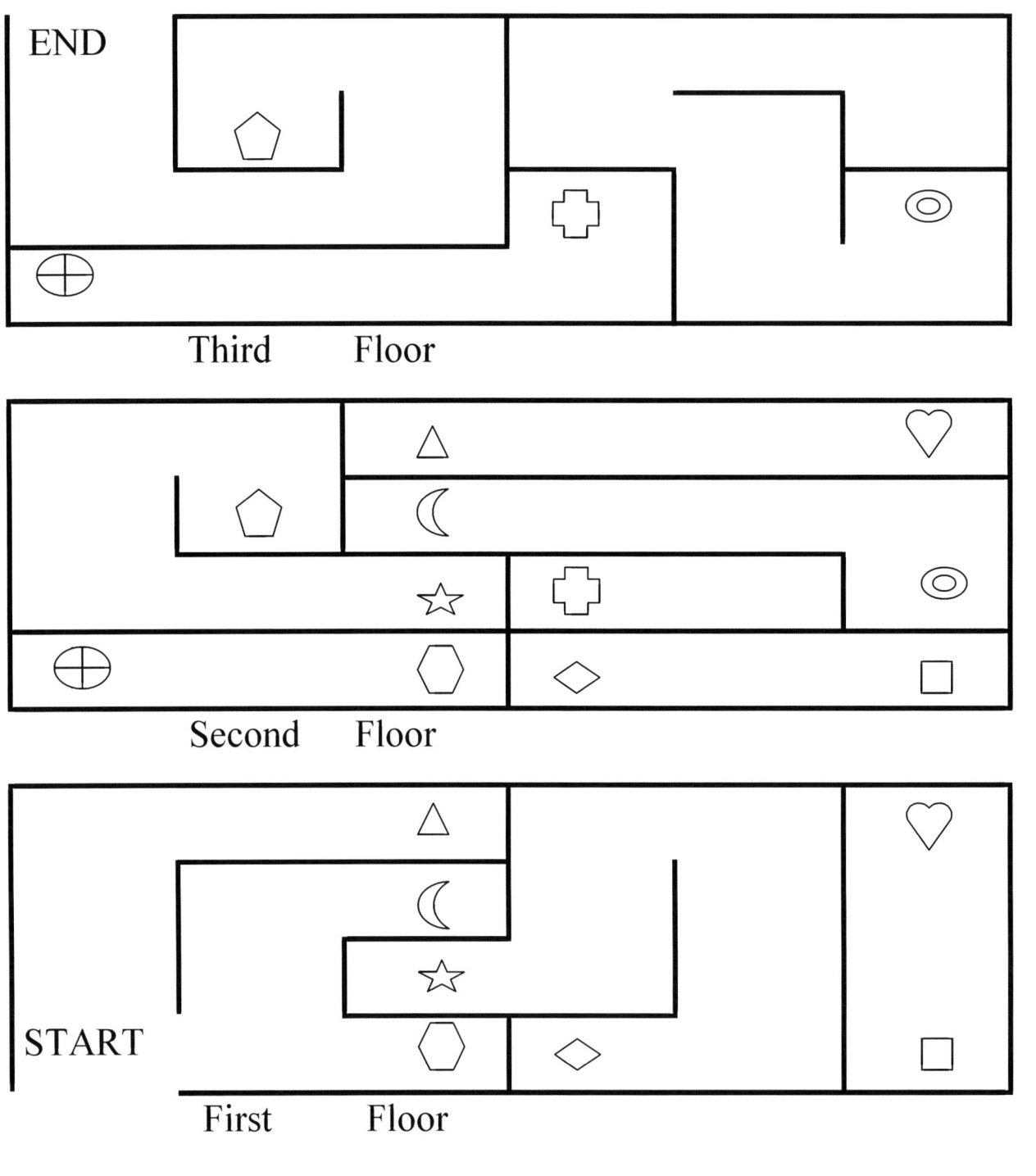

(Answer 10) How many sides does an octagon ⬡ have?

Lightning ⚡ strikes.

Third Floor (maze with END, shapes: ⚡, ✚, △, ◎, ⊕, ⬠)

Second Floor (maze with shapes: ⬡, □, △, ⊕, ⚡, ♡, ✚, ◇, ◎, ☾, ⬠, ☆)

First Floor (maze with START, shapes: ⬡, □, ♡, ◇, ☾, ☆)

(Answer = 8) Concentric circles ◎ are circles that have the same point in the middle or center.

Are you using a crayon or a red pencil? An expert can use ink. Some people just use their finger.

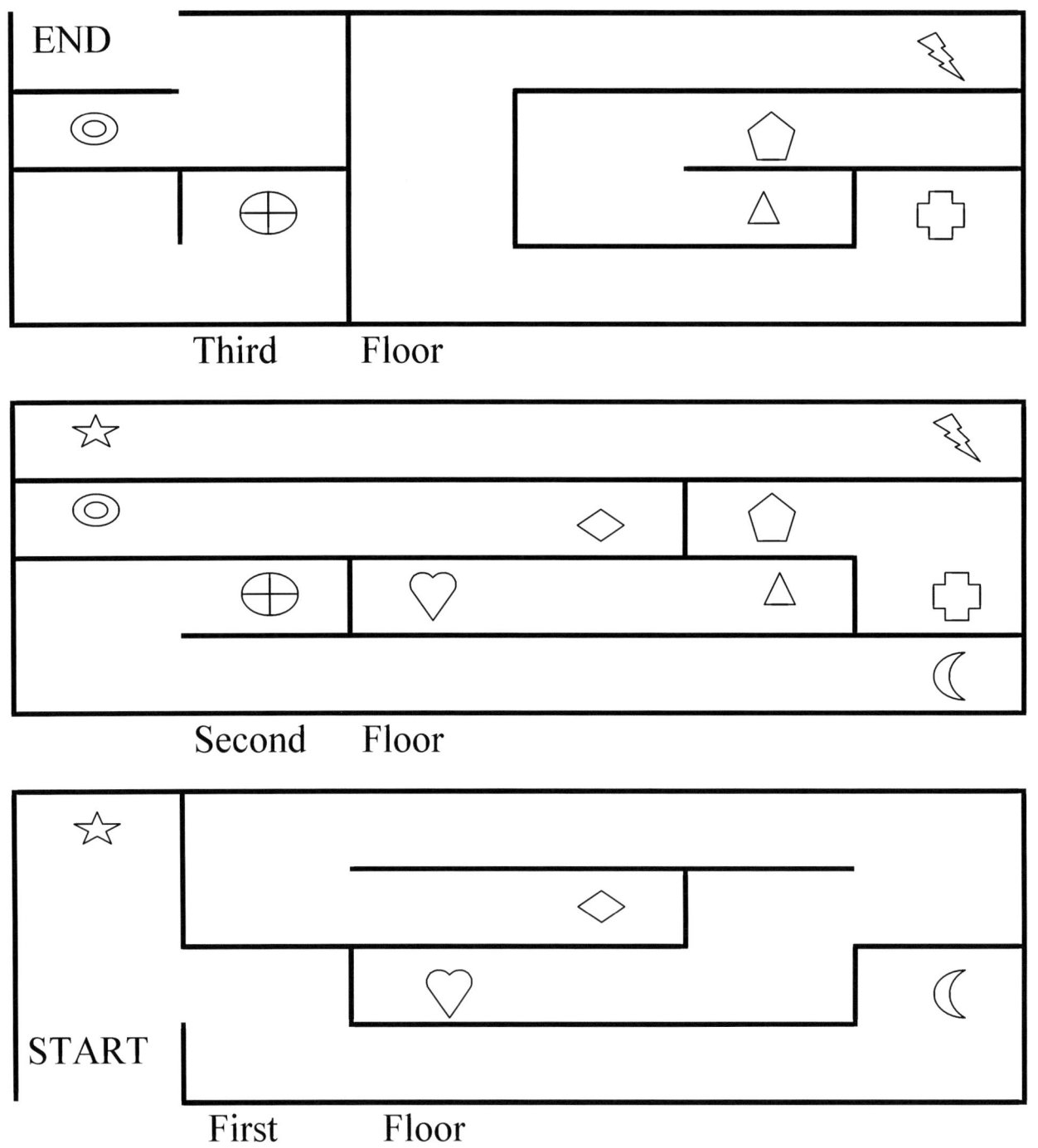

Can you draw 3 concentric circles?

Go fly a kite.

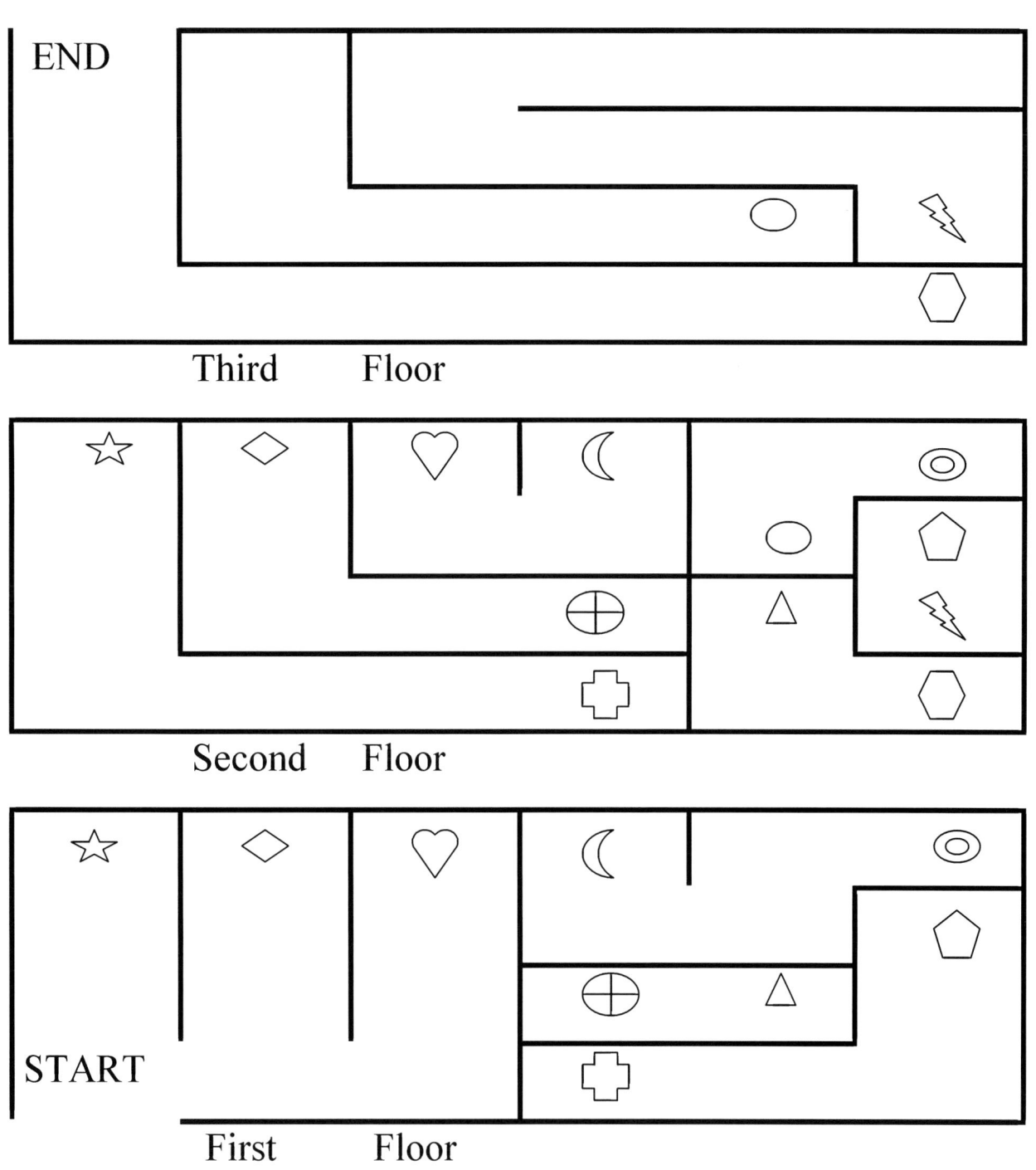

Can you draw a 12 sided figure? What is this called?

There are just a few more 6 by 4 by 3 mazes. Larger mazes are in later chapters.

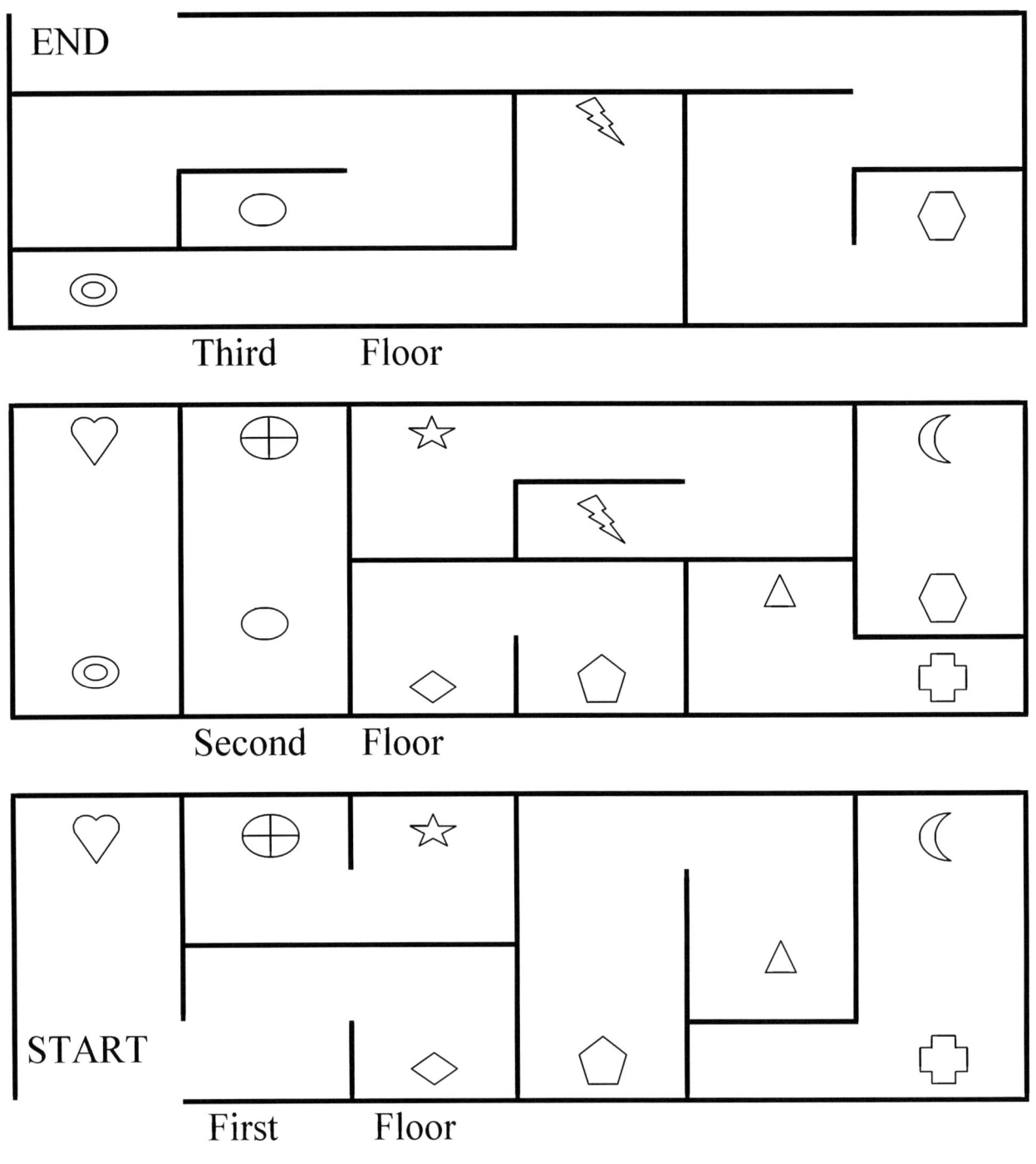

(Answer: a dodecagon) A line segment is the shortest distance between 2 points.

This maze is easier.

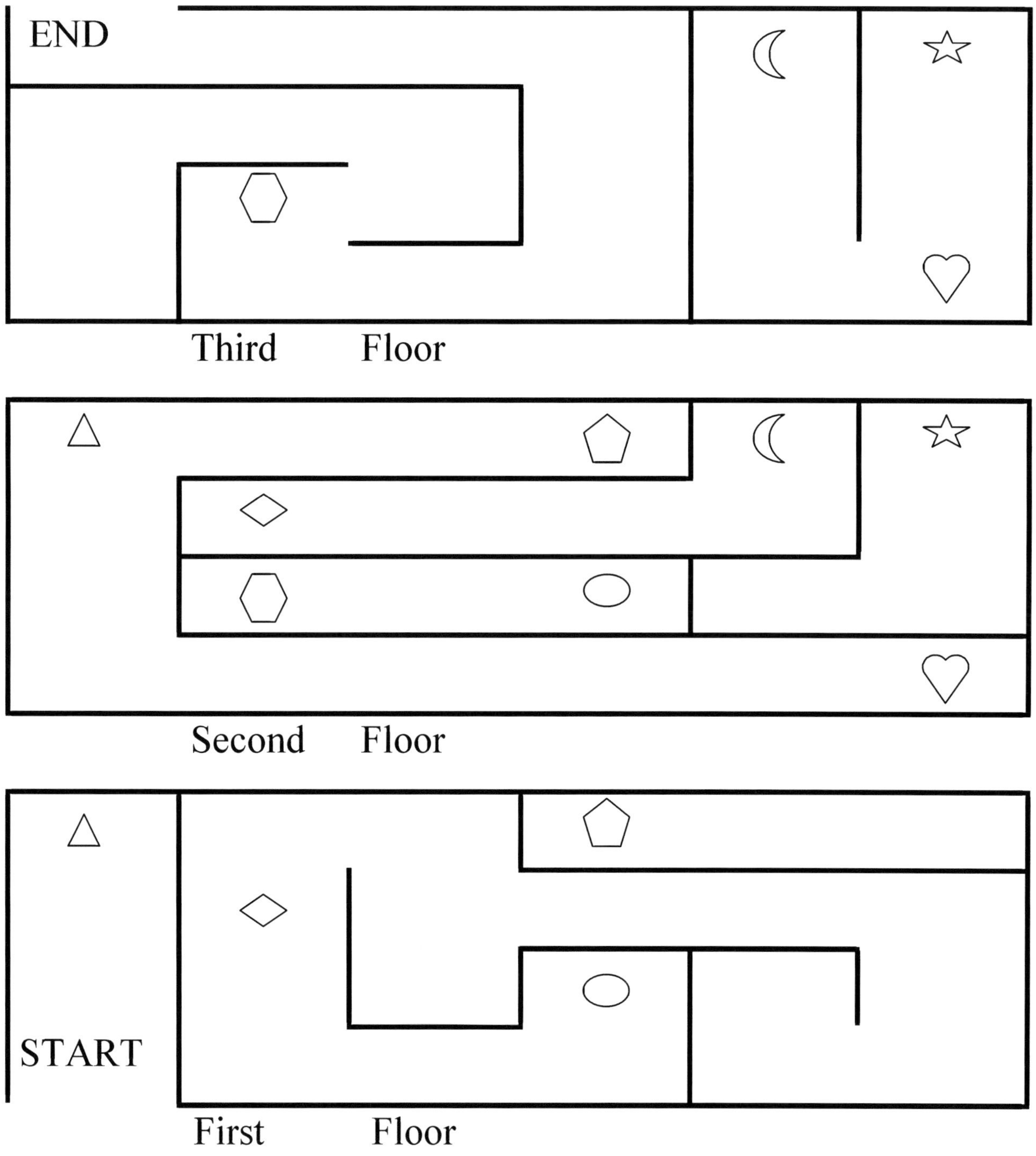
END
Third Floor
Second Floor
START
First Floor

A point is the intersection of 2 lines.

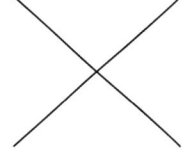

X ⊠   marks the spot.

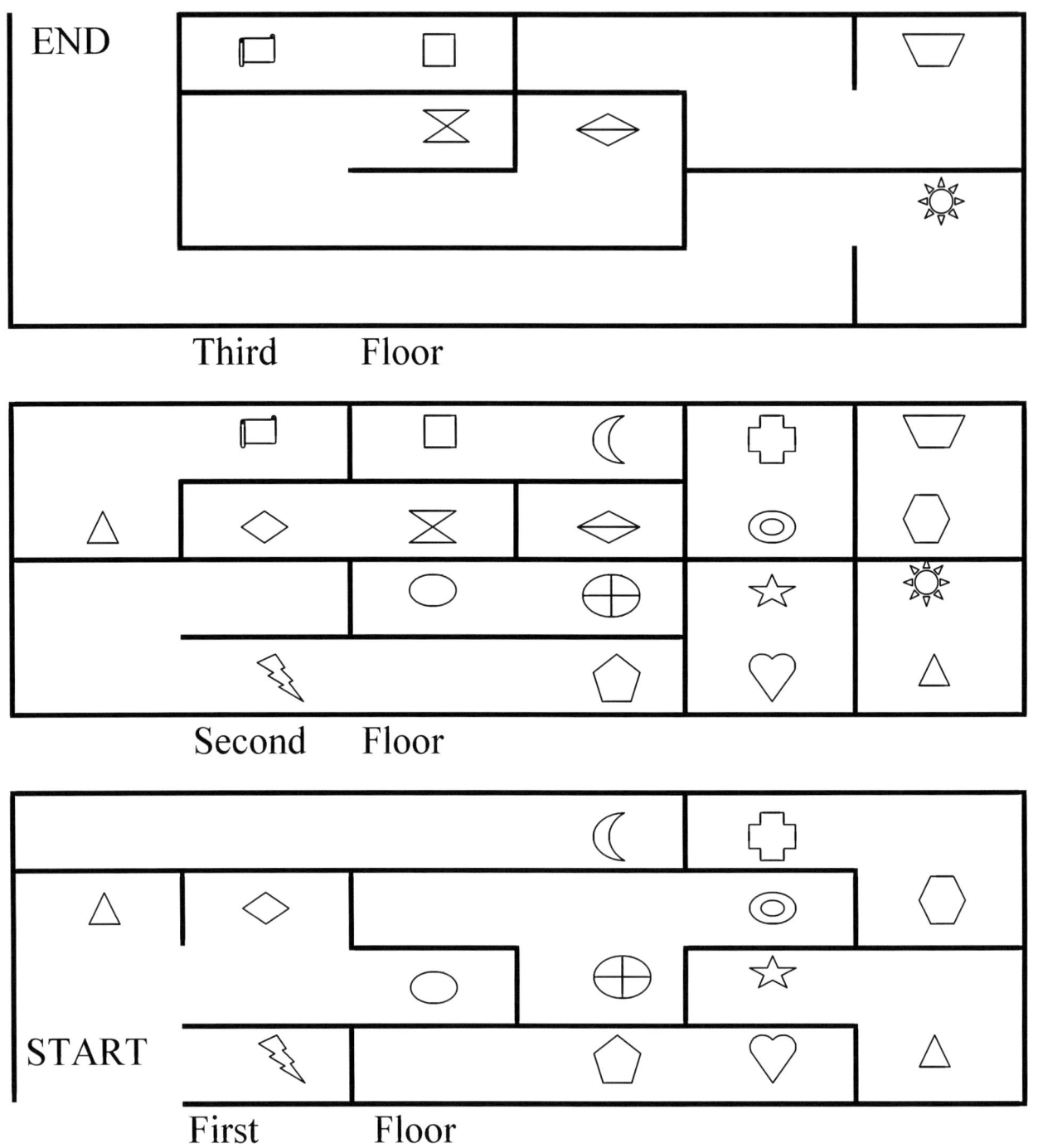

How many sides does a circle have? Buy the next book to find out.

Chapter 8   Subtraction Number Mazes

How do you subtract with a Number Line?
To Add you count up. (move to the right)
To Subract you count down. (move to the left)
For instance, on this Number Line

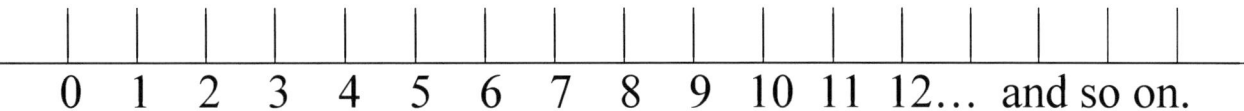

0 1 2 3 4 5 6 7 8 9 10 11 12… and so on.

to subtract 2 from 4 (or take away 2 from 4).
Count up (to the right) 4 from 0, then
Count down (to the left) 2 from 4.
Step up then step down.

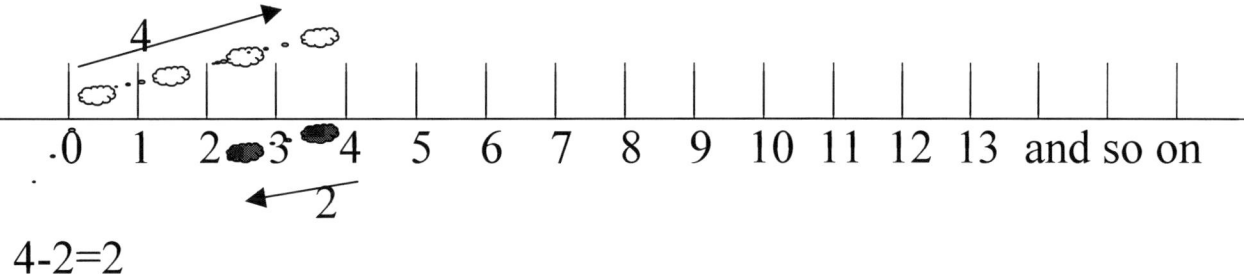

4-2=2

Using a pencil, try subtracting 4 from 7 by your self on the Number Line below.

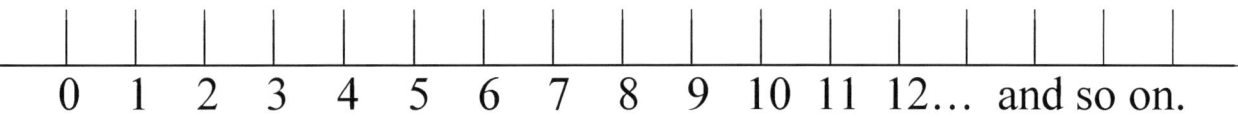

0 1 2 3 4 5 6 7 8 9 10 11 12… and so on.

Here is the solution:

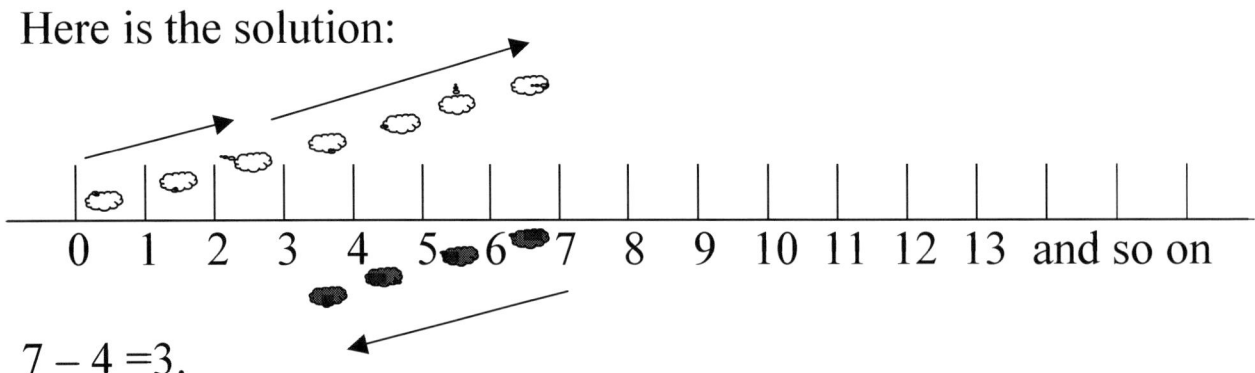

$7 - 4 = 3$.

In a Number Maze, you must subtract when a path goes by a number with a negative sign - . Try to use the Number Line above.

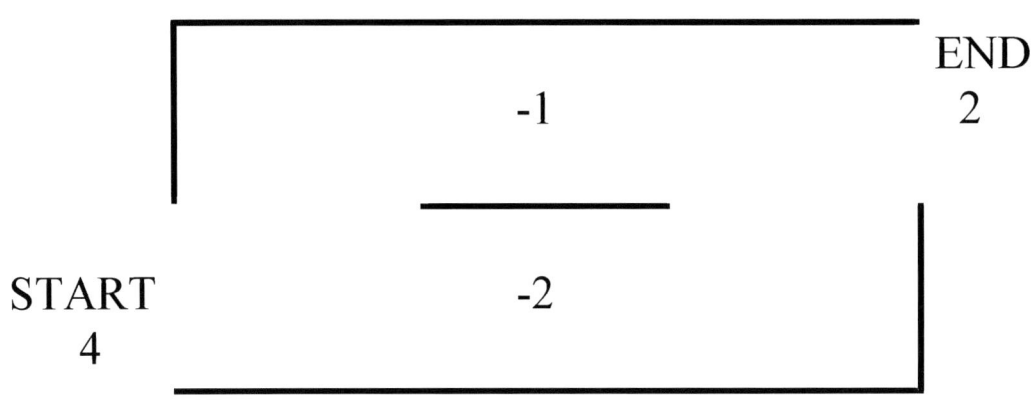

The top path from 4 at the Start to -1 to 2 at the End is wrong because $4 - 1 = 3$, not 2.

The bottom path from 4 to -2 to 2 is correct because $4 - 2 = 2$.

For a picture of the solution follow the arrows on the next page.

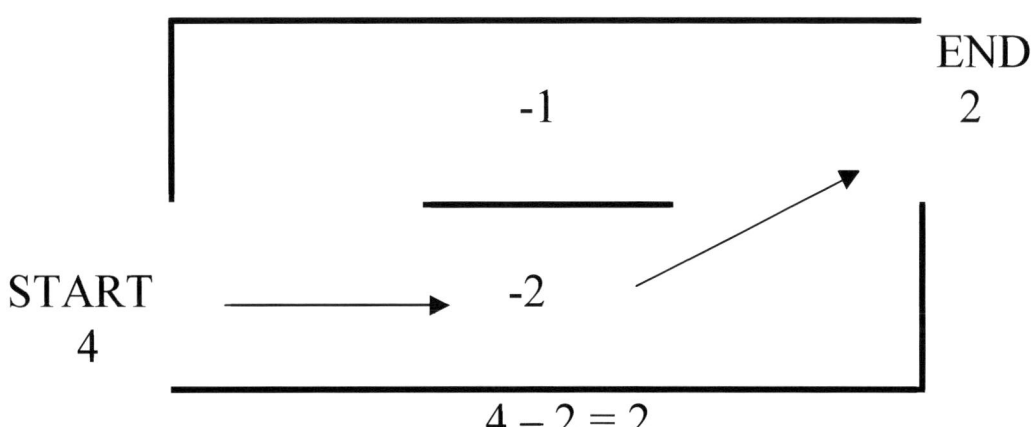

Now just change the END number from a 2 to a 3 and the path to the End changes.

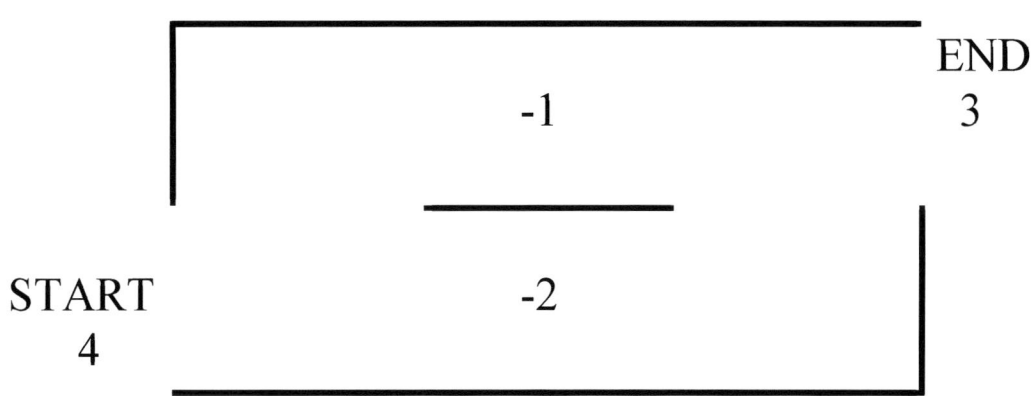

The solution is:

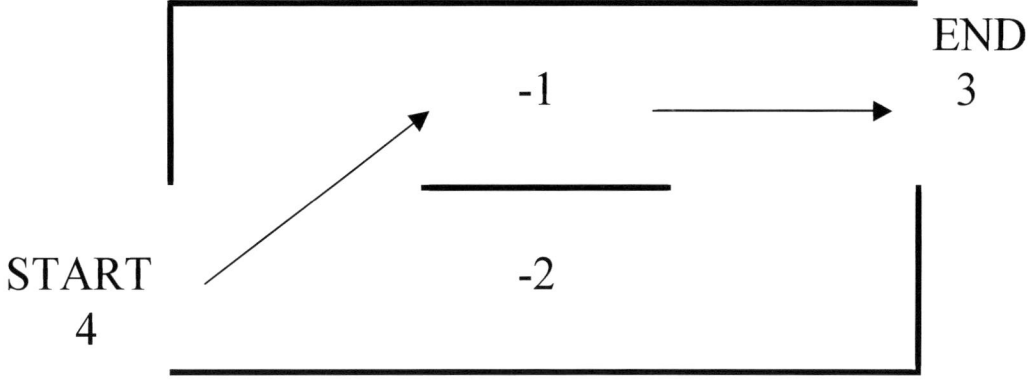

Take the upper path. 4 – 1 = 3.

What is more interesting: Number Mazes with subtraction or Number Mazes with addition.

Start at START. End at END.

```
              3            2         END
                                      3
START        -2           -1
  3
```

The solution is

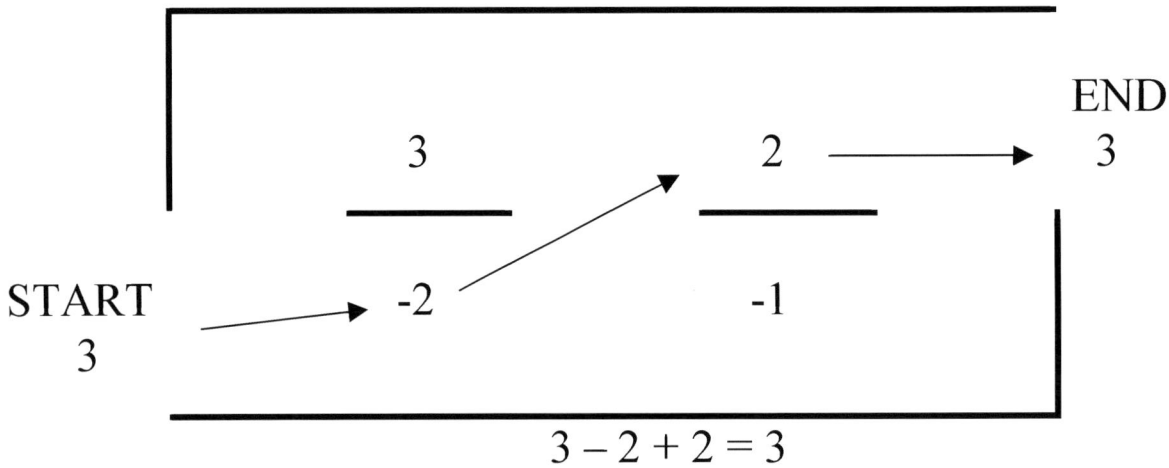

$3 - 2 + 2 = 3$

What is $2 - 2 = ?$
See the bottom of the next page for the answer.

Try

```
           ┌─────────────────────────────────────┐
           │    -2              2           END
           │    ───            ───            3
  START         -1              1
    4      │
           └─────────────────────────────────────┘
```

Or try

```
           ┌─────────────────────────────────────┐
           │    -1        2          4       END
           │    ───      ───        ───        5
  START         1        -2         -3
    2      │
           └─────────────────────────────────────┘
```

Or try

```
           ┌─────────────────────────────────────┐
           │    -2        3         -2       END
           │    ───      ───        ───        1
  START         -1        1          4
    4      │
           └─────────────────────────────────────┘
```

The answer is $2 - 2 = 0$.

The solutions to the Number Mazes on the last page are:

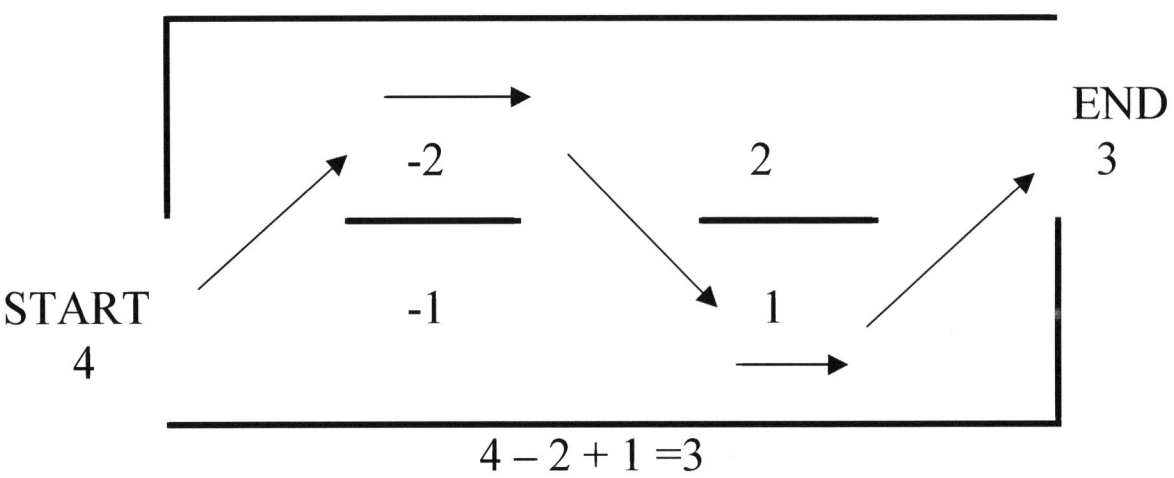

or

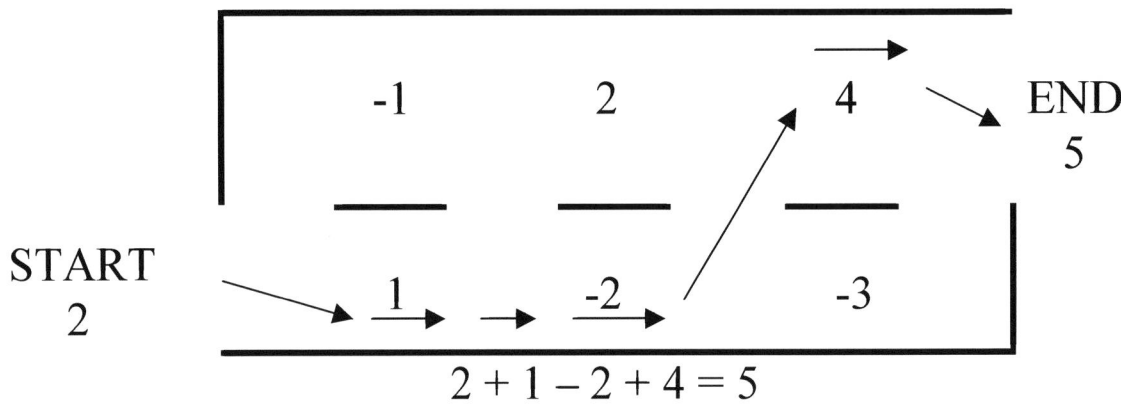

or

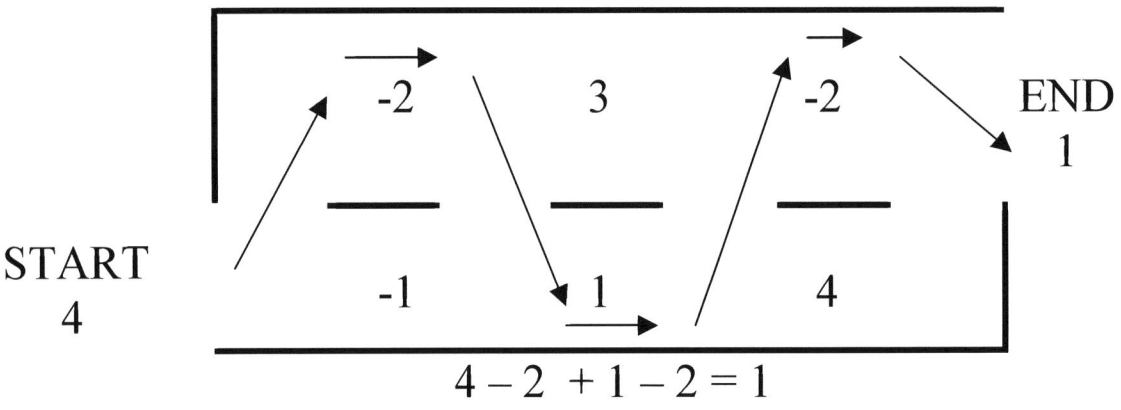

Here are the old shapes of Number Mazes but with subtraction.
Here, the End number is lower than the Start number.
For these Number Mazes, you do not have to use every number.

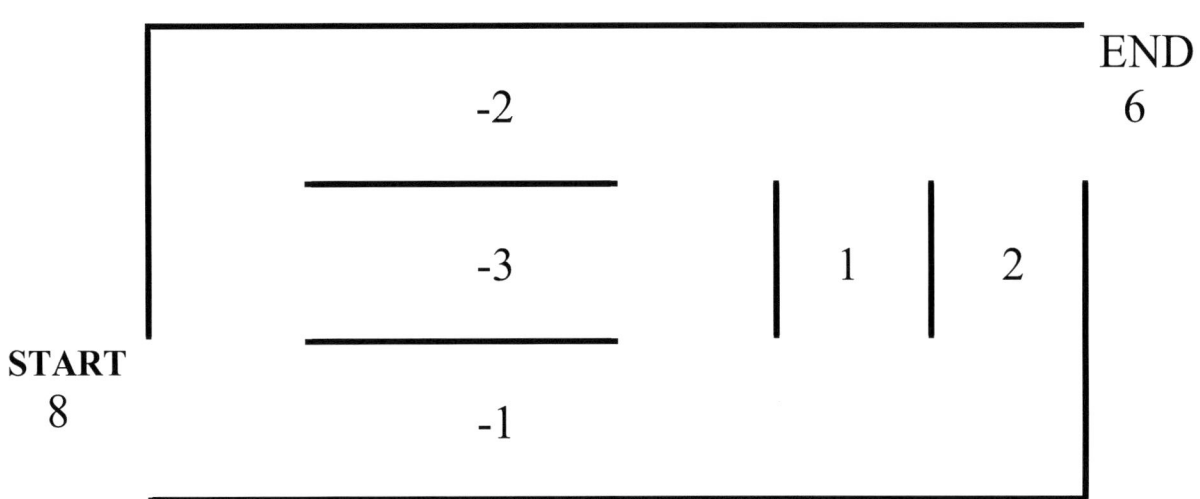

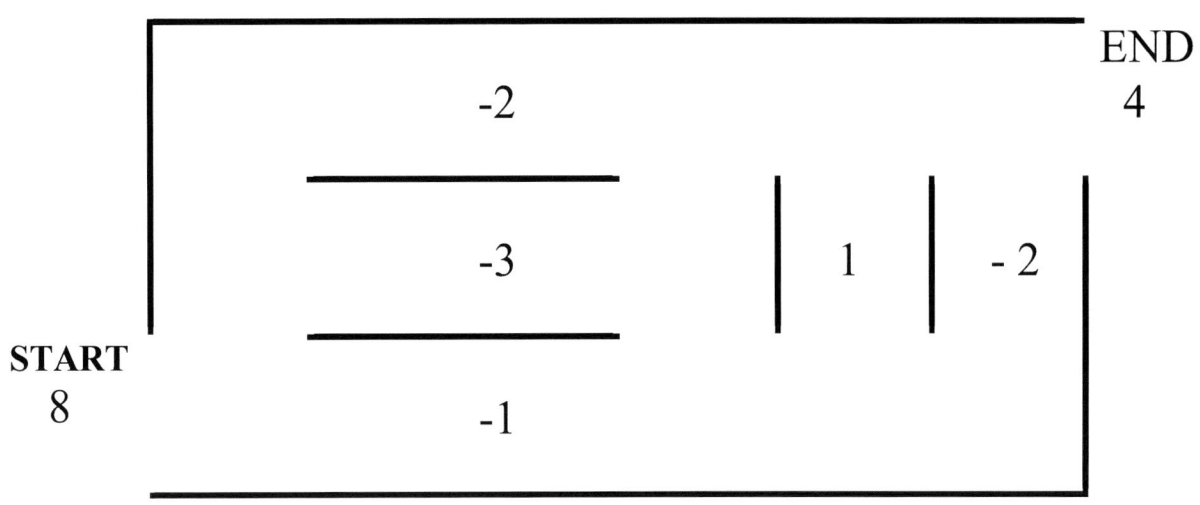

In these Number Mazes you need to use every number.

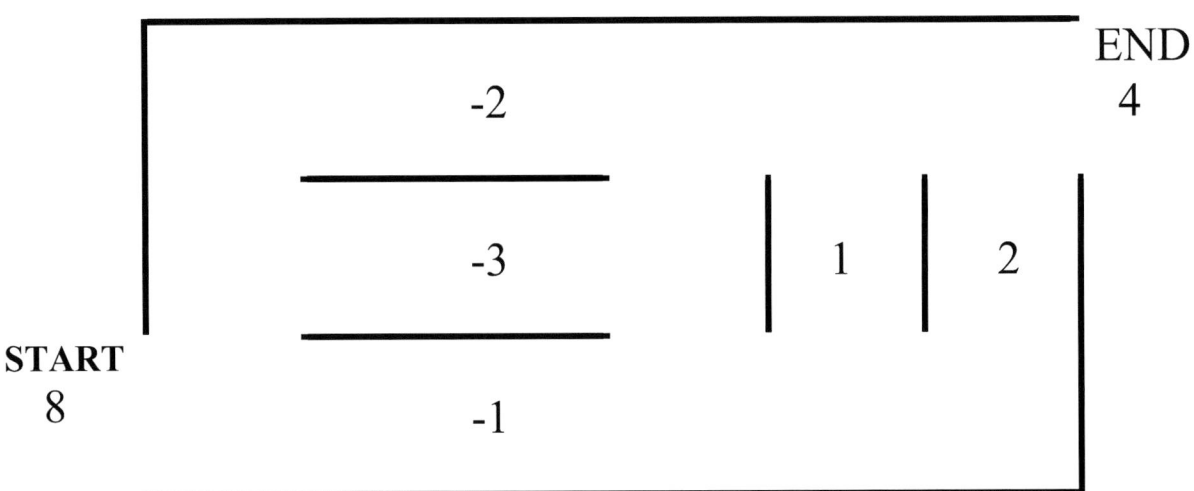

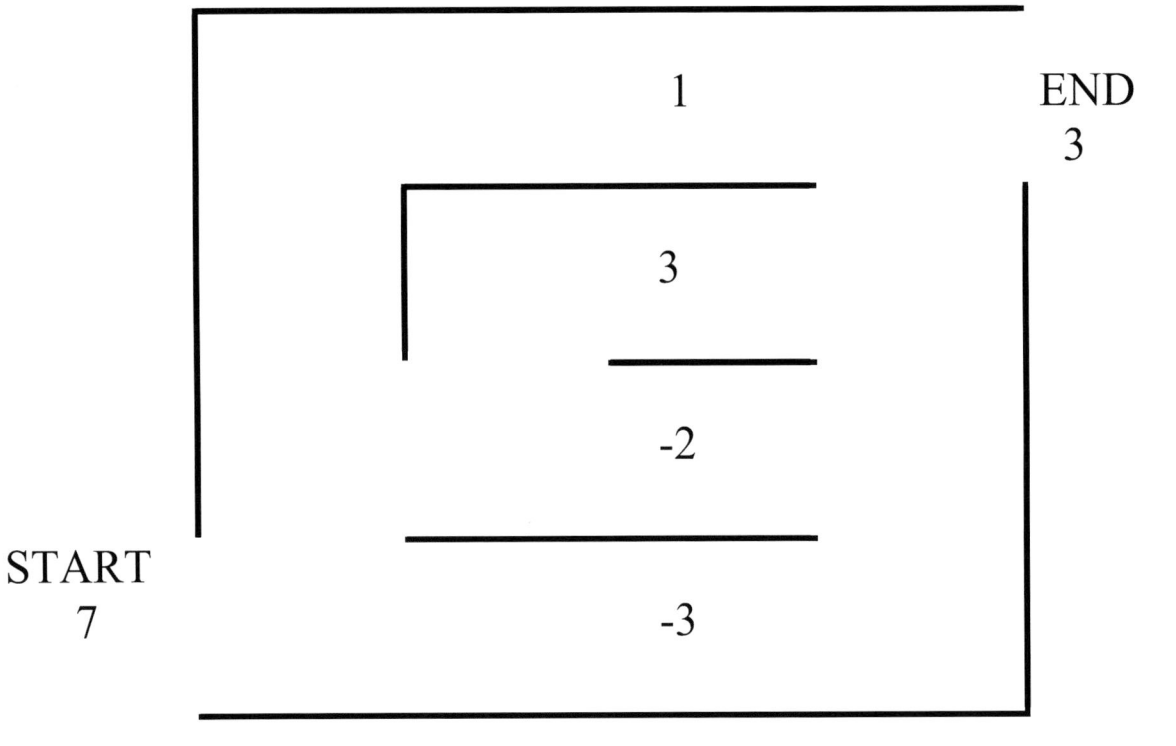

The solutions are on the next page.   Solutions ⟶

These are the solutions of the Number Mazes on the last page.

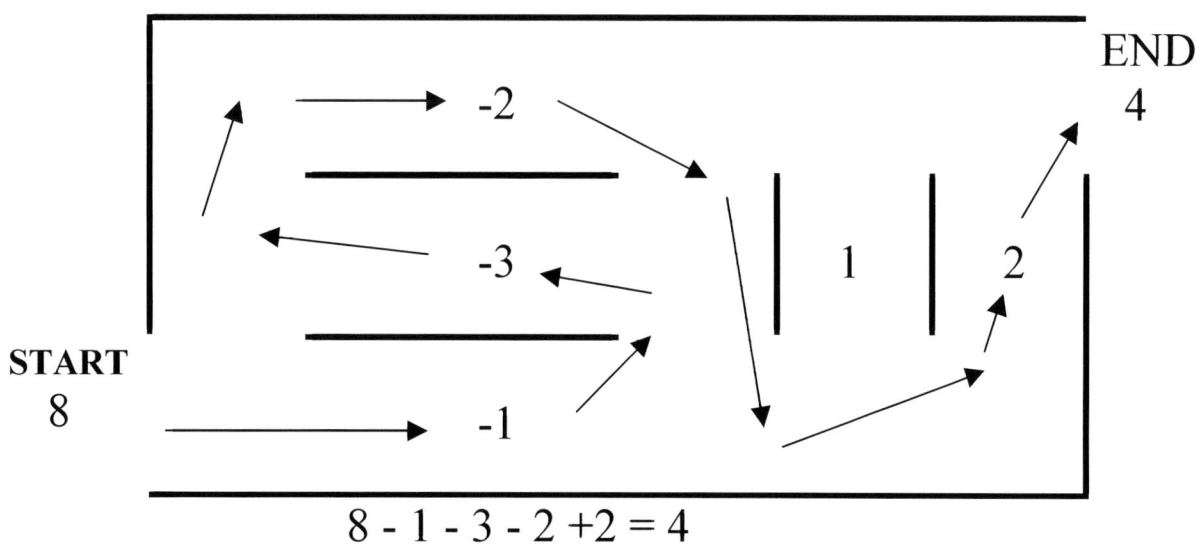

8 - 1 - 3 - 2 + 2 = 4

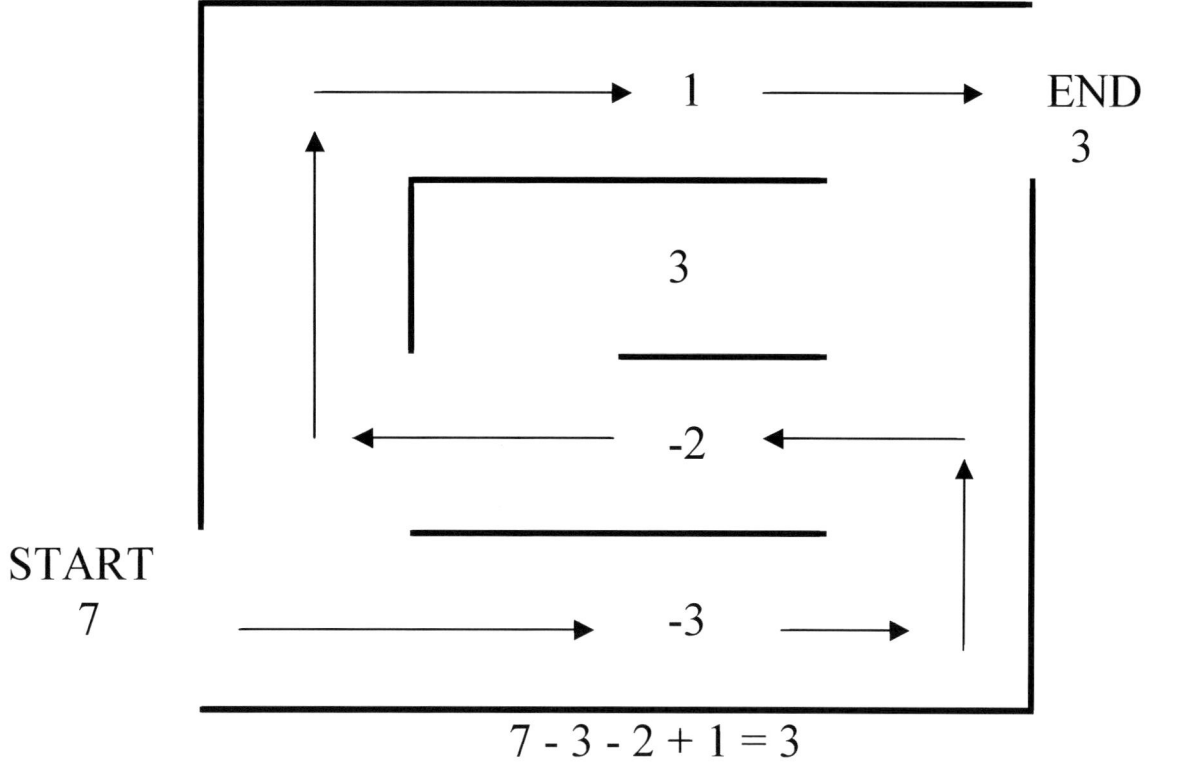

7 - 3 - 2 + 1 = 3

Make your own Subtraction Number maze. Use -1,-2,-3 etc.

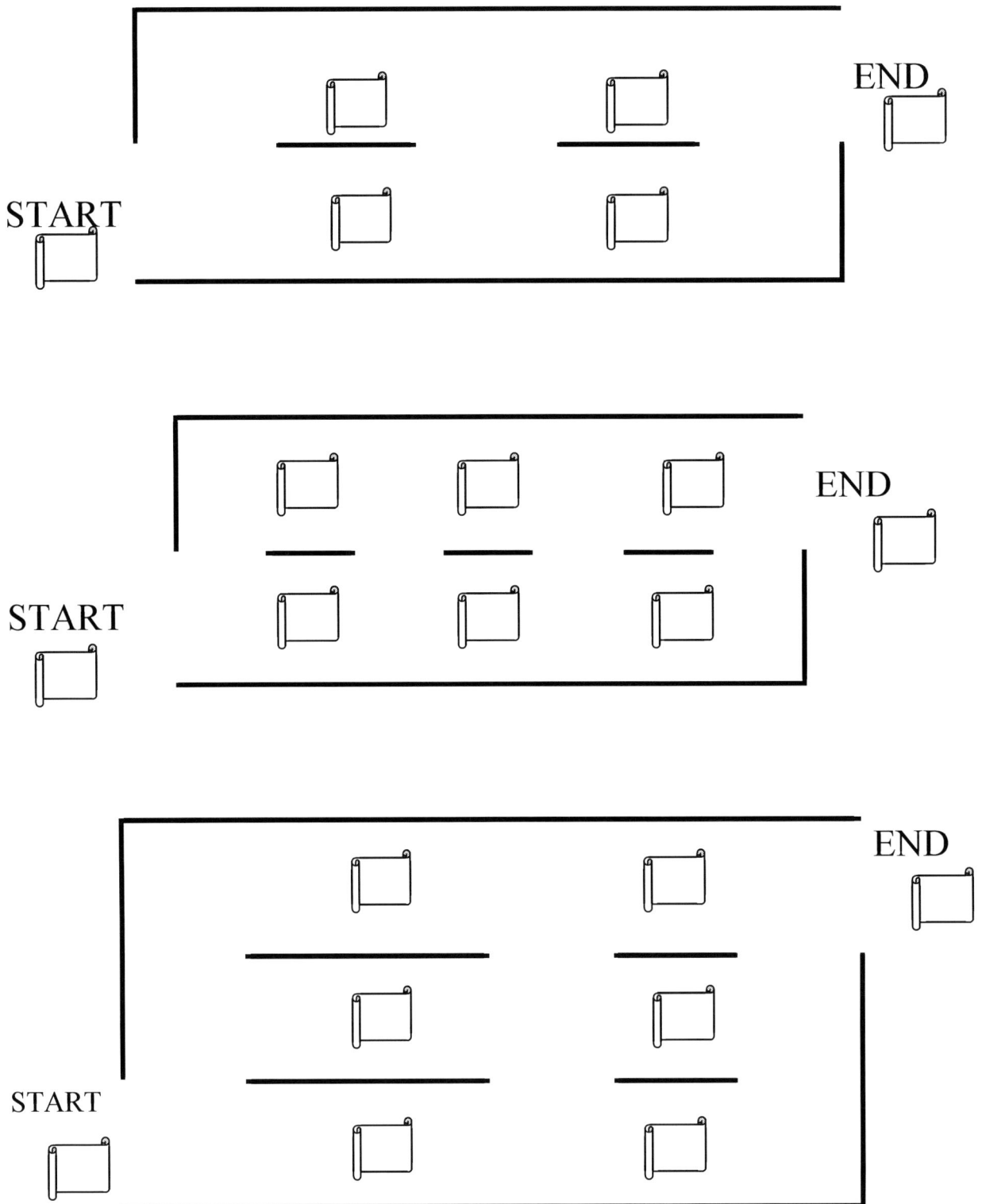

Chapter 9   4 by 4 by 4 Mazes

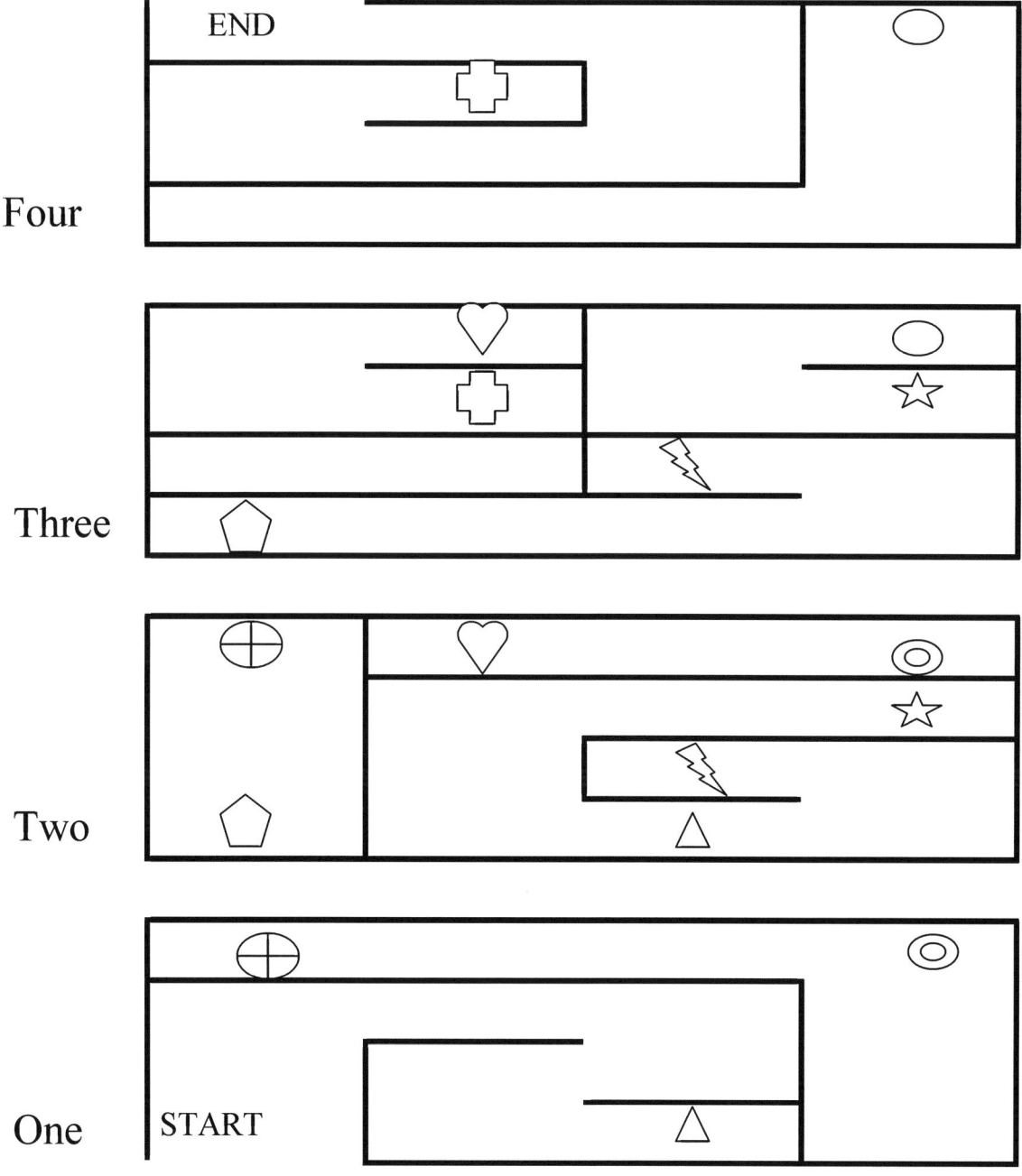

The number 432 means that this number is the sum of 4 hundreds, 3 tens and 2 ones. This is the system of numbers we are used to. It is called base 10. It is like a code. 432=400+30+2.

What does 635 mean? How many hundreds, tens and ones is this number the sum of? Answer: 6 hundreds, 3 tens, and 5 ones.

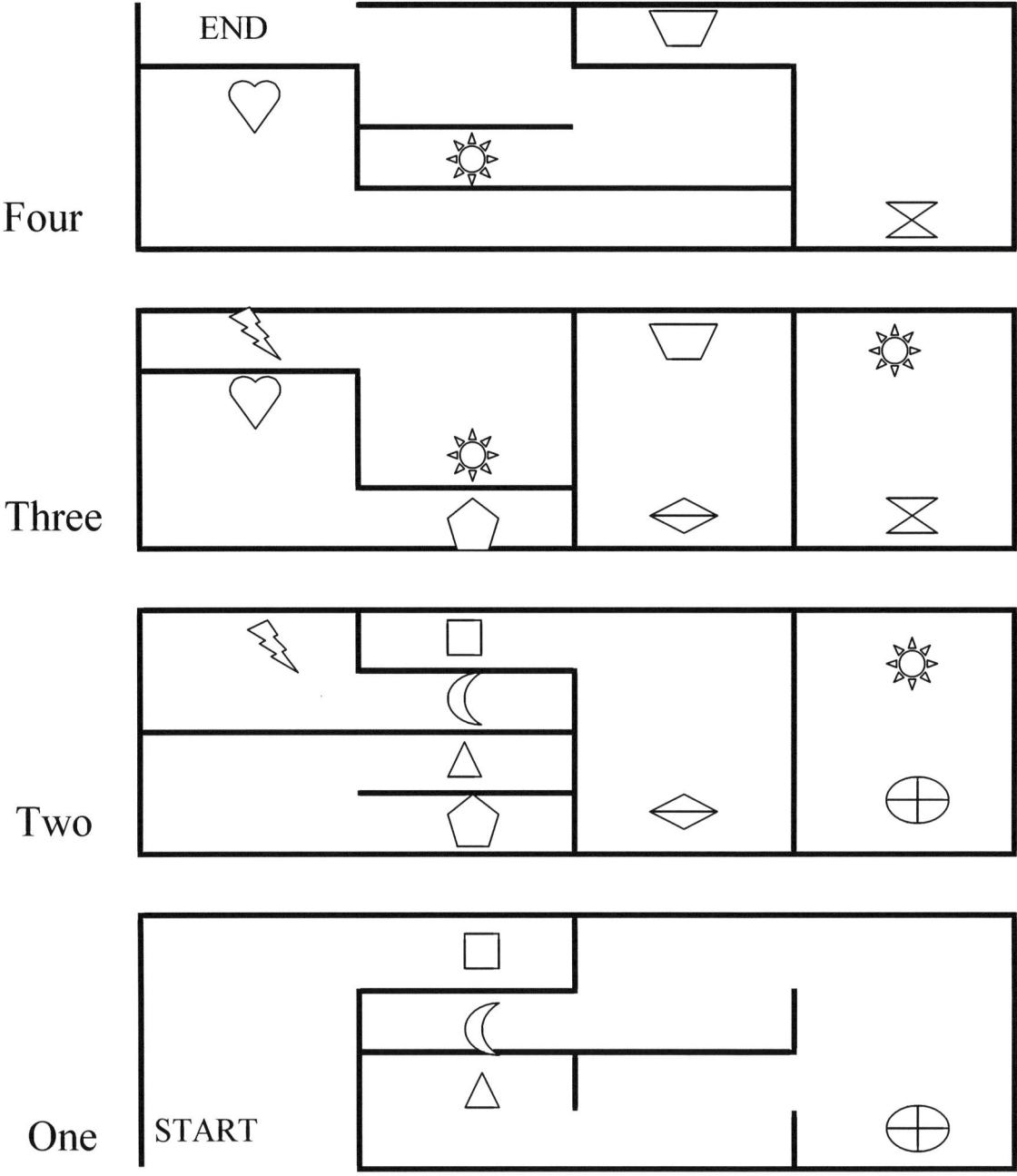

There are other codes. For instance, base 2 is another code used for computers. It consists of just zeros 0 and ones 1.
11001,11, 10011110 and so on.

In a computer, a 0 means a switch is open.
A 1 means a switch is closed.

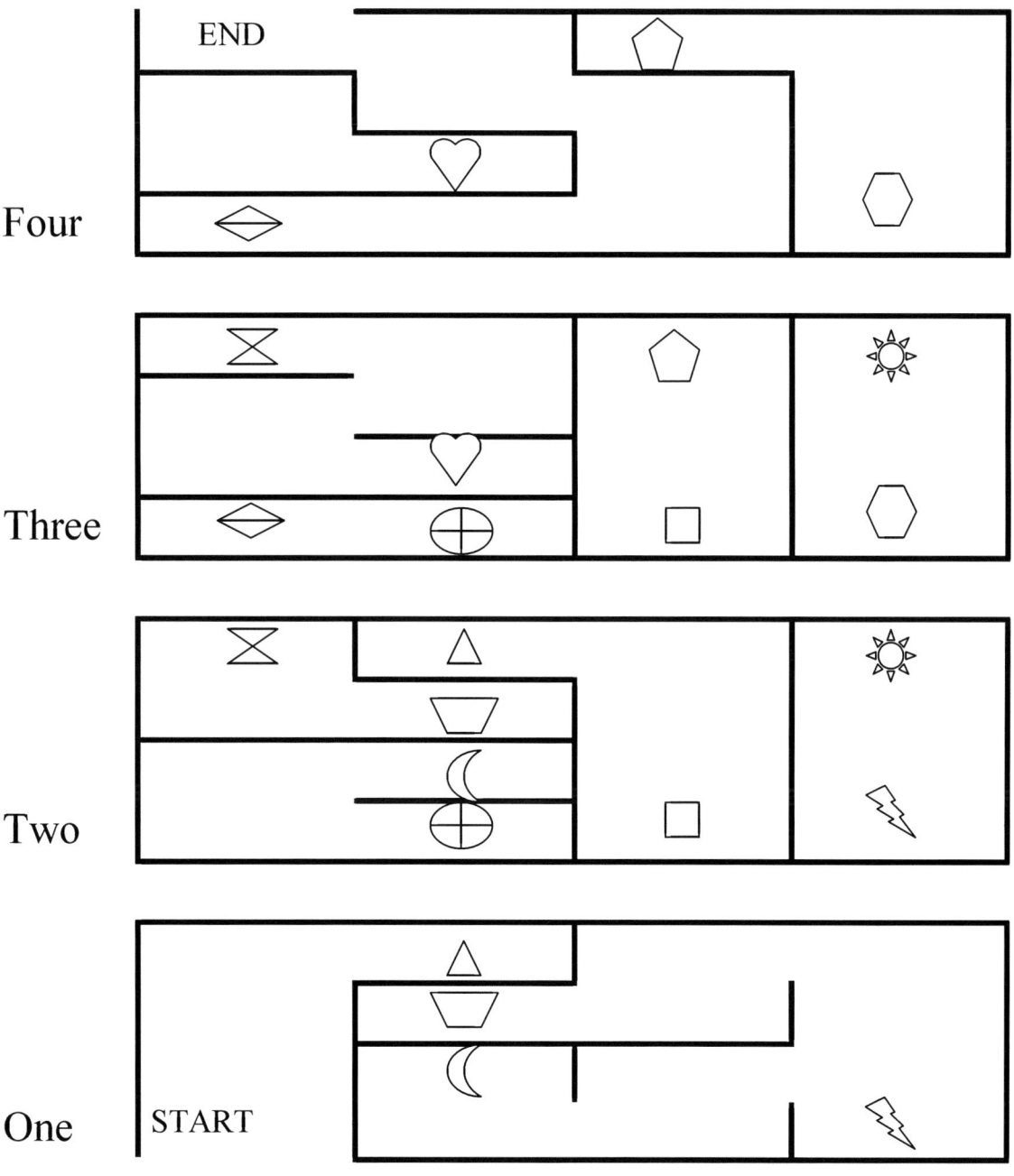

In base 10 where each digit in 346 tells us how many hundreds, tens and ones there are. Using base 2, each digit in 110 tells how many fours, twos and ones there are. Reading from right to left, 110 means 0 ones, 1 two and 1 four.

In base 10, the digits stand for the number of ones, tens, hundreds, thousands, ten thousands, hundred thousands, etc.

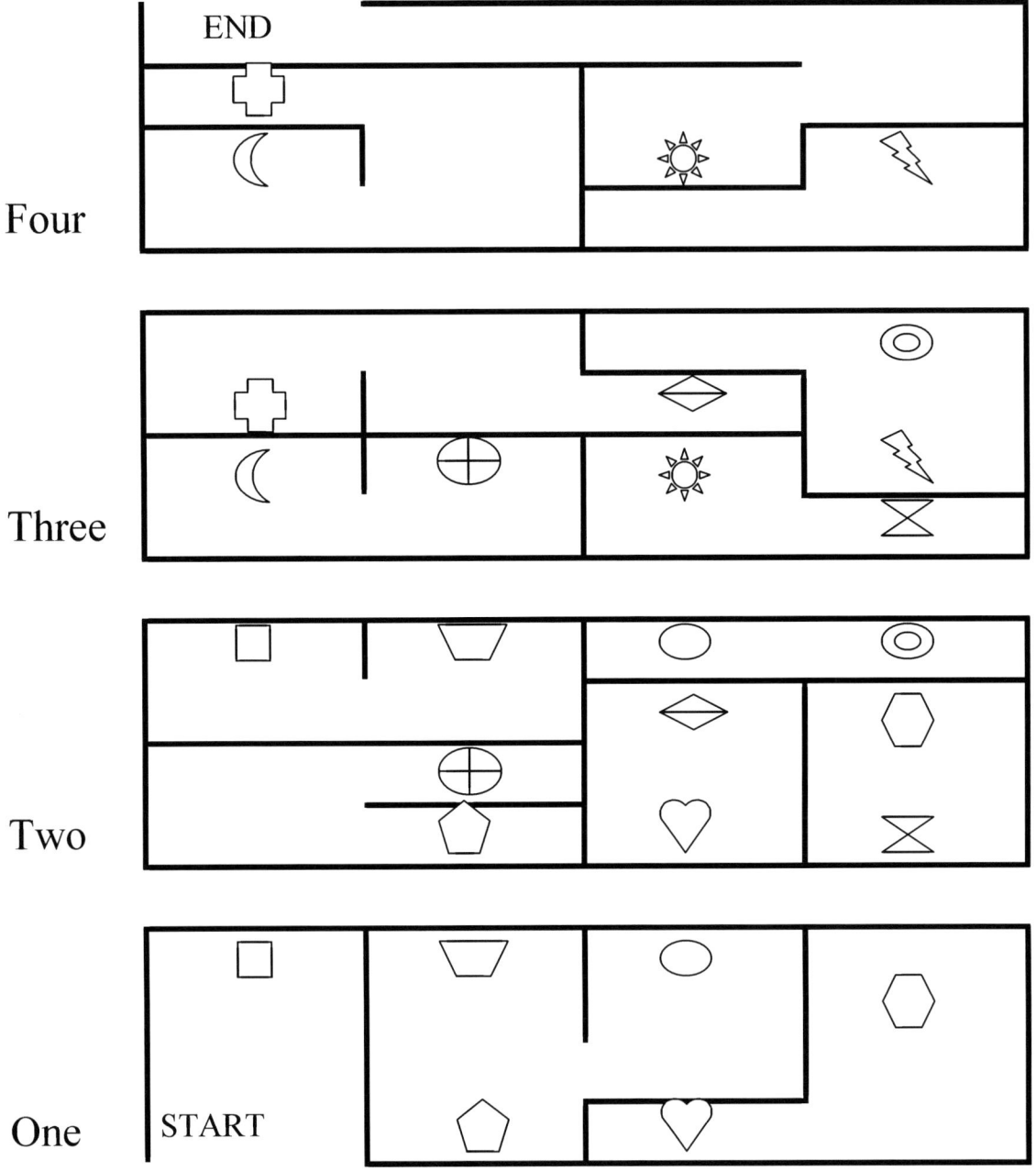

Four

Three

Two

One

In base 2, the digits stand for, (from right to left), ones, twos, fours, eights, sixteens, thirty-twos, sixty-fours, hundred and twenty-eights, two hundred and fifty-sixes, etc. Each digit stands for twice the digit to the right one. In base 10, each digit is 10 times the last.

Try counting in base 2, ….1, 10 (= 1 two +0 ones=2),
11 (=1 two +1 one=3) , 100 (=1 four + 0 twos + 0 ones =4).

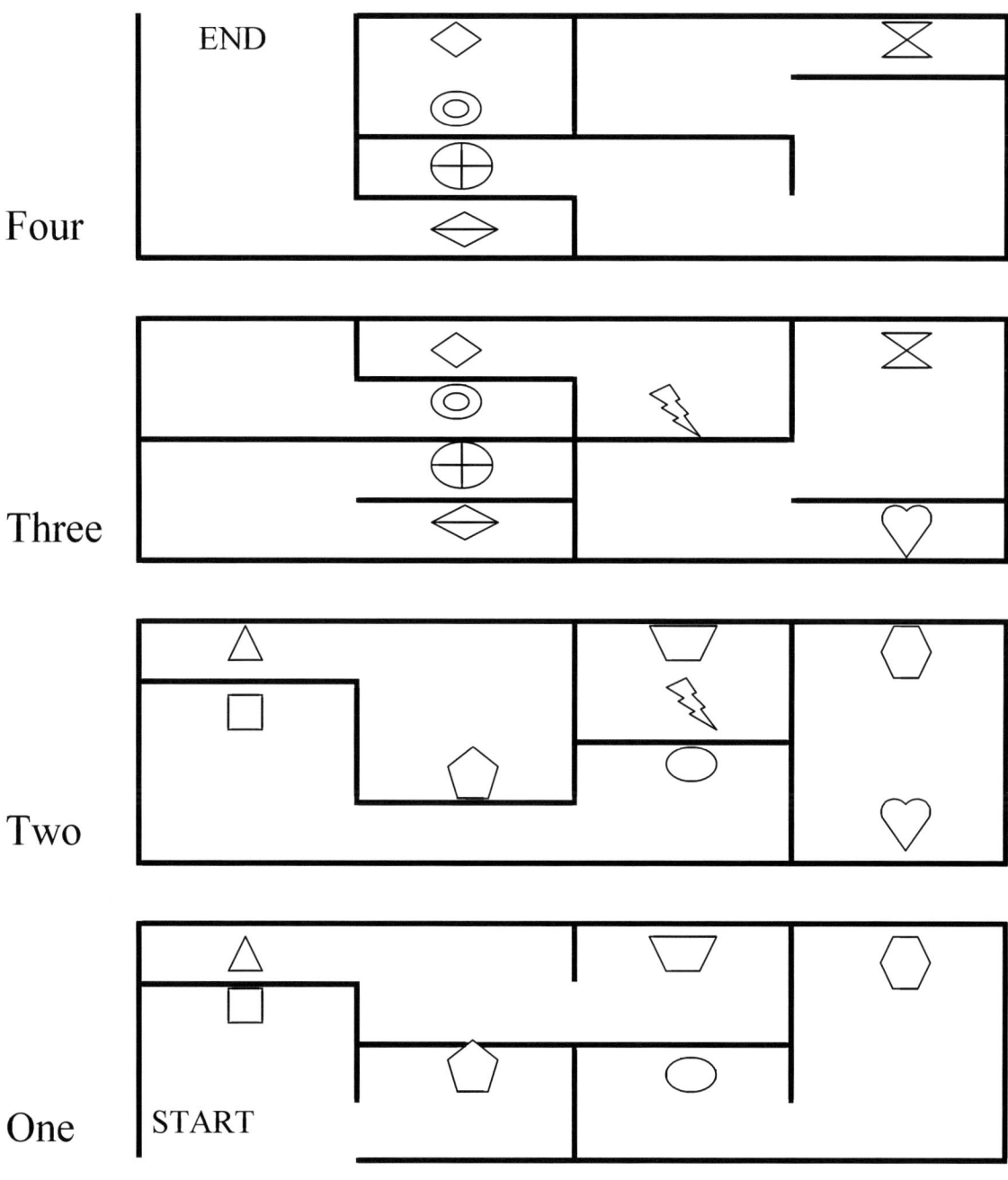

Four

Three

Two

One

In base 2, 101 means 1 four + 0 twos +1 one = 5.
In base 2, 110 means 1 four + 1 two + 0 ones = 6.
In base 2, 111 means 1 four + 1 two +1 one = 7.
What is next?

In base 2, 1000 means 1 eight + 0 fours + 0 twos + 0 ones = 8.
You do not use the numbers 2,3,4,5…. Just use 0 and 1.

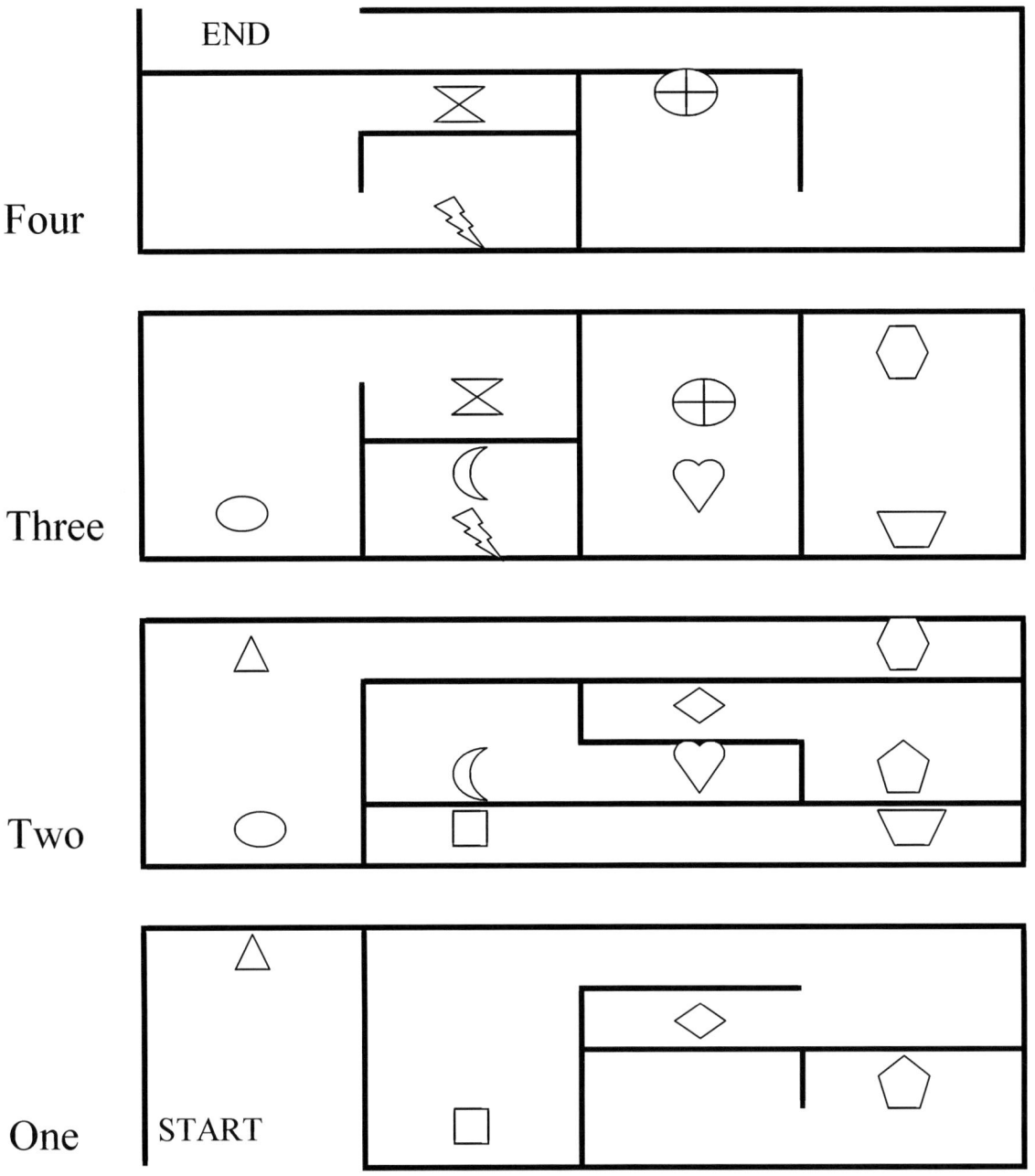

Then, in base 2, 1001 means 1 eight + 0 fours + 0 twos + 1 one = 9.
In base 2, 1010 means 1 eight + 0 fours + 1 two + 0 ones = 10.
In base 2, 1011 means 1 eight + 0 fours + 1 two + 1 one = 11.

1100 means 1 eight + 1 four + 0 twos + 0 ones = 10.
1101, then 1110, 1111 and

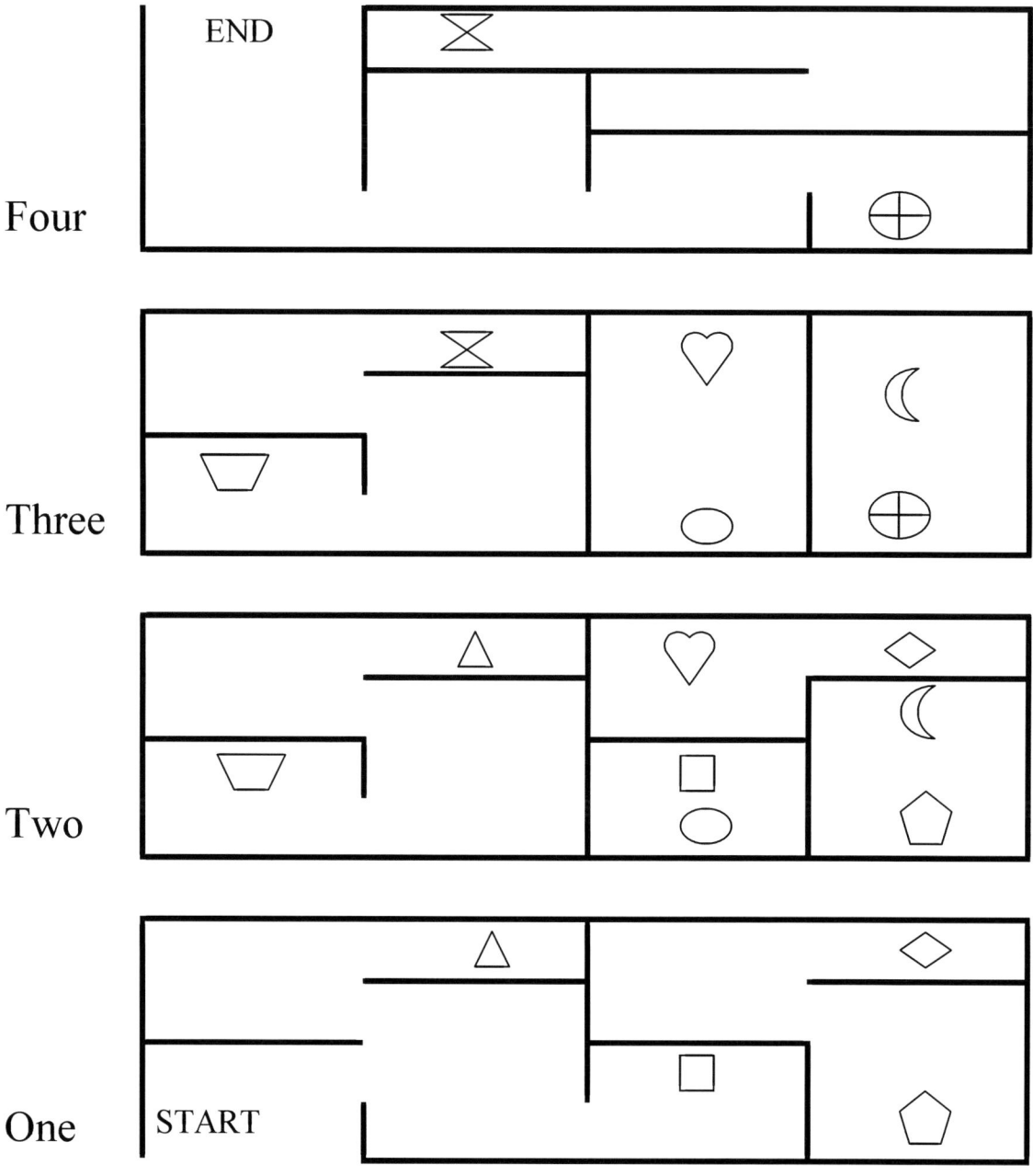

10000 (1 sixteen + 0 eights + 0 fours + 0 twos + 0 ones = 16).
Can you count to 20 in base 2?
Count to 32 in base 2 with your parents. See what they think.

Chapter 10   Negative Number Mazes

On the Number Line

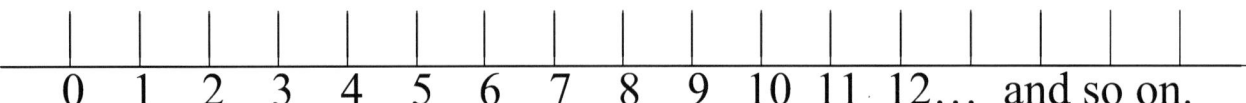

You can count up 1,2,3,4,5,... as high as you want, to infinity.

What happens if you count down 5,4,3,2,1,0,..., to the left of 0 on the Number Line?.
Do you run off the page?

To the left of 0 is –1, called negative 1, then
-2, called negative 2, then –3, then –4, and –5 and so on
to negative infinity. See the picture below.

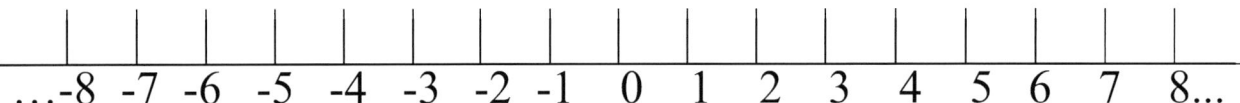

0 is in the middle.
And the number line goes forever in both directions.

Negative numbers are the numbers to the left of 0 on the number line, such as –4, -7, -10,-14 and –100, -1000, -1492, and -1,000,000.

Positive numbers are the numbers to the right of 0 on the number line, such as +4, +10,+100 which are written 4,10,100.

How do you add negative numbers?
5 + (-2) = ?

You count from 0 up 5 spaces to the first number positive 5.
Then count down (or to the left) 2 spaces because it is a negative 2.

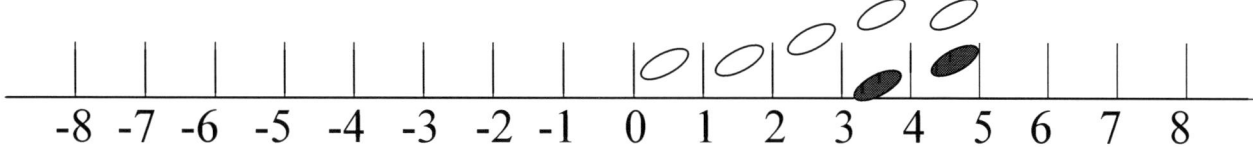

You land on the number 3. So 5 + (-2) = 3.

The next problem is trickier.
2 + (- 4) = ?

You count from 0 up 2 spaces to the first number positive 2,
Then count down 4 spaces (or to the left) because the second number is negative 4. What is the answer?

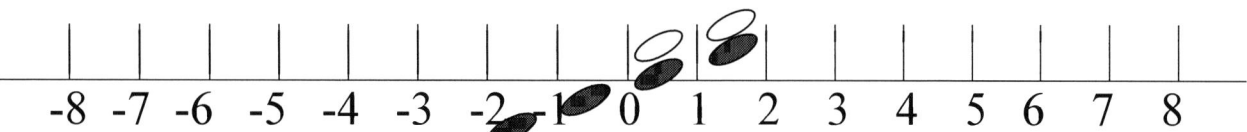

You land on the number -2. So 2 + (-4) = -2.
In this example, you counted back past 0 to -2.

What is 2 + (-3) = ?
What is 2 + (-5) = ?   Answers: -1 and -3.

What are (-4) + 2 = ? and (-4) +(-2) = ?

For the first you go to (-4) on the number line by counting down 4 spaces from 0. Then you count up 2 spaces from (-4) to (-2).

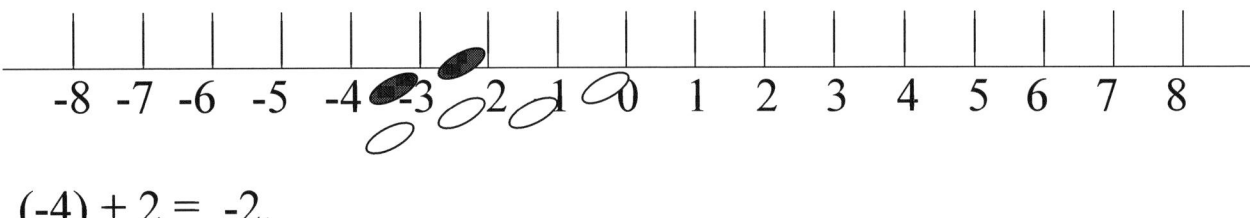

(-4) + 2 = -2.

For the second (-4) + (-2) = you go to (-4) again on the Number Line by counting 4 spaces down from 0 to -4. Then you count down 2 more spaces from (-4) to (-6). You count down or to the left of 0 because (-2) is negative.

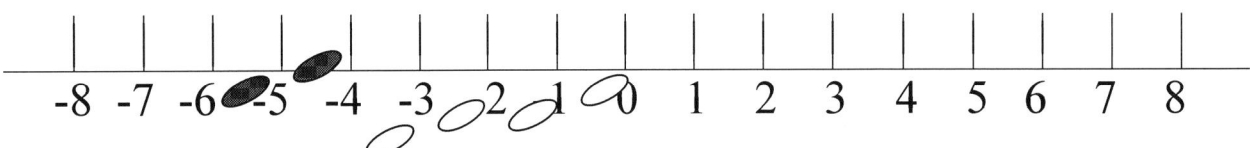

So (-4) +(- 2) = -6.
Also,
(-4) +(-3) = -7,
(-4) + 3 = -1,
(-4) + 4 = 0,
(-4) + 5 = 1,
4 + (-3) = 1,
4 +(-4) = 0,
4 +(-5) = -1.   Do you understand these equations?

This is a Negative Number Maze:

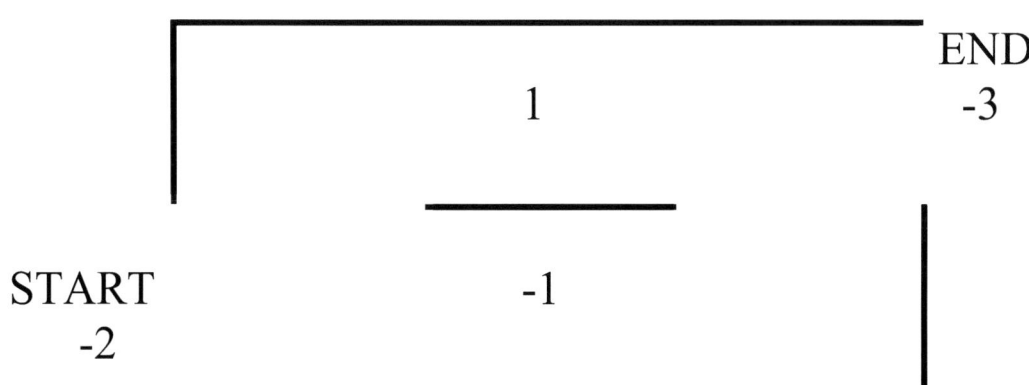

The solution is the bottom path. (-2) + (-1) = -3.

Switch the End number from –3 to –1. Then you have:

```
            ┌──────────────────────────────┐ END
            │              1               │ -1
            │                              │
            │        ──────────            │
            │                              │
   START    │             -1               │
   -2       │                              │
            └──────────────────────────────┘
```

The solution here is to take the top path. (-2) + 1 = -1.

Try

```
            ┌──────────────────────────────┐ END
            │              4               │ 2
            │                              │
            │        ──────────            │
            │                              │
   START    │             -4               │
   -2       │                              │
            └──────────────────────────────┘
```

The solution is the top path. Fun, is it not?

If you are having a problem with negative numbers, ask someone for help. On this page there is a slightly different way of explaining negative numbers, which you probably figured out yourself.

Number Line

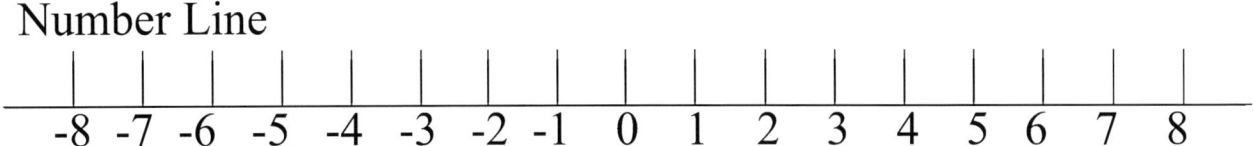

To add two numbers 3 and 2, start at the first number 3 and count up 2 intervals on the Number Line to reach 5. You go up because 2 is positive. 3 +2 =5.

To add the two numbers 3 +(-2), start at the first number 3 and count down on the Number Line to reach 1. You go down because (-2) is negative. 3 + (-2) = 1.

This is the way we add and subtract positive numbers. The same rules work for negative numbers.

To add two numbers (-3) + 2, start at the first number -3 and count 2 up on the Number Line to reach -1. You go up because 2 is positive. (–3) +2 =-1.

To add the two numbers (-3) +(-2), start at the first number -3 and count down on the Number Line to reach -5. You go down because (-2) is negative. (-3) + (-2) = -5.

Try (-3) + 4 = ___? and (-3) + (- 4) = ___?

The answers are 1 and -7.

What is (-1) + 10 =___? The answer is 9.
What is 5 + (-10) =___ ? The answer is -5.

Do these for practice before going on to more difficult ones.

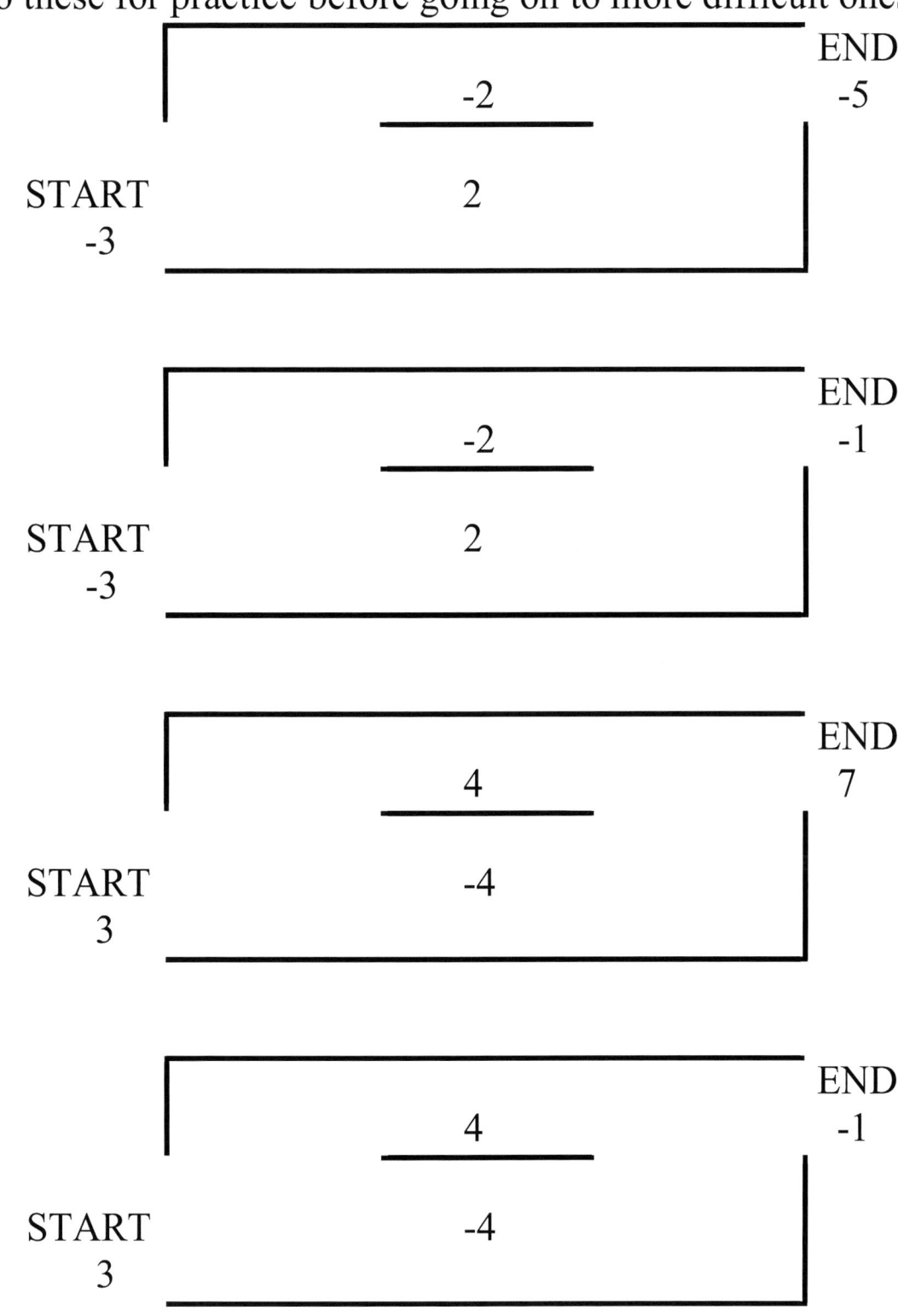

The solutions to the Negative Number Mazes on the last page are the paths that make
(-3) + (-2) = -5, (-3) + 2 = -1, 3 + 4 = 7, 3 + (-4) = -1.

Here we go.

Solutions (read from left to right): (-2) + (-2) + 1 = -3, (-2) + (-1) + 1 = -2, (-2) + (-1) + 4 = 1.

In these Negative Number Mazes, Start with a positive number.

	2	4	END 4
START 1	-1	-3	

	2	4	END -3
START 1	-1	-3	

	2	4	END 0
START 1	-1	- 3	

Solutions (read from left to right): 1 + (-1) + 4 = 4, 1 + (-1) + (-3) = -3, 1+ 2 + (-3) = 0.

These Negative Number Mazes are harder.

```
                ┌─────────────────────────────────────┐
                │    3          2          -4         │  END
                │    ─          ─          ─          │   0
   START        │                                     │
     2          │   -3          1          -6         │
                └─────────────────────────────────────┘
```

or

```
                ┌─────────────────────────────────────┐
                │    3          2          -4         │  END
                │                                     │  -4
                │    ─          ─          ─          │
   START        │                                     │
     2          │   -3          1          -6         │
                └─────────────────────────────────────┘
```

or

```
                ┌─────────────────────────────────────┐
                │    3          2          -4         │  END
                │                                     │  -5
                │    ─          ─          ─          │
   START        │                                     │
     2          │   -3          1          -6         │
                └─────────────────────────────────────┘
```

Solutions: 2 +3+1 + (-6) = 0, 2 +(-3) + 1 + (-4) = -4, 2 + (-3) + 2 + (-6) = -5.

These Negative Number Mazes Start with a negative number.

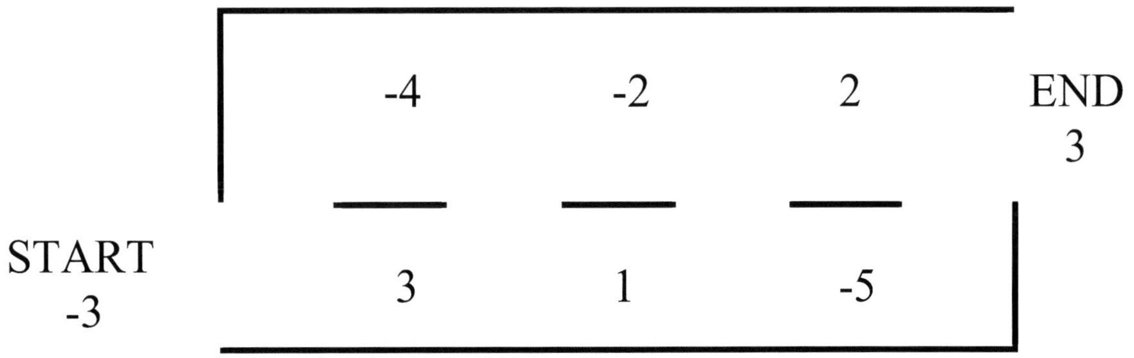

START
-3

| -4 | -2 | 2 | END 3 |
| 3 | 1 | -5 | |

or

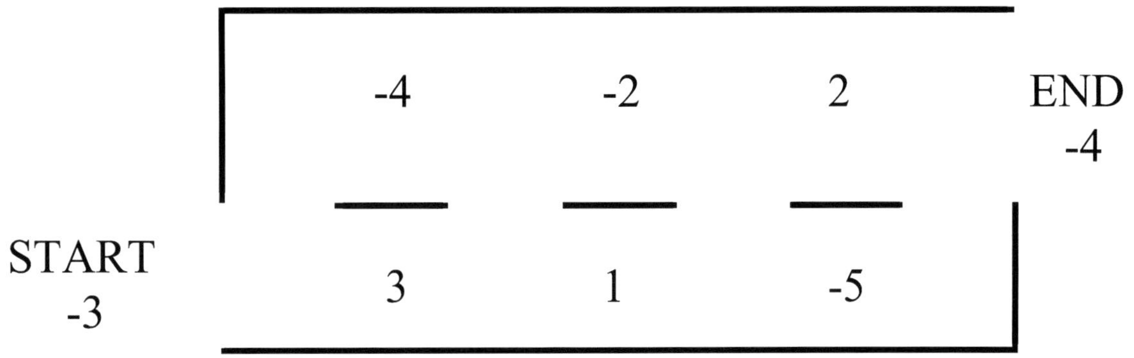

START
-3

| -4 | -2 | 2 | END -4 |
| 3 | 1 | -5 | |

or

START
-3

| -4 | -2 | 2 | END -14 |
| 3 | 1 | -5 | |

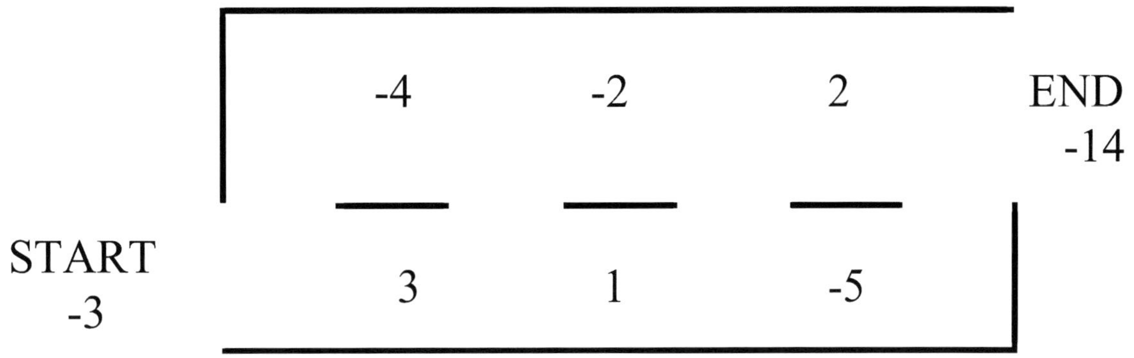

Solutions: (-3) +3+1 + 2 = 3, (-3) +(-4) + 1 + 2 = -4, (-3) + (-4) + (-2) + (-5) = -14.

Can you find your way through theses Negative Number Mazes?

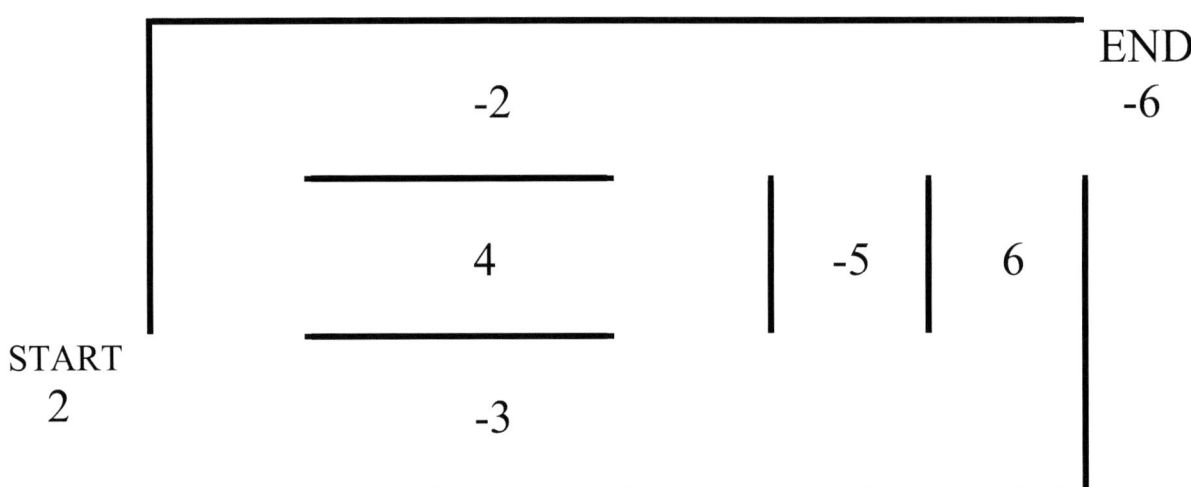

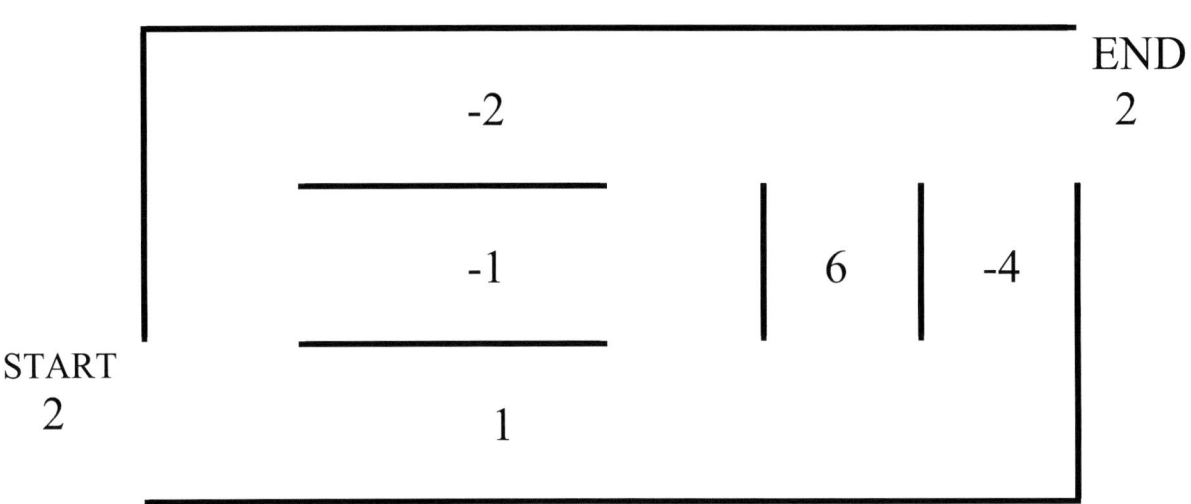

Solutions: (2) + (-3) +(-5) = -6.   2 + 1+ (-1) + (-2) +6 + (-4) = 2.

Make your own Negative Number Maze. Use -1,-2,-3 etc.

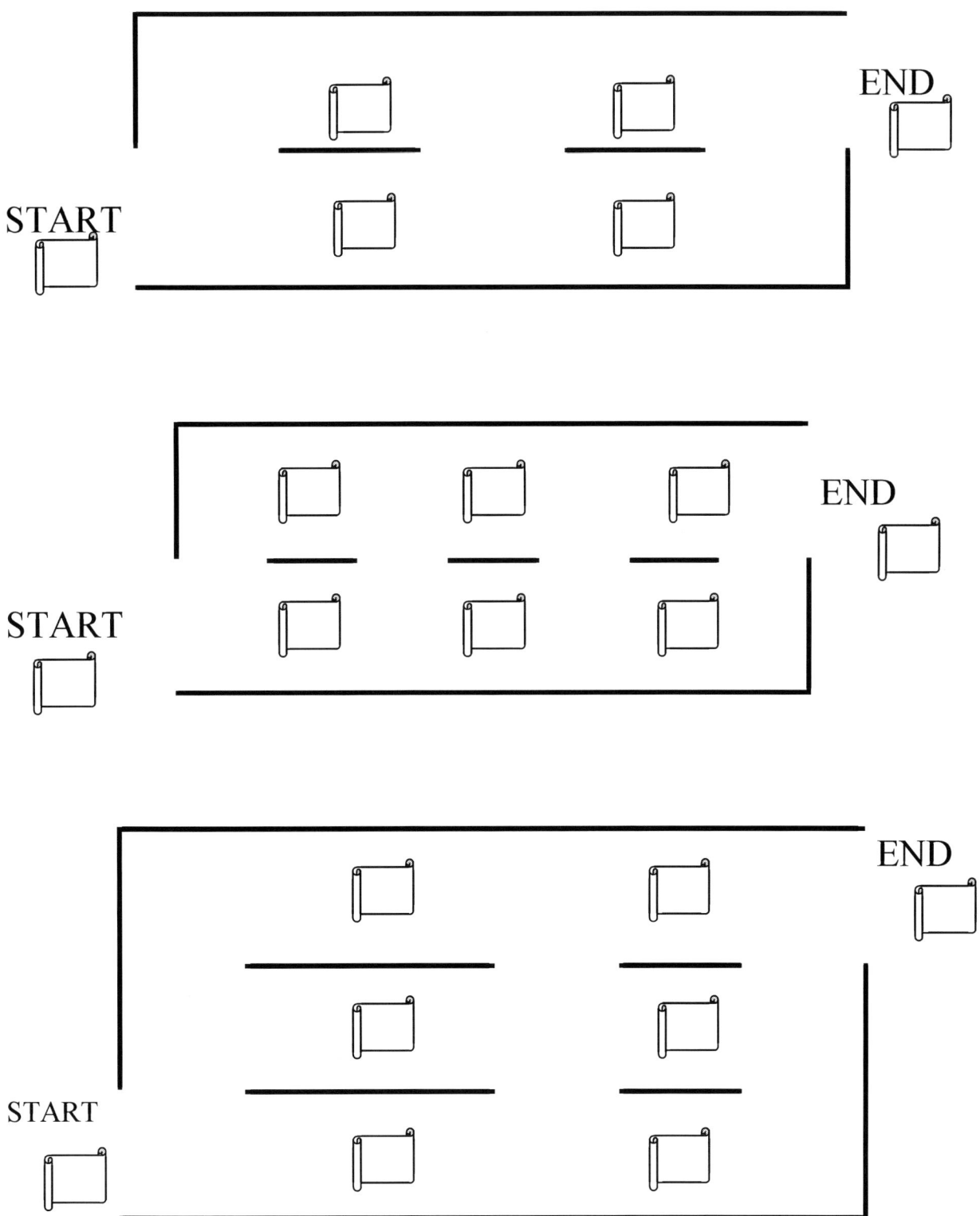

Chapter 11   6 by 4 by 4   Mazes

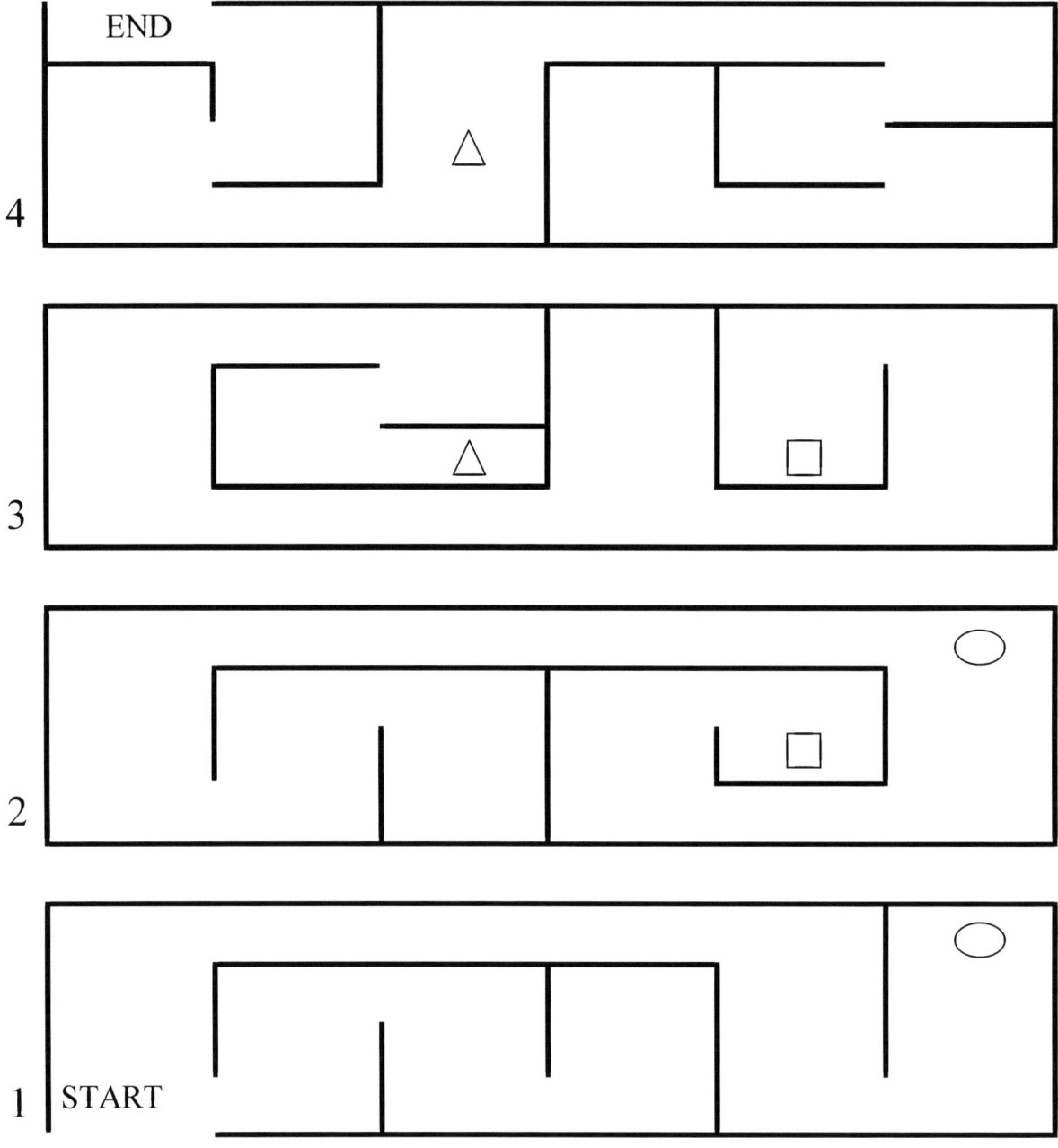

At 10 o'clock, I read for 4 hours. What time will it be when I stop reading? It will be 2 o'clock. 10 + 4 = 2.

At 6 o'clock I wake up. If I have slept for 8 hours, when did I go to sleep? 10 o'clock. 6 – 8 = 10.

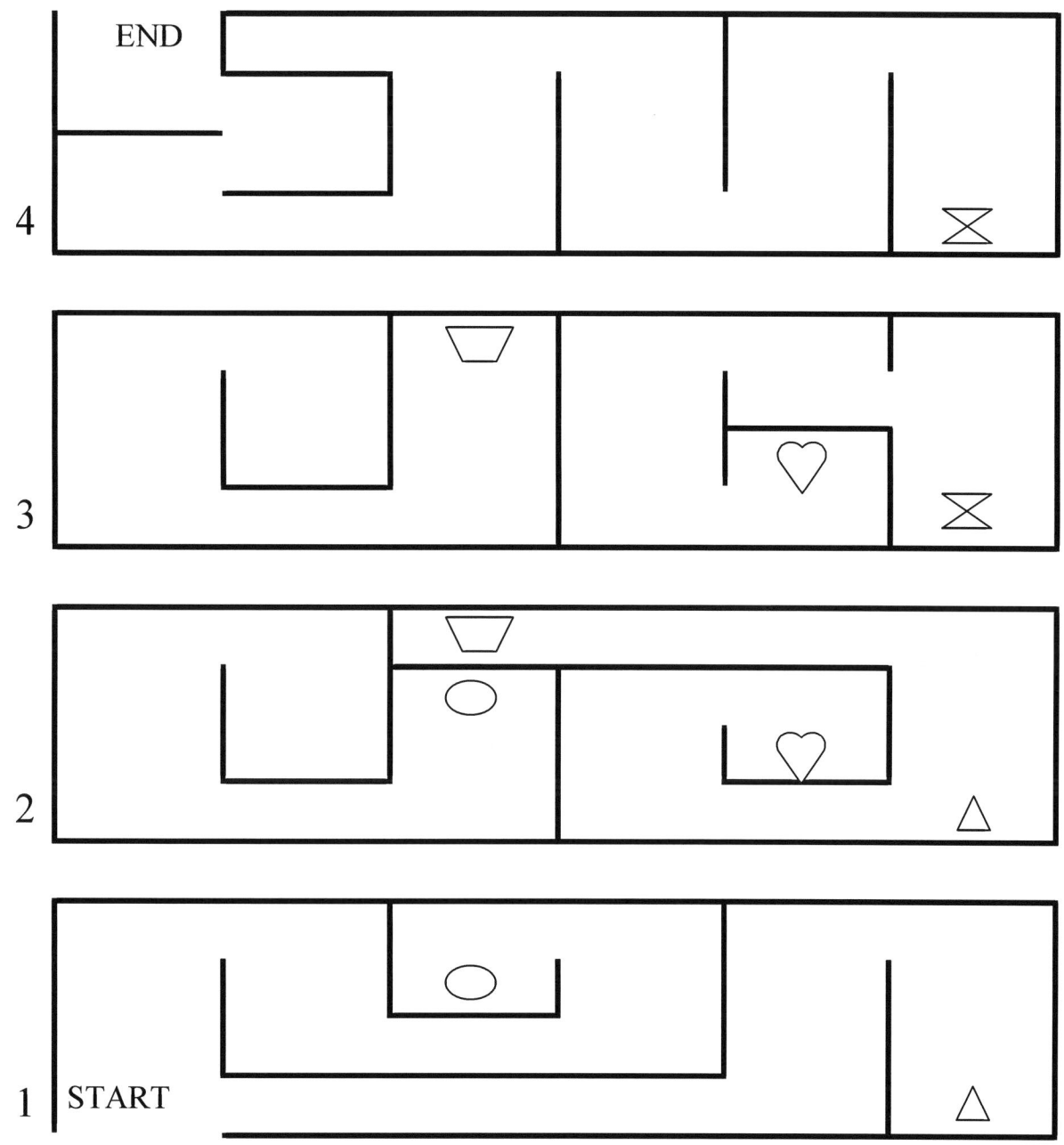

This is called clock arithmetic. 11 + 2 = 1. 11 + 3 = 2.
1 – 2 = 11. 1 – 3 = 10 on the clock on the wall.

Clock

On a Clock with 4 numbers 0,1,2,3 what is 2 + 1?

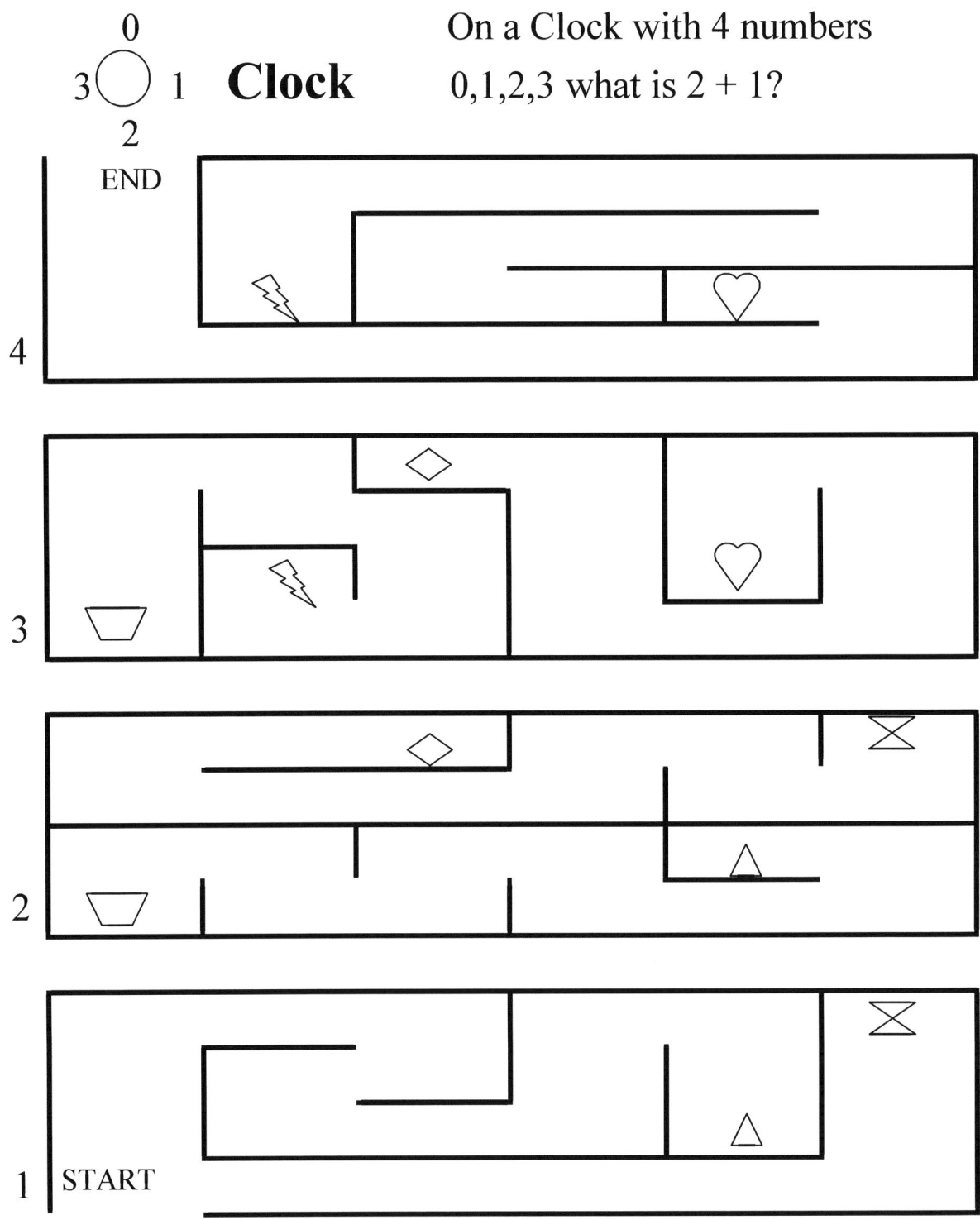

To do this, go to 2 and then count 1 hour clockwise.
You land on 3. So 2 + 1 = 3.
But what happens when you add 3 + 1?

To add 3 + 1, go to 3 and then count 1 hour clockwise. You land on 0. So 3 + 1 = 0. Surprise!

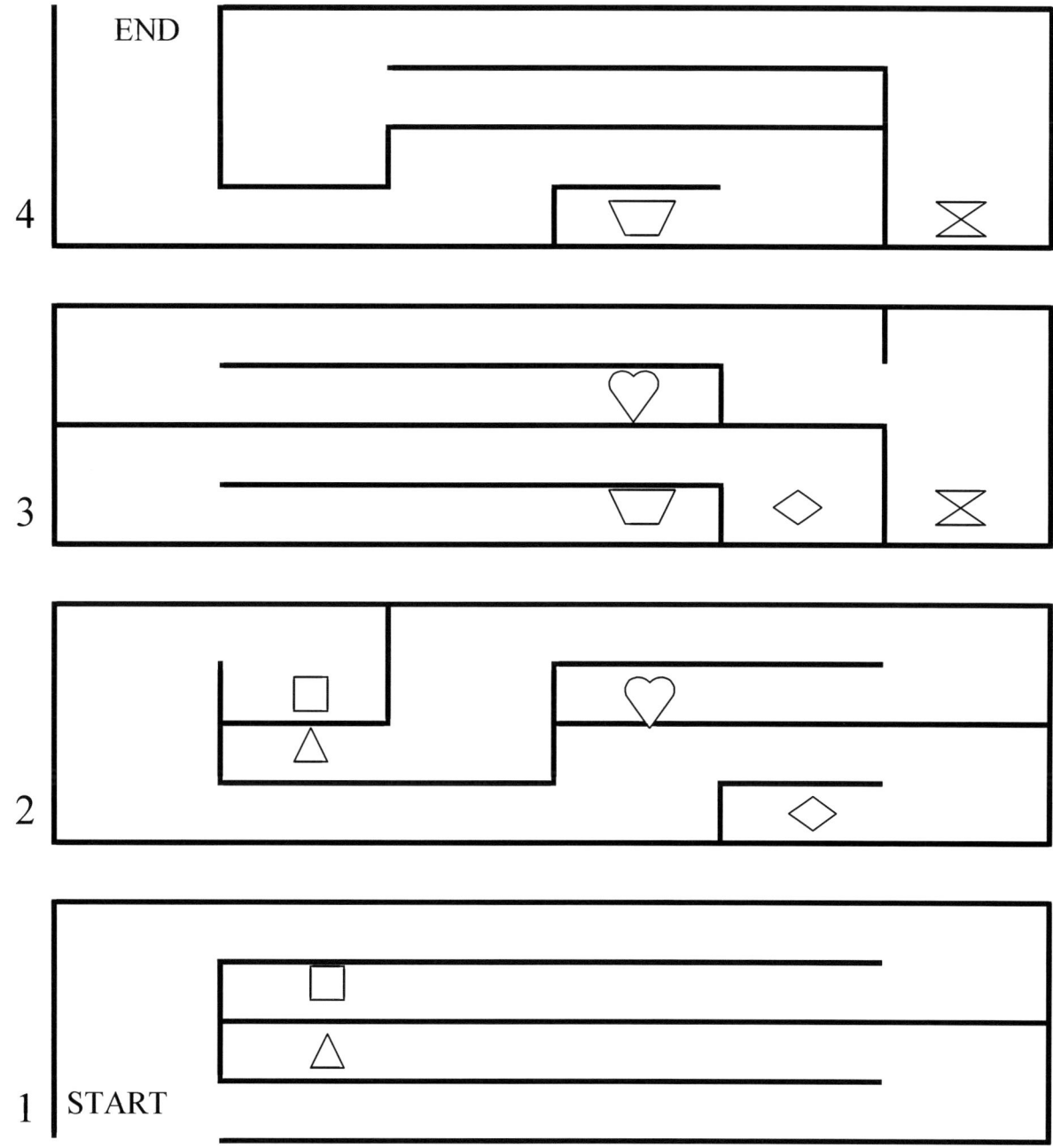

What is 3 + 2 ? Start on 3 and count 2 clockwise. You land on 1. 3 + 2 = 1. The teacher has a lump in his throat. Your Dad says, "What are they teaching you at school! "

But 3 + 2 = 1 on a clock with 4 numbers. This is a special type of thinking that you and your friends can understand.

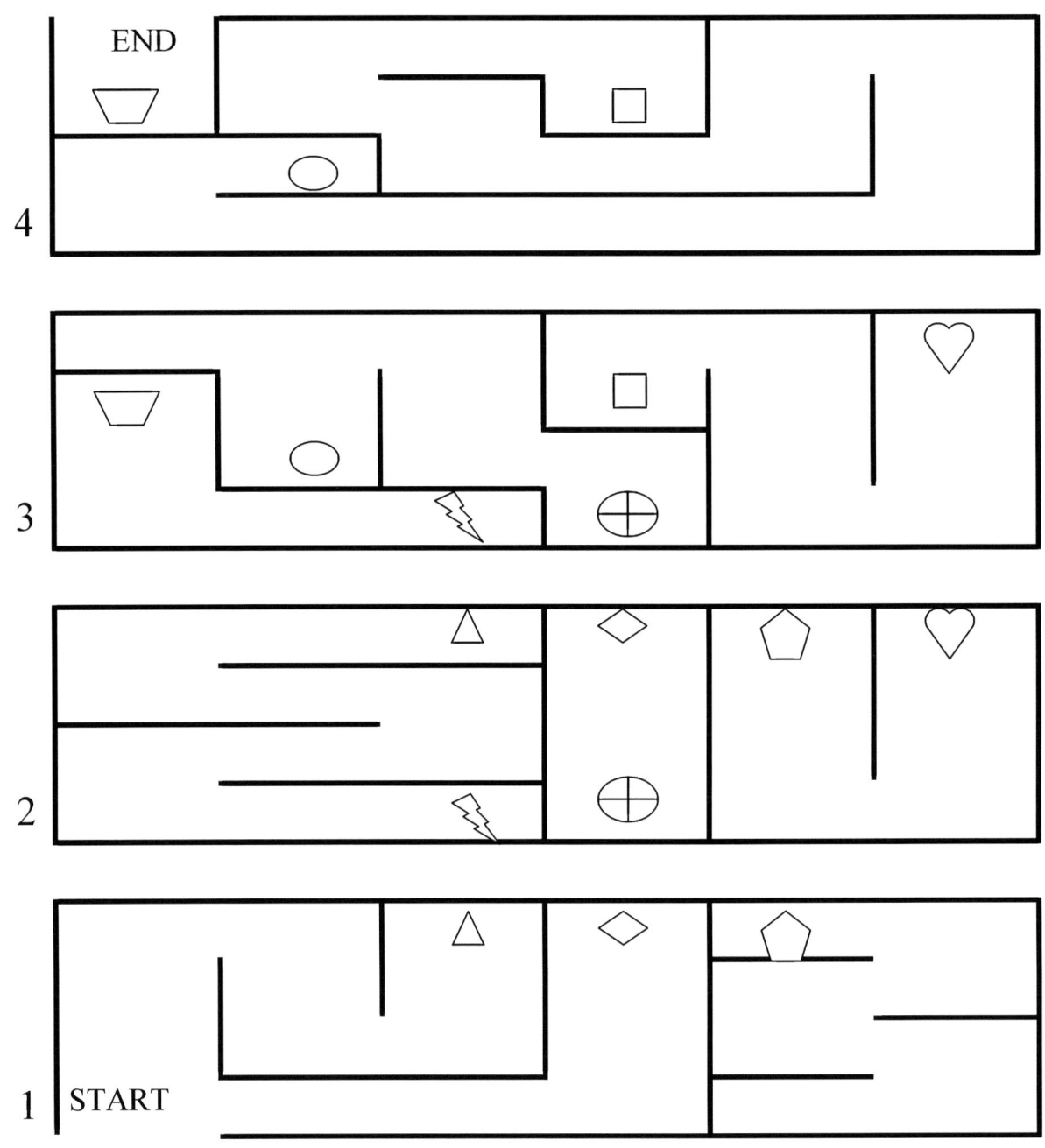

3 + 3 = What?
6? No. Not on a clock with 4 numbers.

To add 3 + 3, go to 3 and then count 3 hours clockwise.
3 + 3 = 2.

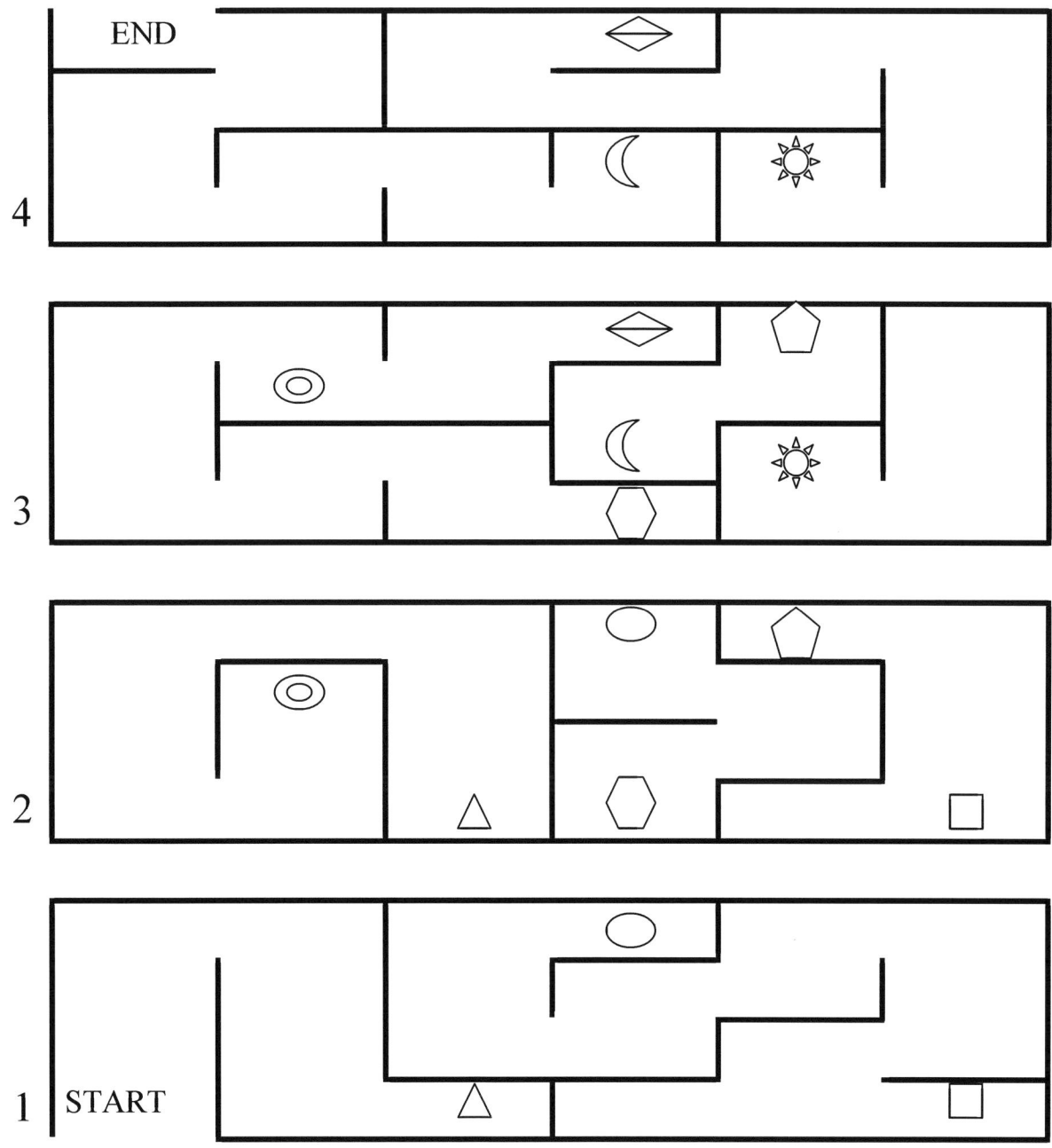

How about subtraction? To subtract 2 – 1, go to 2 and then count 1 hour counterclockwise (backwards). What is 2 – 3 on a clock with four numbers.

To subtract 2 – 3, go to 2 and then count 3 hours counterclockwise to 3. 2 – 3 = 3 on a clock with 4 numbers.

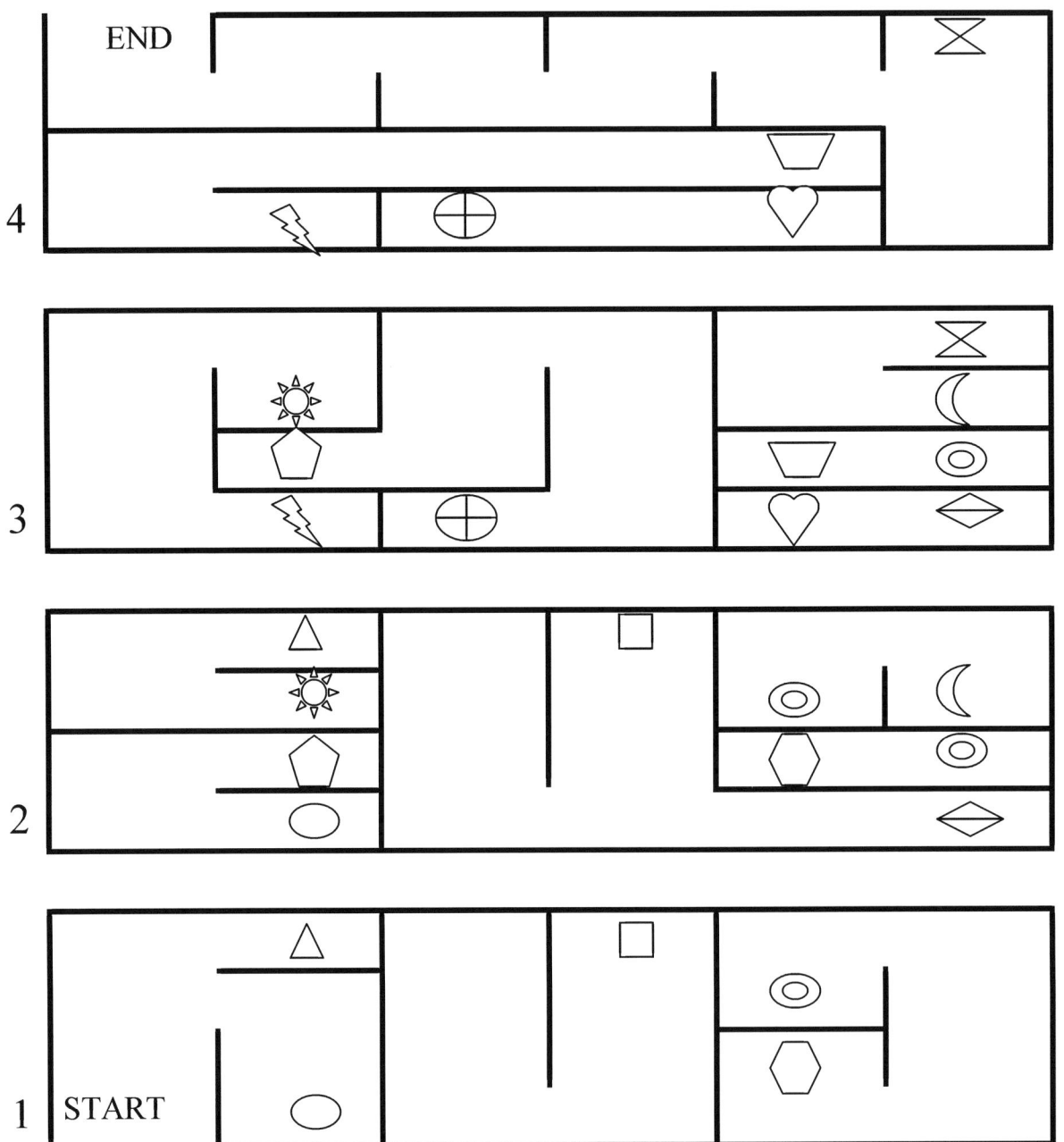

What is 2 – 3 on the Number Line? Go to 2 and then count down 3 spaces to –1. So 2 – 3 = -1.

What is 1 −3 on the clock with 4 numbers? Go to 1 and then count 3 hours counterclockwise to 2.   1 − 3 = 2.

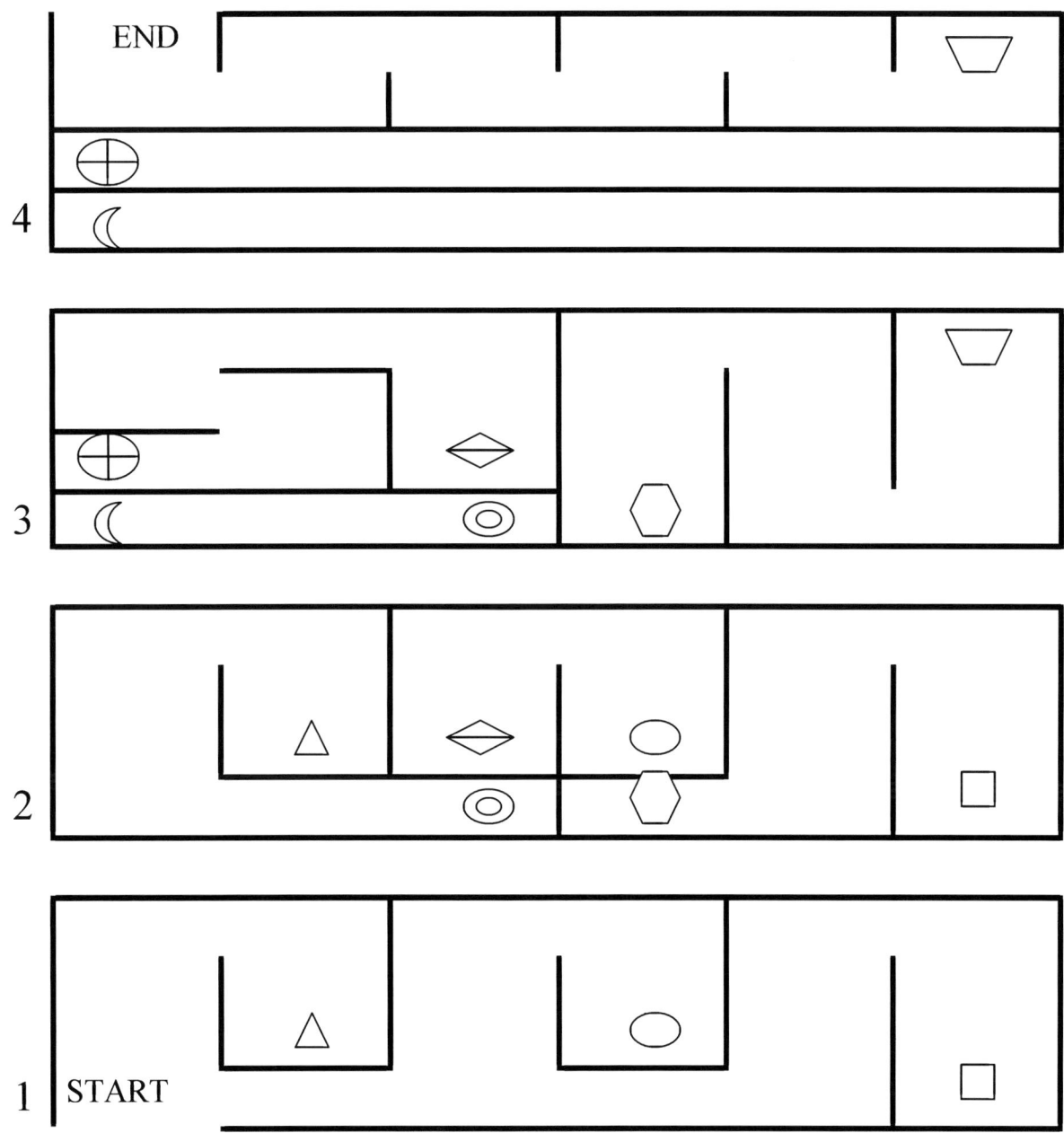

Addition and subtraction on a clock with 4 numbers has different answers than addition and subtraction on a Number Line.
Yet, the mathematical ideas similar!

Clock

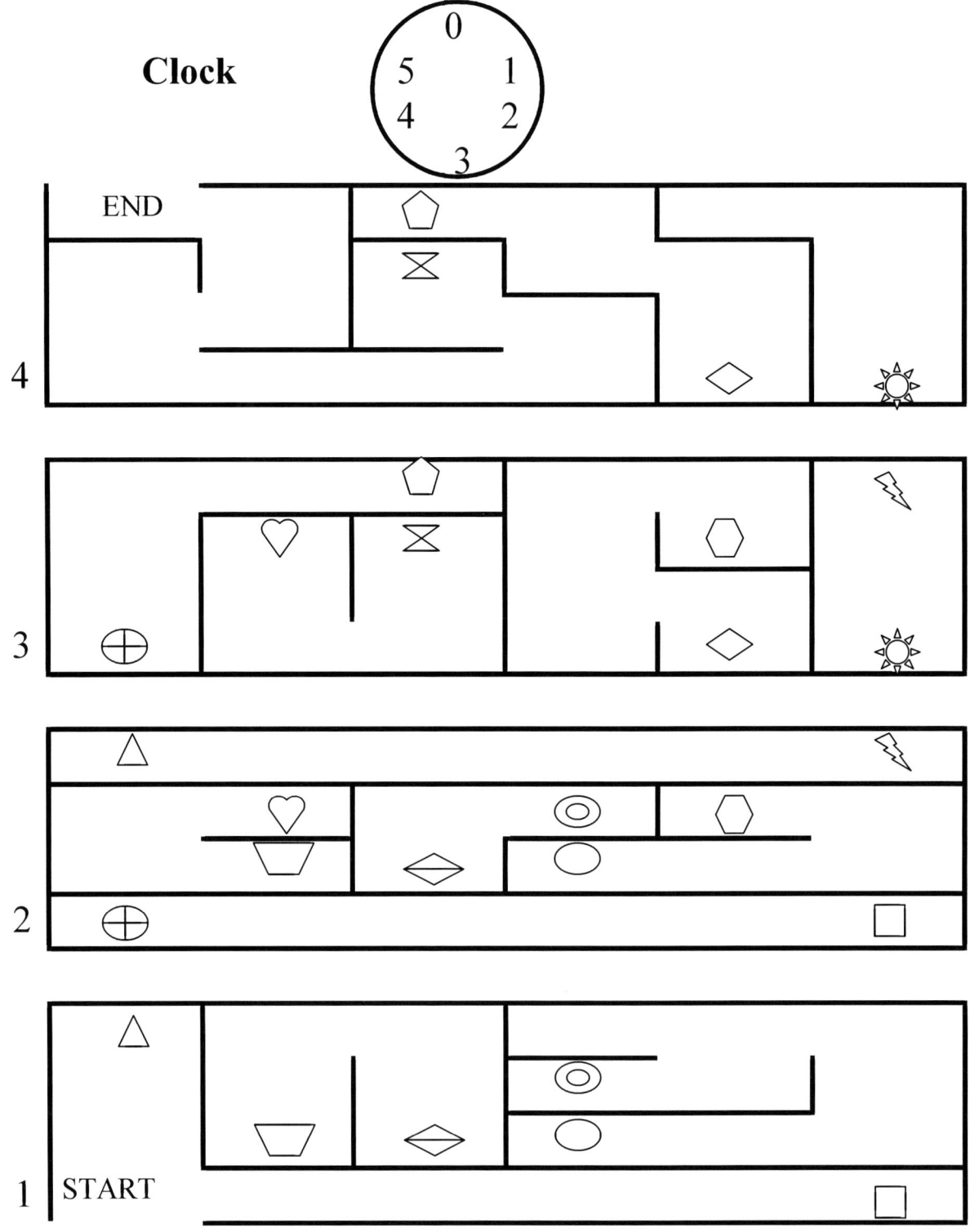

On the clock with 6 numbers at the top of the page, apply the same reasoning you used on a clock with 4 numbers.

Add 5 + 2 on a clock with 6 numbers. Go to 5 and then count 2 hours clockwise to 1. 5 + 2 = 1.

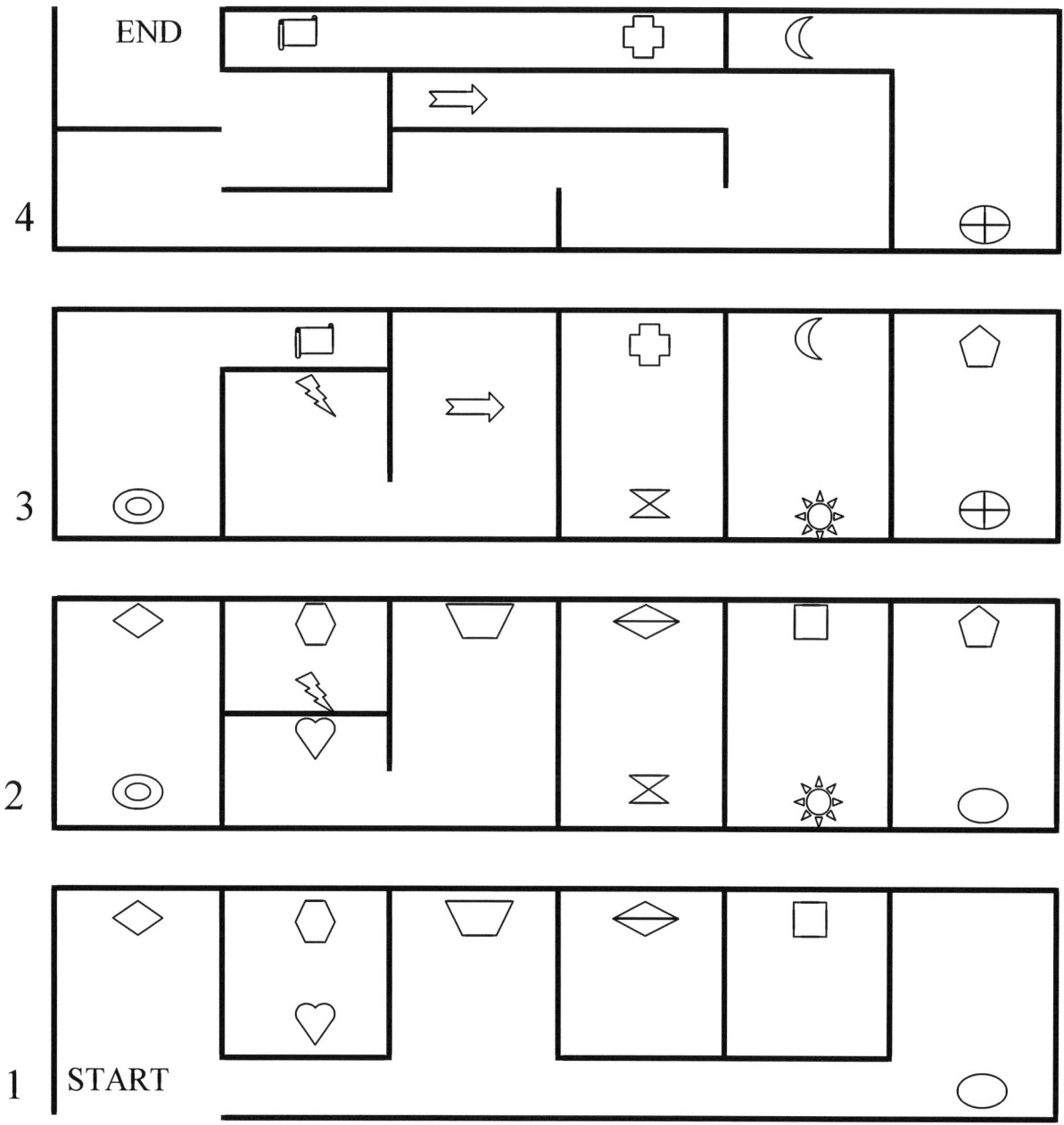

What is 4 + 2? 4 + 3? 4 + 4? 4 + 5?
0,1,2, and 3 are the answers on a clock with 6 numbers.

On a clock with 6 numbers what is 5 + 2? 5 + 3? 5 + 4? 5 + 5? 1, 2, 3 and 4 are the answers.

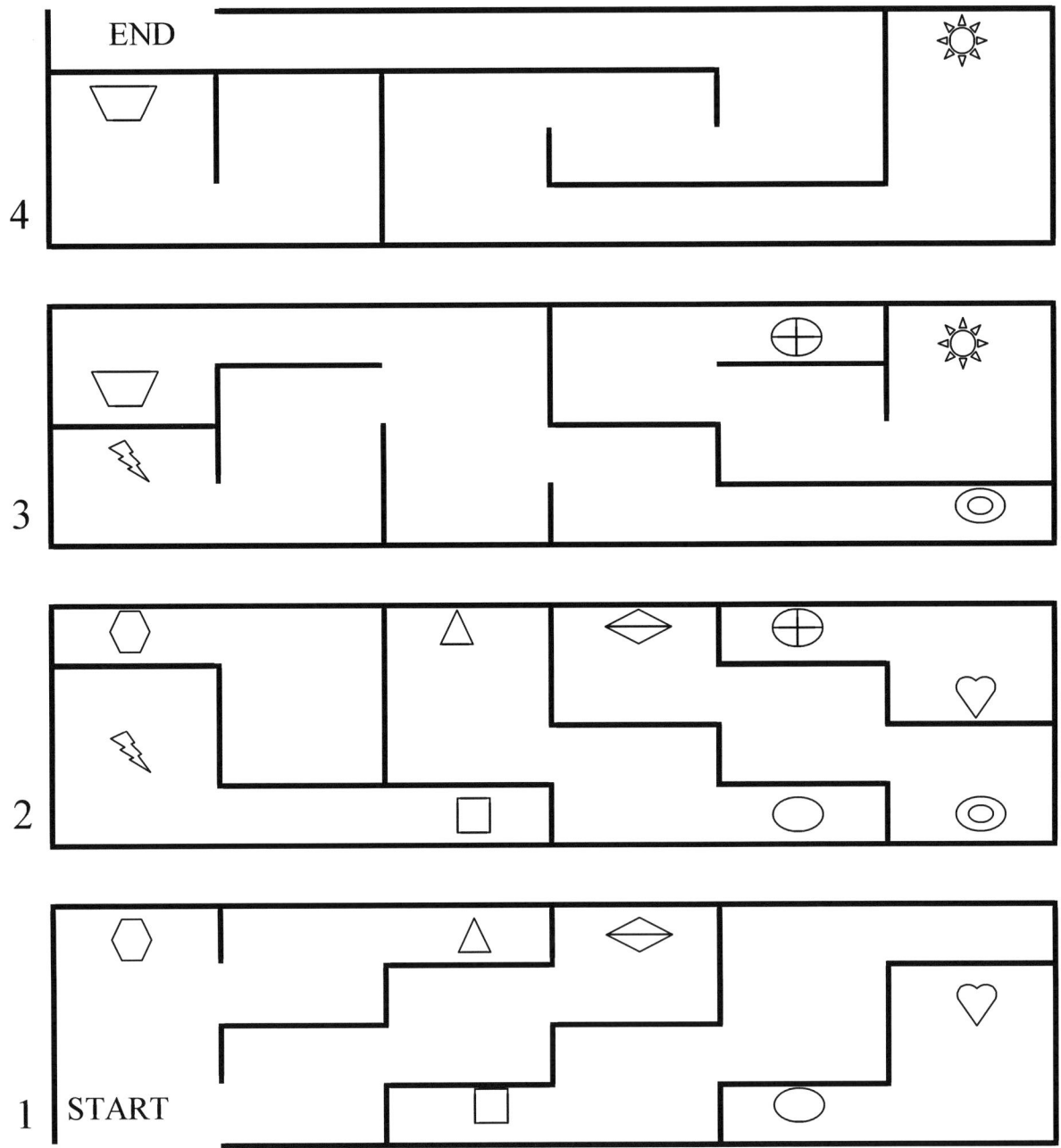

Try subtraction on a clock with 6 numbers.
Find 3 – 4? Go to 3 and then count 4 hours counterclockwise to 5. So 3 – 4 = 5.

What are 3 – 5 ? 2 – 2 ? 2 – 3 ? 2 – 4 ? 2 – 3 ? on a clock with 6 numbers. The answers are 4,0,5,4, and 5.

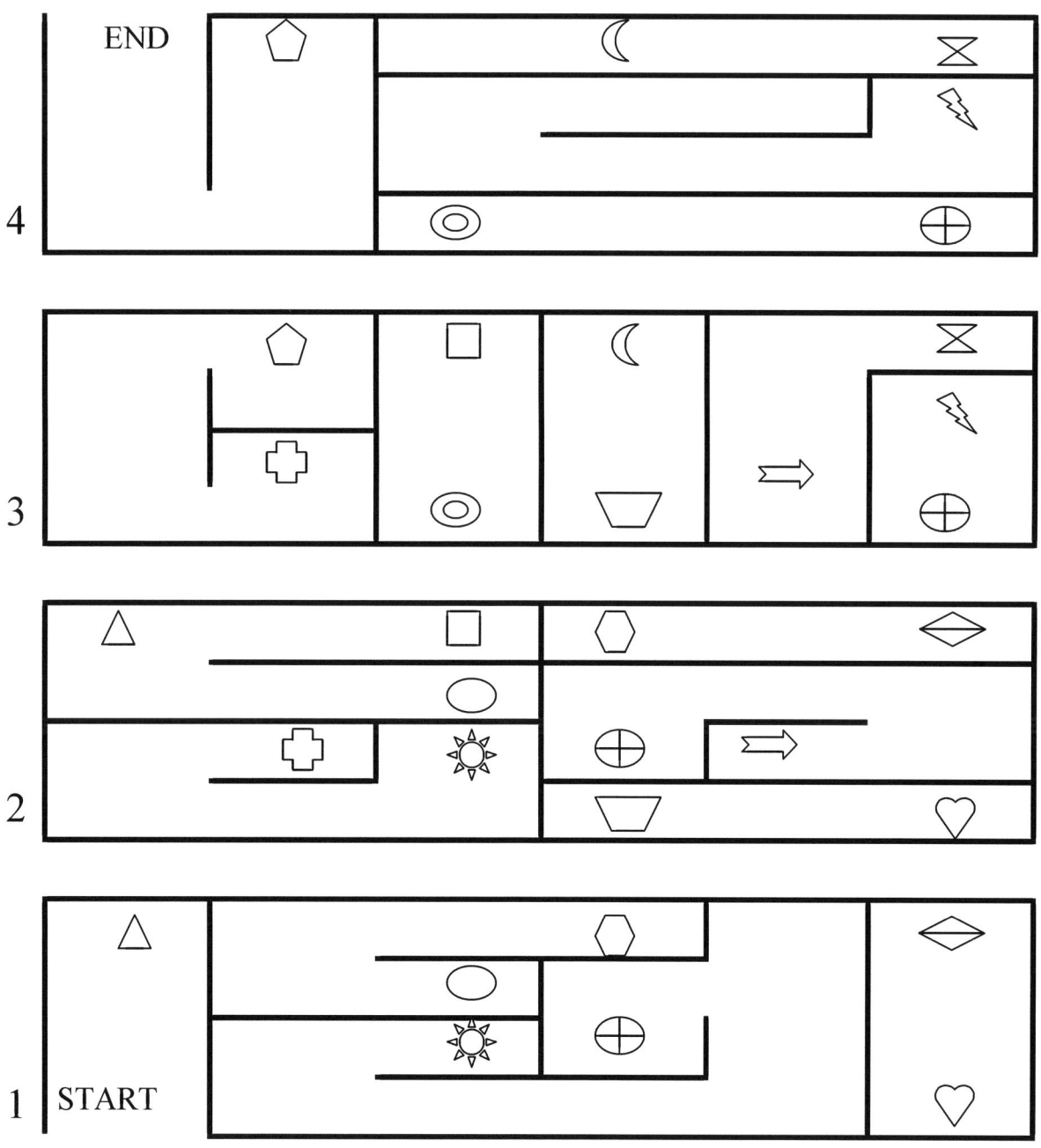

Clocks can have any amount of numbers. A clock can have 5 numbers, 7 numbers or 19 numbers. The same principles of addition and subtraction apply to each.

On a clock with 7 numbers, try 5 + 4 or 1 − 3 .
The answers are 2 and 5.

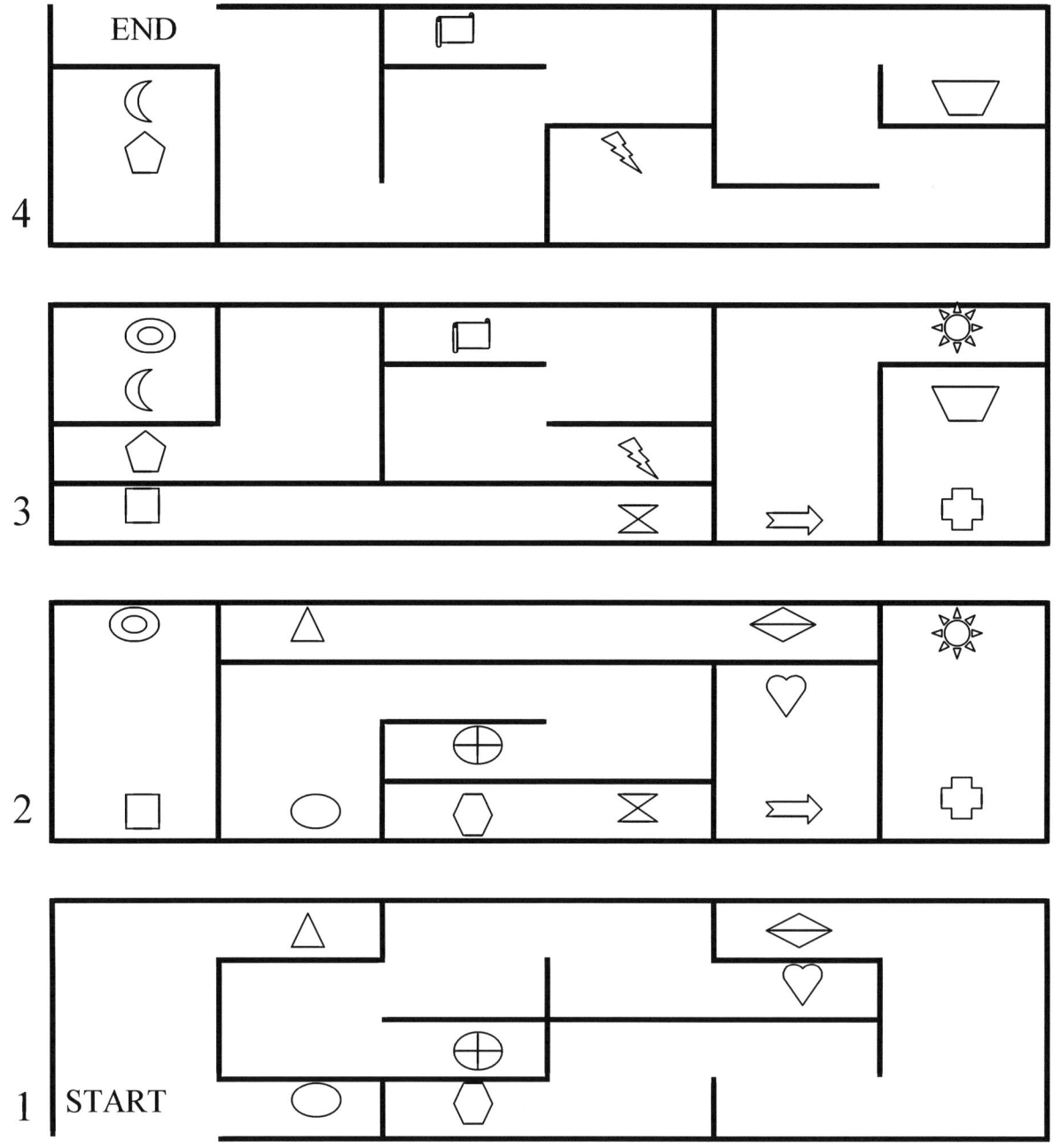

How do we find what the number 7 is in base 2?

We find out how many ones, twos or fours are in 7. There is 1 four, 1 two and 1 one. 7 = 4 + 2 + 1.

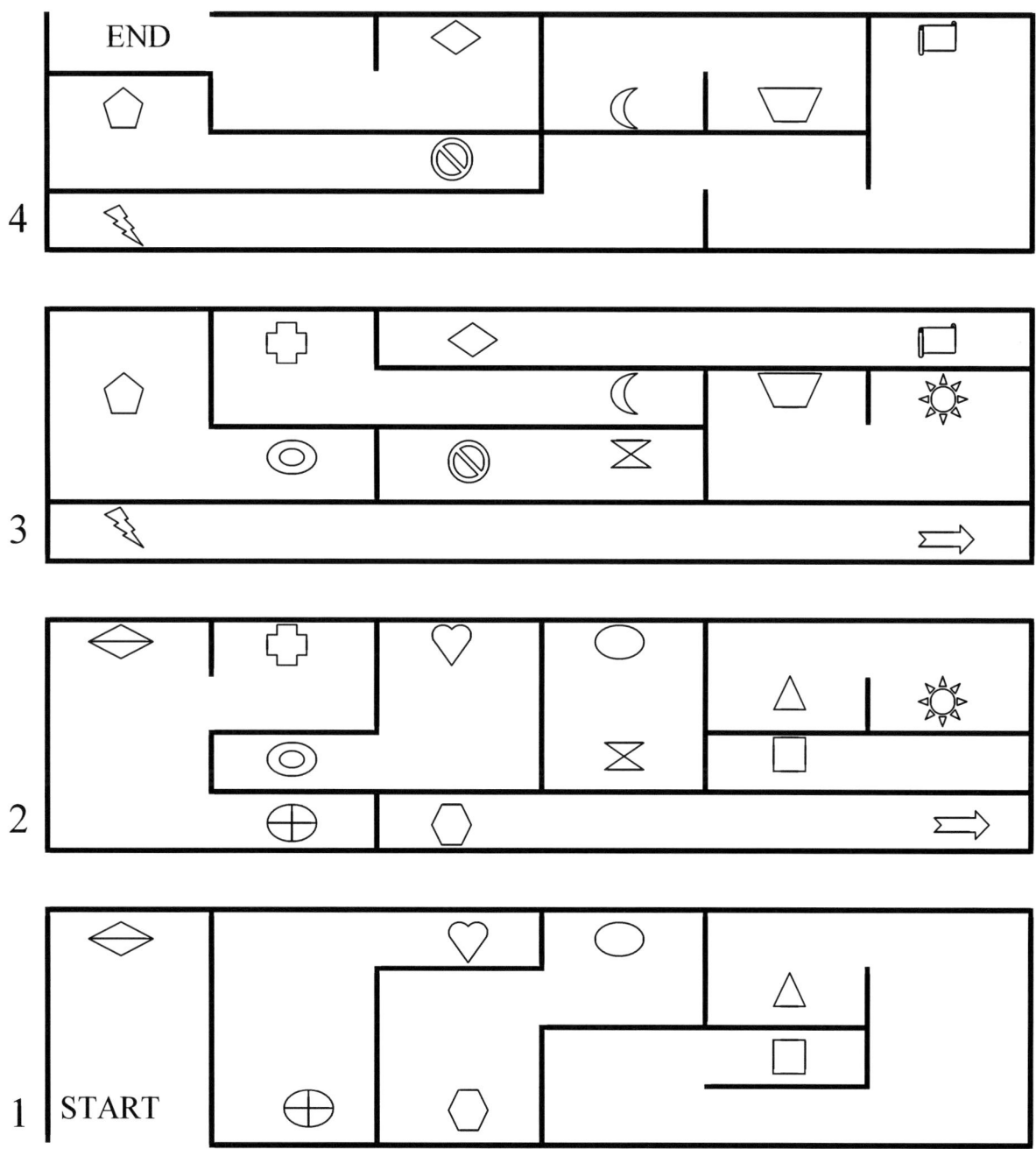

So 7 in base 10 is 111 in base 2.

What is 5 in base 2? 5 = 4 + 1. Therefore 5 (in base 10) is 101 in base 2. In general, to find out what a number is in base 2,

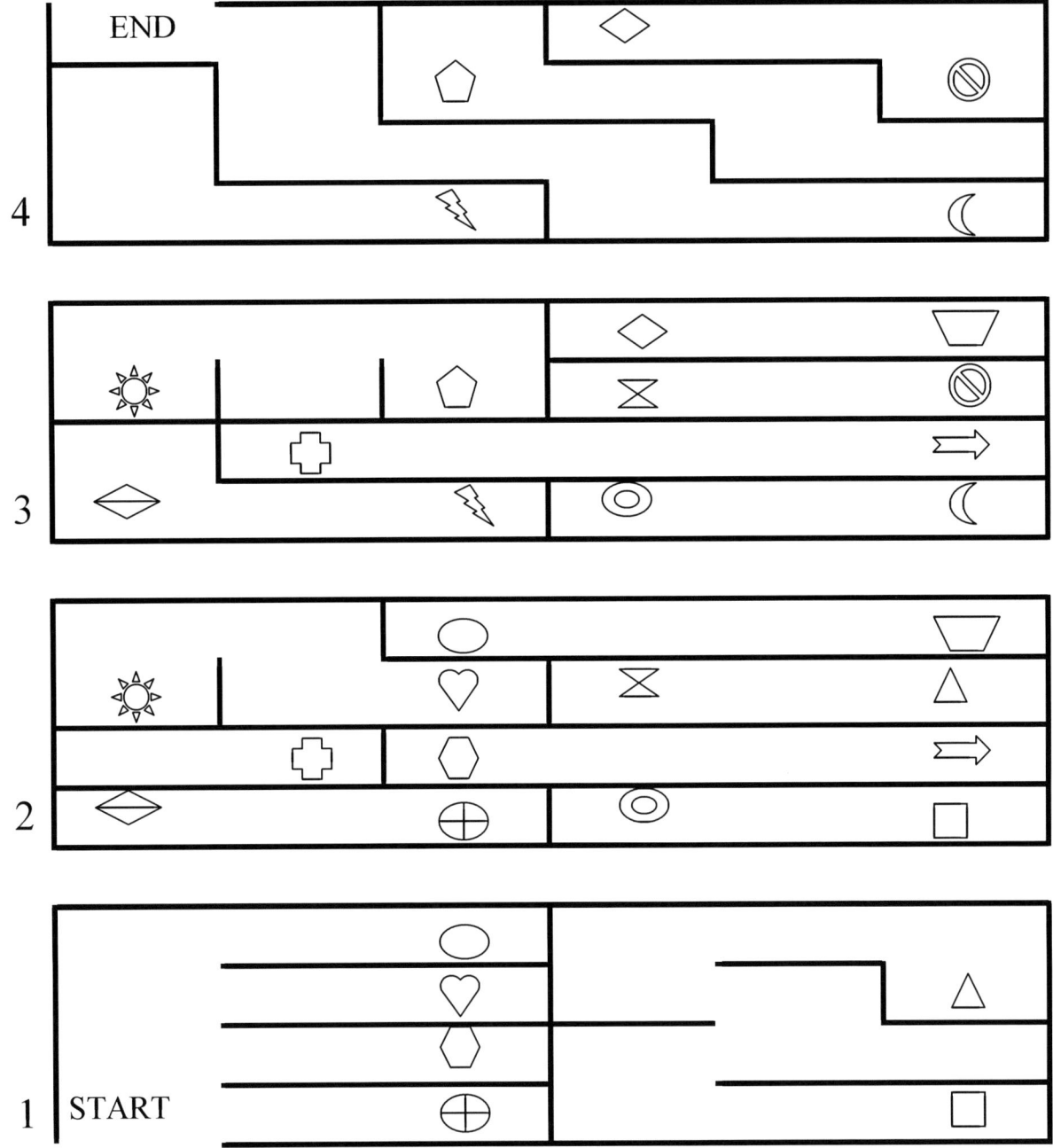

we must first find out how many ones, twos, fours, eights, sixteens, thirty-twos, sixty-fours, one hundred and twenty-eights …and so on are in the number.

Each time we find one of these, we put a 1 in the correct place. For example 17 has 1 sixteen and 1 one.

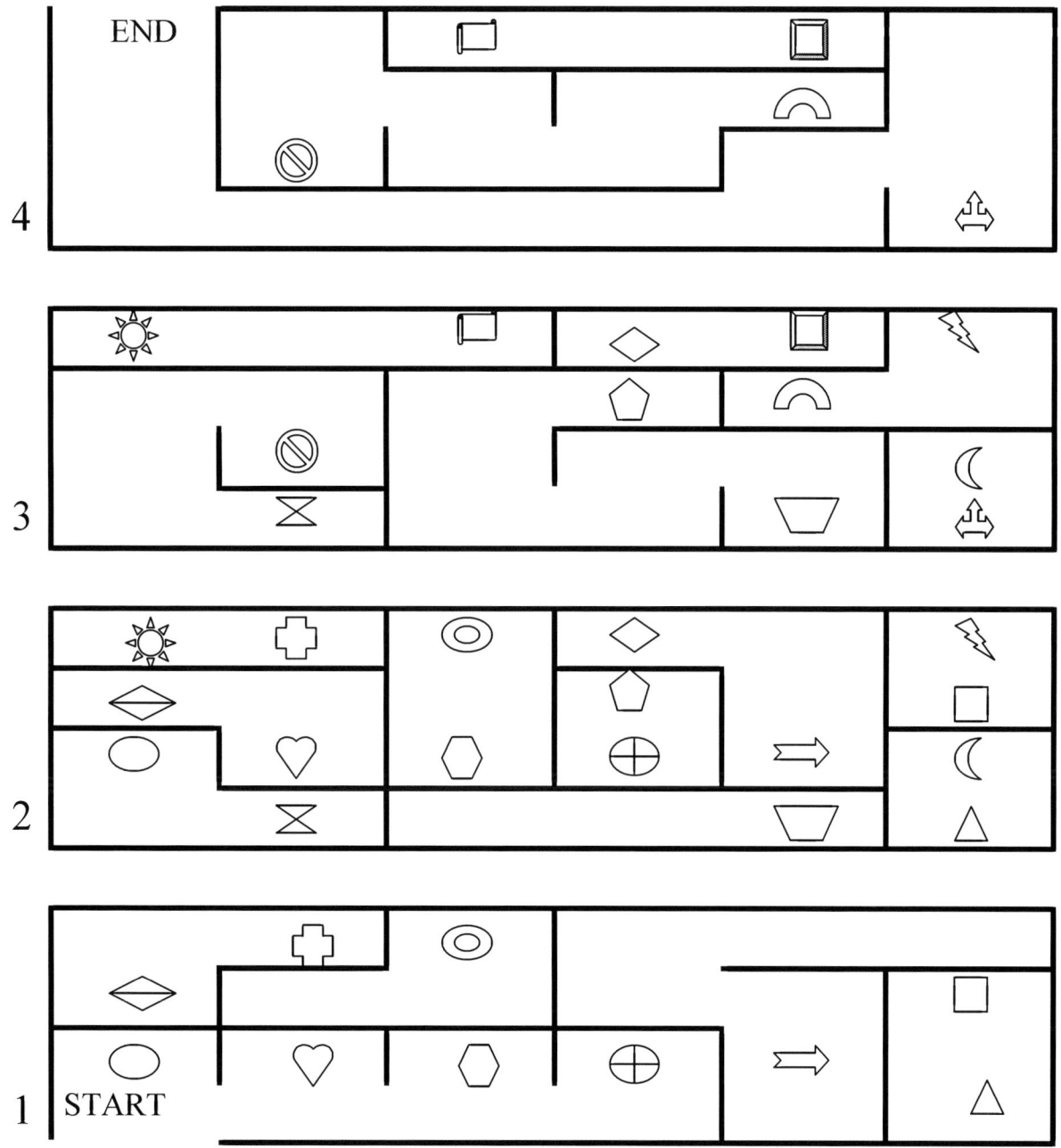

So 17 in base 10 is 10001 in base two. Reading from right to left, the first 1 is in the one's place and the last 1 is in sixteen's place.

Start with a number in base 10 and convert it to base 2. If you convert it back to base 10, it is the same number.

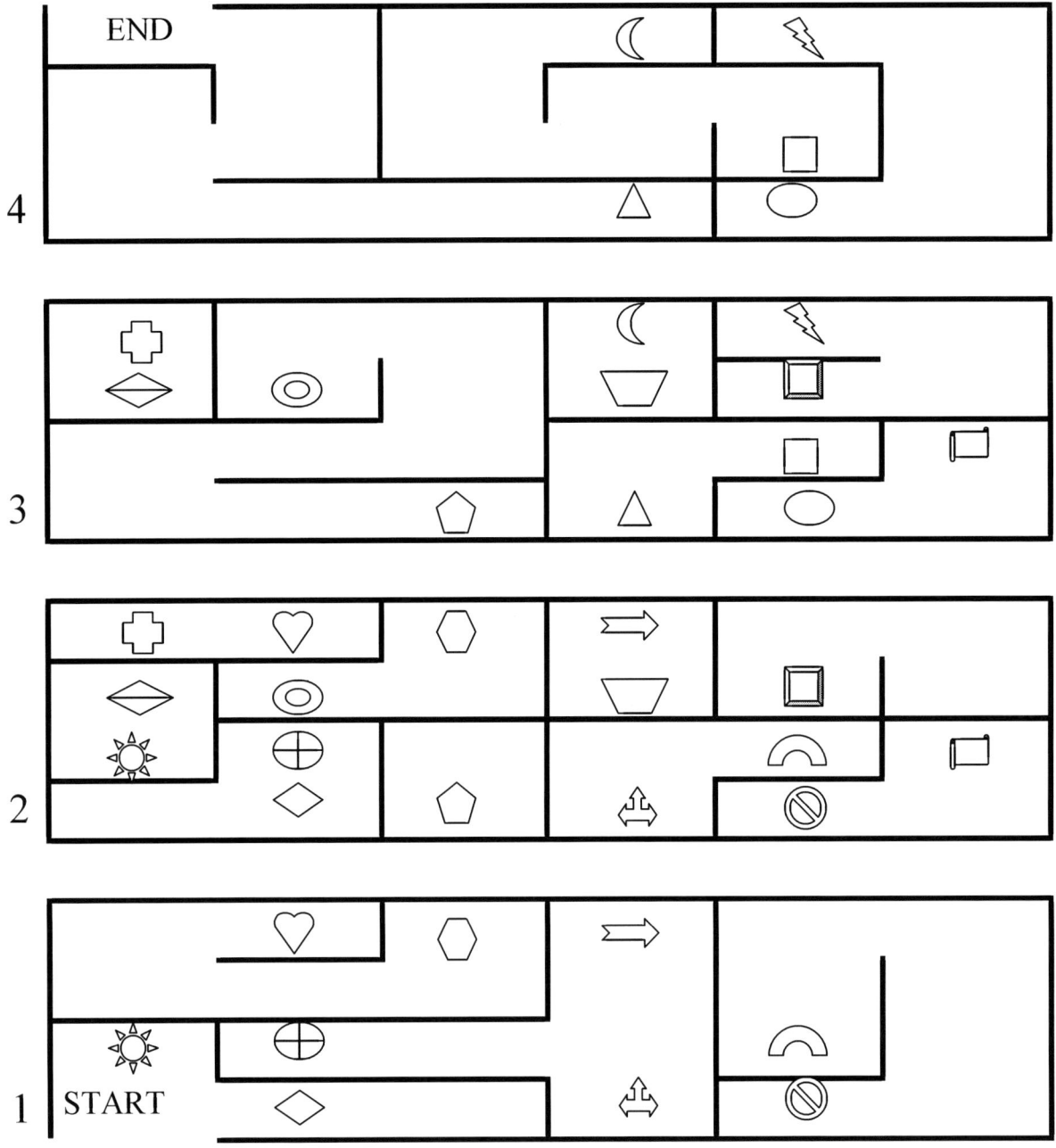

5 in base 2 is 101. And 101 in base 10 is 5 because 5=4 + 1. Start with 7 in base 10. In base 2 it is 111. Convert 111 back to Base 10, 4 + 2 +1 =7.

In base 2, what is 1 + 1? 2 of course. But in base 2 you may not use a 2 for a digit. 2 in base 2 is 10.
1 + 1 = 10.

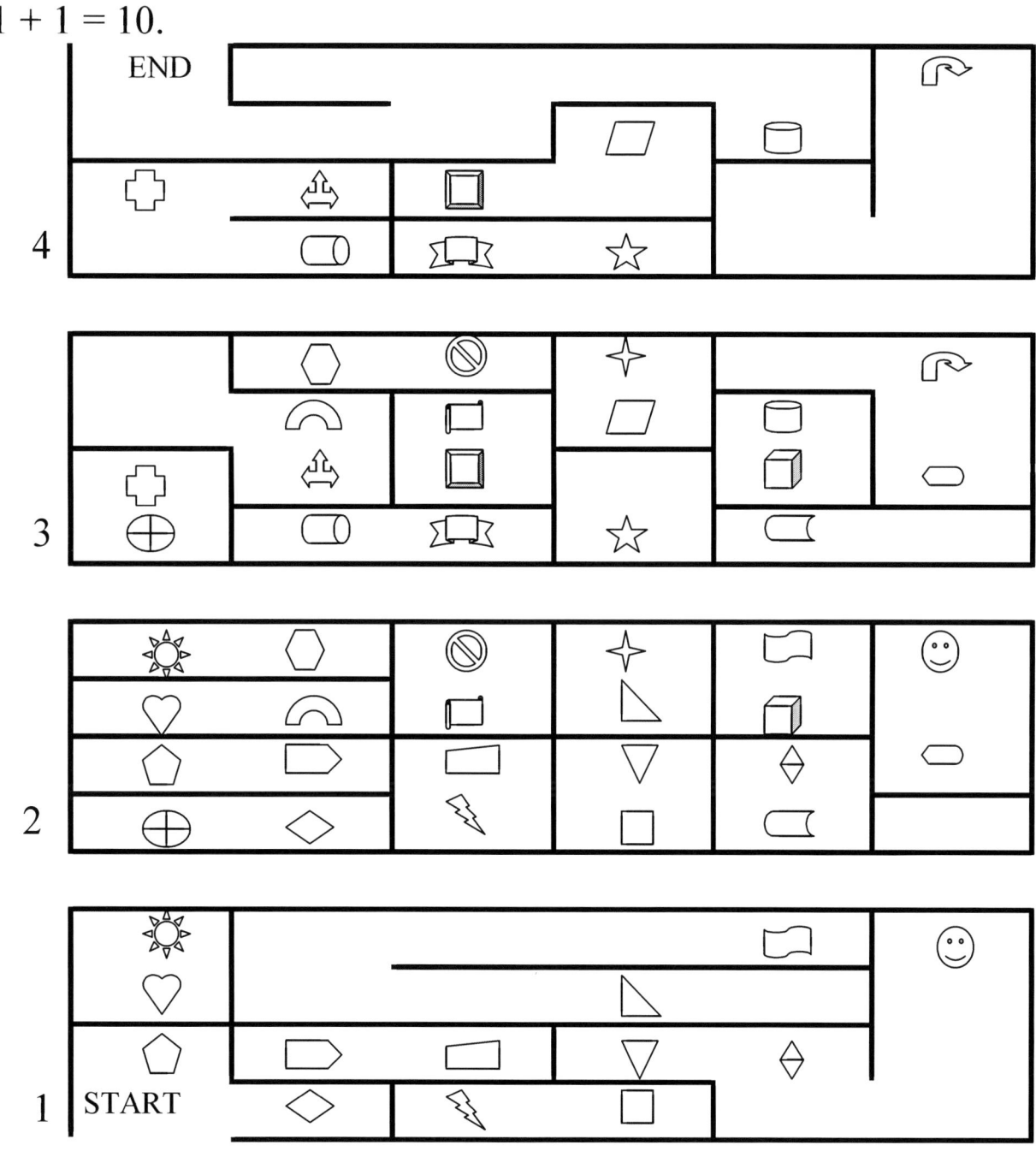

What is 10 + 1 in base 2? 10 + 1 = 11 (3).
11 + 1 = 100(4). 11 + 10 = 101.

Chapter 12   Coordinates in 3 Dimensional Mazes

Coordinates show you exactly where you are in the world. They are the best way to locate position. We use coordinates everyday. For example, your distance from something is a coordinate. If your team is 6 yards from the goal line, 6 is the value of a 1 dimensional coordinate. You can locate this 6 on the Number Line below.

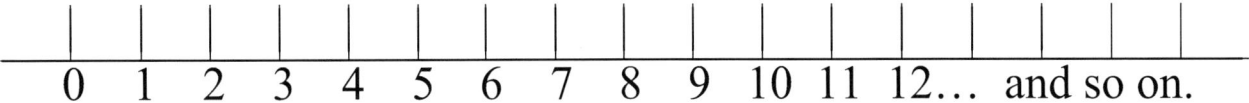

The number 6 tells you how far along a line you are from 0, the starting point.

Height is another example of a 1 dimensional coordinate. When you say that a tall building is 1000 feet high, you describe how far above the ground the roof is. The 14th floor is only 200 feet above the ground. You can use the 1 dimensional coordinate to find out which is higher, the roof or the 14th floor.

What are some more examples of 1 dimensional coordinates in life? Age is a 1 dimensional coordinate. Who is older, you or your parent? Your age is a number that can be thought of as a point on a Number Line. On the Number Line, your parent's age is to the right of yours because they are older than you.

As the mazes in this book become more complicated, coordinates will help you keep track of where you are in the maze.

If you put 2 Number Lines together like a jigsaw puzzle, then you have 2 dimensional coordinates. Place one Number Line along the bottom and one Number Line along the side.

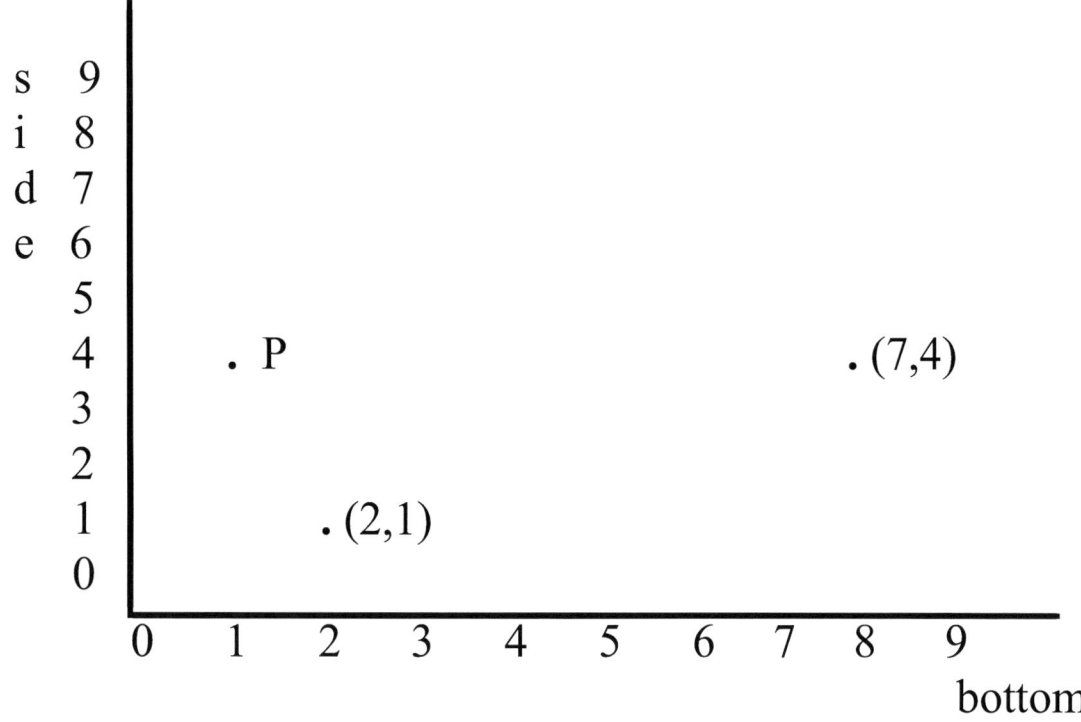

A place or position on a graph is given by 2 numbers, one along the bottom and one along the side. The point 2 along the bottom and 1 along the side is the point . (2,1) shown above. The point 7 along the bottom and 4 along the side is the point . (7,4) shown above. The 2 numbers that determine a point . are called 2 dimensional coordinates of that point. What are the coordinates of the point above labeled P? They are (1,4).

How does a compass give 2 dimensional coordinates?

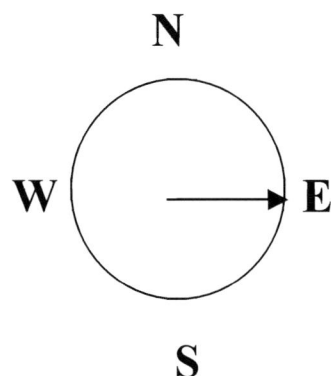 A compass uses 2 directions to describe position. Boston is 160 miles north and 180 miles east of New York City.

For another example, think of your bedroom.

6 yards	Bed				
5 yards				Stool	
4 yards		Light			
3 yards					
2 yards					
1 yard					Chair
	Door	1 yard	2 yards	3 yards	4 yards

Standing at the Door the Stool is 3 yards toward the Chair and 5 yards toward the Bed. Where is the light?

The New York City roads have natural 2 dimensional coordinates: the numbered streets and the avenues. 5th Avenue and 57th Street are the 2 dimensional coordinates of a block just south of Central Park on the East side. What are the 2 dimensional coordinates of the Empire State Building?

2 dimensional mazes have 2 dimensional coordinates. What size is this maze?

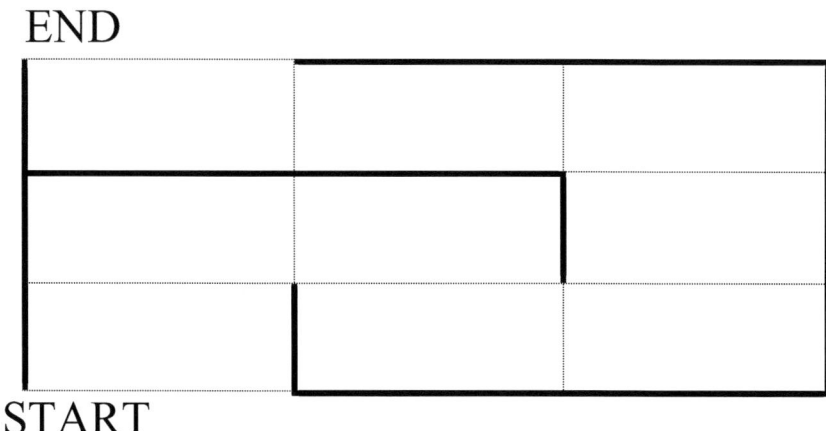

This maze has size 3 by 3. To see the 2 dimensional coordinates, first number the columns along the bottom 1,2,3 and number the rows along the side 1,2,3.

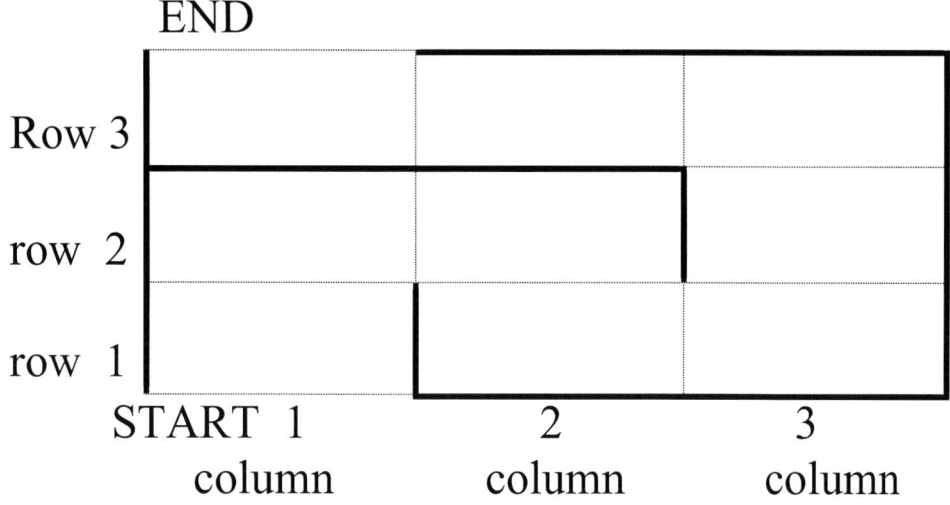

Imagine that you are at the movies and that the seats are represented by the boxes in the picture below.
Each seat is in a row and a column.
Each row and each column has a number.
So two numbers determine the position of a seat.

```
        END
         | (1,3)    (2,3)    (3,3) |
row 3    |                         |
         | (1,2)    (2,2)  | (3,2) |
row 2    |                 |       |
         | (1,1) | (2,1)    (3,1)  |
row 1    |       |                 |
        START  1        2        3
```

The box next to the START has the 2 dimensional coordinates (1,1).
The first "1" means the "1st column".
The second "1" means the "1st row".

The box next to the END has the coordinates (1,3).
The "1" means the "1st column".
The "3" means the "3rd row".

What are the coordinates of the middle box?   (2,2).

To describe the solution to the maze, you may list the boxes in the order you move through the maze. Above, the path is described by the list (1,1) to (1,2) to (2,2) to (2,1) to (3,1) to (3,2) to (3,3) to (2,3) to (1,3). Draw the ARROWS.

	1	2	3	4
4	(1,4) END	(2,4)	(3,4)	(4,4)
3	(1,3)	(2,3)	(3,3)	(4,3)
2	(1,2)	(2,2)	(3,2)	(4,2)
1	(1,1) START	(2,1)	(3,1)	(4,1)

For this 2 dimensional maze, draw the arrow showing the solution and then list the coordinates of the boxes that the arrows go through. The solution is on the bottom of the next page.

3 dimensional coordinates are used to show the solution of 3 dimensional mazes. The three coordinates determine a position in 3 dimensional space.

For example, my office in New York City might be at Third Avenue and 65th Street on the 31st Floor. This location is represented by the 3 coordinates of the point (3,65,31).
Where in the city is (5,34,102)?
It is the top of the Empire State Building.
The position of an airplane is given by 3 coordinates: distance North or South of a given city, distance East or West of a given city and the distance up above the ground.
What can you see if the given city is New York, and you are at (0 miles North, 200 miles East, 3 miles up)? You see just water.

As you move from box to box - whether vertically or horizontally - only one coordinate changes at a time. The first coordinate identifies the "row". The second coordinate identifies the "column". And the third coordinate identifies the "floor".

Look at the 3 dimensional coordinates on this maze.

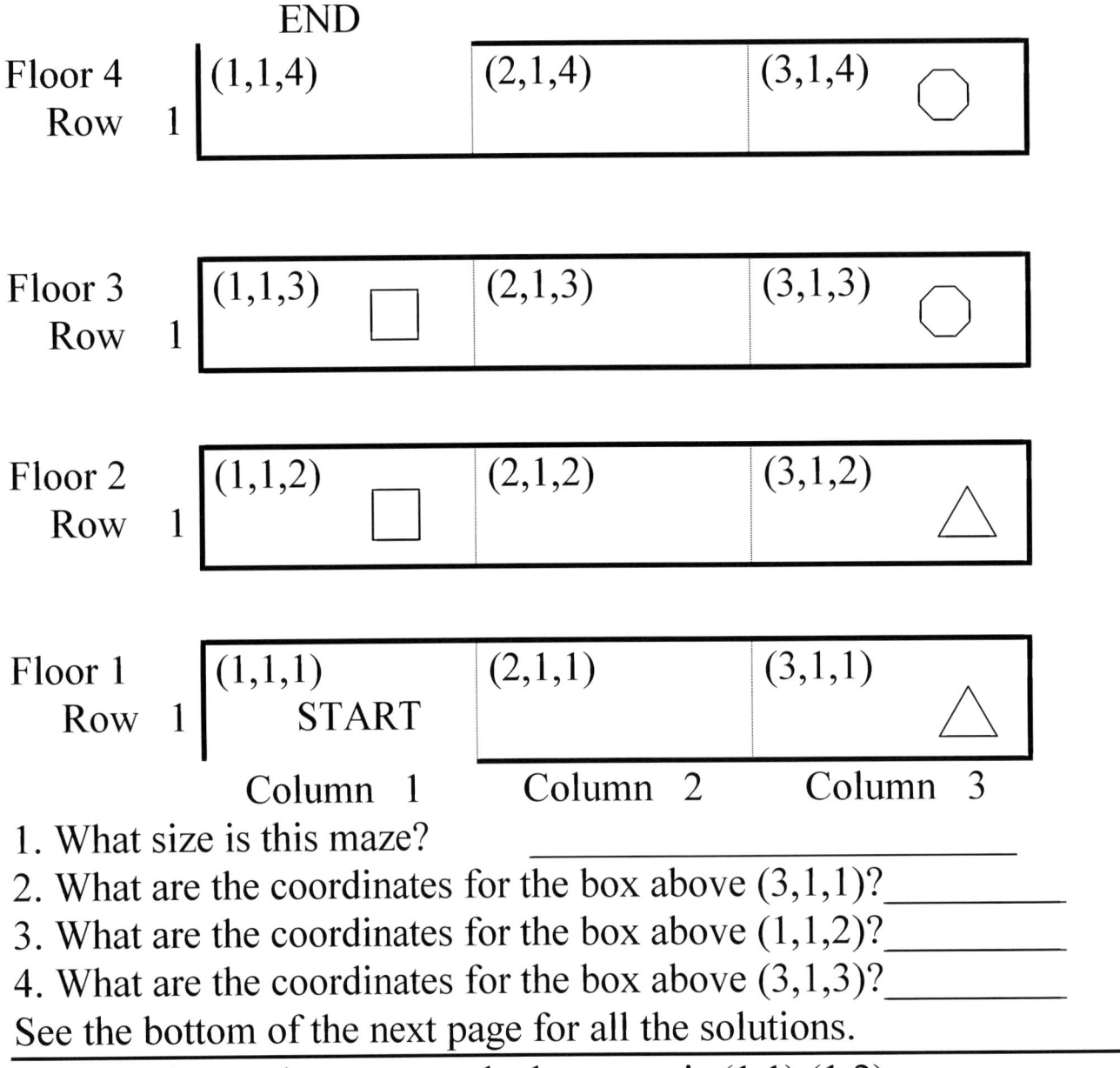

1. What size is this maze? _____
2. What are the coordinates for the box above (3,1,1)? _____
3. What are the coordinates for the box above (1,1,2)? _____
4. What are the coordinates for the box above (3,1,3)? _____
See the bottom of the next page for all the solutions.

The solution to the maze on the last page is (1,1),(1,2), (1,3),(1,4),(2,4),(3,4),(4,4),(3,4),(2,4),(1,4). Draw Arrows. Notice as you move only one coordinate changes at a time.

The same thinking applies to the maze on this page except there are 2 rows on each floor. When you move up a floor, make sure you move up to a box with the same row and column.

	END		
Floor 3, Row 2	(1,2,3)	(2,2,3)	(3,2,3)
Row 1	(1,1,3) ◇	(2,1,3)	(3,1,3)

Floor 2, Row 2	(1,2,2)	(2,2,2)	(3,2,1) ▱
Row 1	(1,1,2) ◇	(2,1,2)	(3,1,2) △

Floor 1, Row 2	(1,2,1)	(2,2,1)	(3,2,1) ▱
Row 1	(1,1,1) START	(2,1,1)	(3.1.1) △

Column 1   Column 2   Column 3

On the sides, put in the numbers of the rows, columns and floors.
Then in each box put in the 3 numbers giving the coordinates.
The 3rd coordinate is the Floor.
Draw the Arrows. Write the solution. (See bottom of next page)

The solution to the maze on the last page is (1,1,1),(2,1,1),(3,1,1), (3,1,2),(2,1,2),(1,1,2),(1,1,3),(2,1,3),(3,1,3),(3,1,4),(2,1,4),(1,1,4).
1. 3 by 1 by 4   2. (3,1,2)   3. (1,1,3)   4. (3,1,4)

Using 3 dimensional coordinates to navigate your way though a 3 dimensional mazes, makes it easier to move accurately from Floor to Floor. It is difficult without coordinates to know which box is above a given box on a lower floor.

Floor 3

	(1,3,3) **END**	(2,3,3)	(3,3,3) ◎
3	(1,2,3) ⊗	(2,2,3)	(3,2,3)
2	(1,1,3)	(2,1,3)	(3,1,3) □
1			

Floor 2

	(1,3,2) ▽	(2,3,2)	(3,3,2) ◎
3			
2	(1,2,2) ⊗	(2,2,2) ▱	(3,2,2)
1	(1,1,2)	(2,1,2)	(3,1,2) □

Floor 1

	(1,3,1) ▽	(2,3,1)	(3,3,1)
3			
2	(1,2,1)	(2,2,1) ▱	(3,2,1)
1	(1,1,1)	(2,1,1)	(3,1,1)

START   1   2   3

Solution: (1,1,1), (2,1,1), (3,1,1), (3,1,2), (2,1,2), (1,1,2), (1,1,3),(2,1,3), (3,1,3), (3,2,3), (2,2,3), (1,2,3).

Draw Arrows below to solve the maze. Then write the coordinates of the boxes you move through. (See page 162 for the solution.)

END

Floor 3,2

Floor 2,2

Floor 1,2

START

Solution to maze on the last page:
(1,1,1),(2,1,1),(3,1,1),(3,2,1),(3,3,1), (2,3,1),(2,2,1),(2,2,2), (1,2,2), (1,2,3), (1,1,3), (2,1,3), (2,2,3), (2,3,3), (1,3,3).

CHAPTER 13   8 by 4 by 5 MAZES (practicing coordinates)

(1,4,5) END	(2,4,5)	(3,4,5)	(4,4,5)	(5,4,5)	(6,4,5)	(7,4,5)	(8,4,5)
(1,3,5) ☆	(2,3,5)	(3,3,5)	(4,3,5)	(5,3,5)	(6,3,5) △	(7,3,5)	(8,3,5)
(1,2,5)	(2,2,5)	(3,2,5)	(4,2,5)	(5,2,5)	(6,2,5)	(7,2,5)	(8,2,5)
(1,1,5)	(2,1,5)	(3,1,5)	(4,1,5)	(5,1,5)	(6,1,5)	(7,1,5)	(8,1,5) ♡

(1,4,4)	(2,4,4)	(3,4,4)	(4,4,4)	(5,4,4)	(6,4,4)	(7,4,4)	(8,4,4)
(1,3,4) ☆	(2,3,4)	(3,3,4)	(4,3,4) □	(5,3,4)	(6,3,4) △	(7,3,4)	(8,3,4)
(1,2,4)	(2,2,4) ⊗	(3,2,4)	(4,2,4)	(5,2,4)	(6,2,4)	(7,2,4)	(8,2,4)
(1,1,4)	(2,1,4)	(3,1,4)	(4,1,4)	(5,1,4)	(6,1,4)	(7,1,4)	(8,1,4) ♡

(1,4,3) ▽	(2,4,3)	(3,4,3)	(4,4,3)	(5,4,3)	(6,4,3)	(7,4,3)	(8,4,3)
(1,3,3)	(2,3,3)	(3,3,3)	(4,3,3) □	(5,3,3)	(6,3,3)	(7,3,3)	(8,3,3) ⚡
(1,2,3)	(2,2,3) ⊗	(3,2,3)	(4,2,3)	(5,2,3)	(6,2,3)	(7,2,3)	(8,2,3)
(1,1,3)	(2,1,3)	(3,1,3)	(4,1,3)	(5,1,3)	(6,1,3)	(7,1,3)	(8,1,3)

(1,4,2) ▽	(2,4,2)	(3,4,2)	(4,4,2)	(5,4,2)	(6,4,2)	(7,4,2)	(8,4,2) ☺
(1,3,2)	(2,3,2)	(3,3,2)	(4,3,2)	(5,3,2)	(6,3,2) ◎	(7,3,2)	(8,3,2) ⚡
(1,2,2)	(2,2,2) ⬠	(3,2,2)	(4,2,2)	(5,2,2)	(6,2,2)	(7,2,2)	(8,2,2)
(1,1,2)	(2,1,2)	(3,1,2)	(4,1,2)	(5,1,2)	(6,1,2)	(7,1,2)	(8,1,2)

(1,4,1)	(2,4,1)	(3,4,1)	(4,4,1)	(5,4,1)	(6,4,1)	(7,4,1)	(8,4,1) ☺
(1,3,1)	(2,3,1)	(3,3,1)	(4,3,1)	(5,3,1)	(6,3,1) ◎	(7,3,1)	(8,3,1)
(1,2,1)	(2,2,1) ⬠	(3,2,1)	(4,2,1)	(5,2,1)	(6,2,1)	(7,2,1)	(8,2,1)
(1,1,1) START	(2,1,1)	(3,1,1)	(4,1,1)	(5,1,1)	(6,1,1)	(7,1,1)	(8,1,1)

Solution on page 162.

154

Solution on page 162.

155

Solution on page 162.

Solution on page 162.

Solution on page 162.

Chapter 14   3 by 3 by 3 by 2 Mazes
(The only 4 dimensional maze in print)

What is a 4 dimensional maze?
The maze on pages 160 and 161 is 4 dimensional because each box depends on 4 numbers or coordinates.

Your position on a Number Line depends on 1 number, the distance from 0. There is 1 coordinate on a Number Line.

Your position on the streets of New York City depends on 2 numbers, the street number and the avenue. These 2 coordinates can be visualized on a flat surface.

Your position in space depends on 3 numbers, the distance east, the distance west and the height above ground. There are 3 coordinates in space.

Your position in 4 dimensions depends on 4 numbers. For example, sometimes the number that is the time on a clock together with the 3 numbers determining your position in space are thought of as the 4 numbers of 4 dimensional space. This is called space-time. If you are on the Empire State Building, your position in space-time could by given by the four numbers,
(34 Street, 5th Avenue, 102 floor, 3 p.m. Oct.14, 2006).

A year later your coordinates would be
(34 Street, 5th Avenue, 102 floor, 3 p.m. Oct.14, 2007).

How to move through a 4 dimensional maze:

In order to understand a maze in 4 dimensions, remember that a 3 dimensional maze has several floors of 2 dimensional mazes; whereas, a 4 dimensional maze has several floors of 3 dimensional mazes called "slices". The number of the slice is the fourth coordinate of the 4 dimensional maze.

On page 162, each box on the lower slice has the 4th coordinate "1" such as (3,2,2,1). As the first three coordinates vary, the box moves over the whole 3 dimensional maze on the lower slice. You solve the maze on the first slice in the same way that you would solve any 3 dimensional maze.

On page 163, each box on the upper slice has the 4th coordinate "2" such as (3,1,1,2). As the first three coordinates vary, the box moves over the whole 3 dimensional maze on the upper slice. You solve the maze on the upper slice in the same you would solve any 3 dimensional maze.

You can move between the slices by traveling on imaginary ladders connecting a shape on the lower slice to the same shape on the upper slice. Notice that when you move from one box to another only one coordinate changes at a time, just as it did for 3 dimensional mazes. When you move from the lower slice to the upper slice, this is a useful method to make sure that you are moving correctly. For instance, when you move from the triangle shape on the lower slice to the triangle shape on the upper slice, only the 4th coordinate changes. That is, the coordinates change from (1,3,1,1) to (1,3,1,2).

Lower Slice

Solution on page 162.

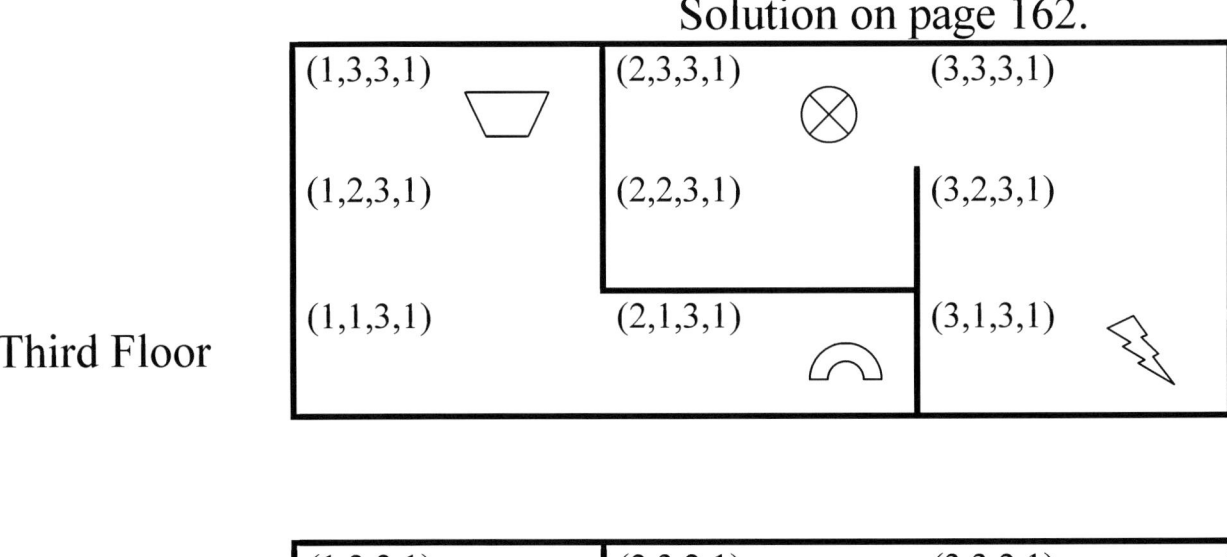

Third Floor

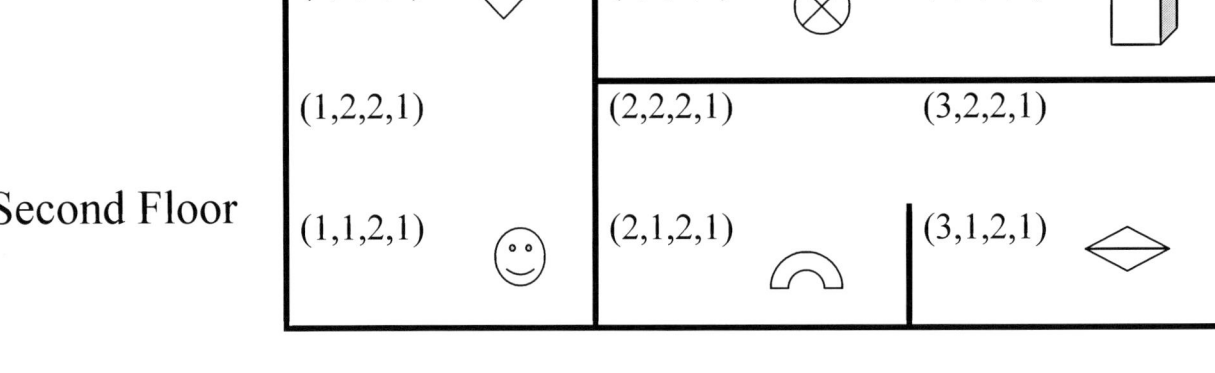

Second Floor

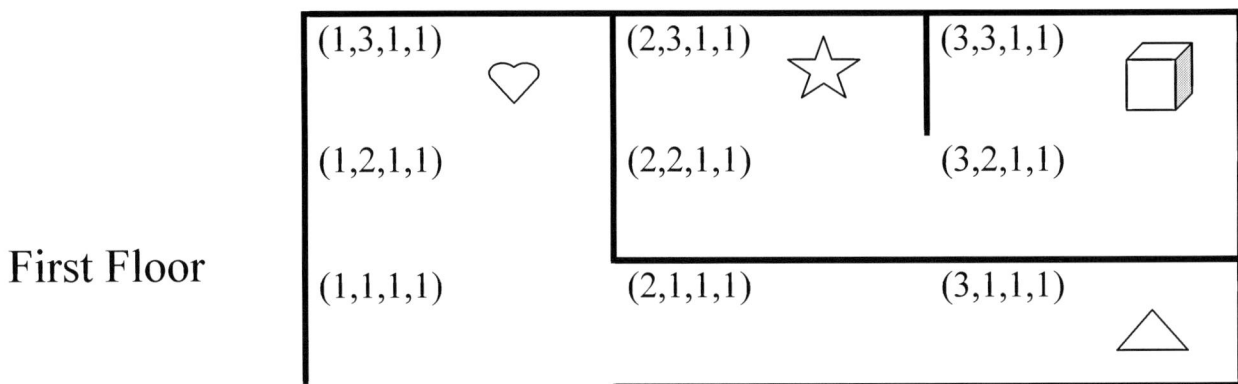

First Floor

Start

Upper Slice

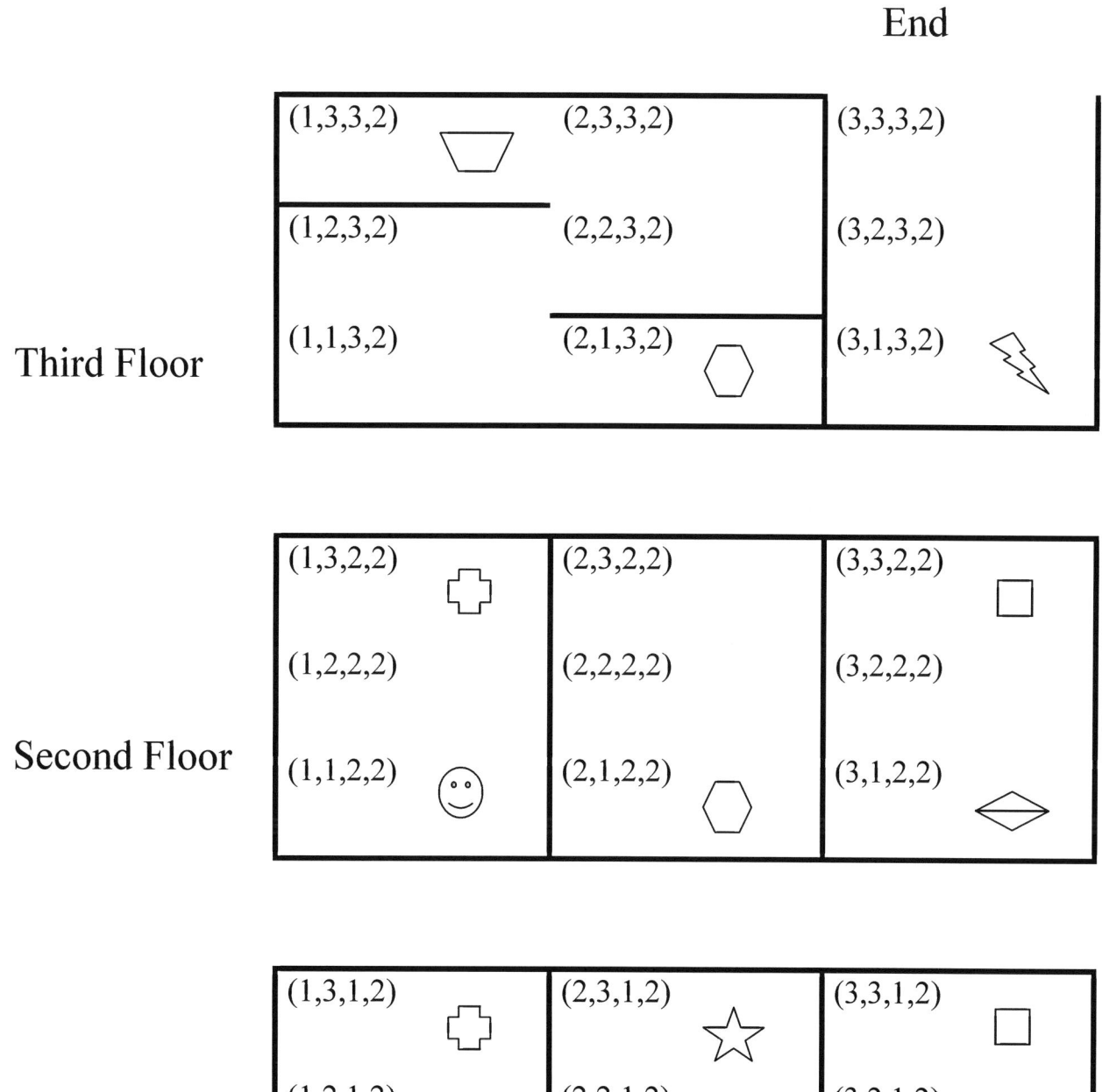

Solution to mazes:

Note that as you go through the maze only one coordinate changes one number at a time.

On page 151, Start at (1,1,1), go to (2,1,1),(3,1,1),(4,1,1),(4,1,2),(3,1,2), (2,1,2),(1,1,2),(1,1,3),(2,1,3),(3,1,3), (4,1,3),(4,2,3),(4,2,2),(3,2,2),(2,2,2),(1,2,2),((1,2,1),(1,3,1),(1,4,1),(2,4,1),(2,3,1),(3,3,1),(3,4,1),(4,4,1),(4,4,2),(3,4,2),(3,4,3),(4,4,3),(4,4,3),(4,3,3),(3,3,3),,(2,3,3),(2,4,3),(1,4,3)End.

On page 152, Start at (1,1,1), go to (1,2,1),(1,3,1),(1,4,1),(2,4,1),(3,4,1),(4,4,1),(5,4,1),(6,4,1),(7,4,1),(8,4,1),(8,4,2),(7,4,2),(6,4,2),(5,4,2),(4,4,2),(3,4,2),(2,4,2),(1,4,2),(1,4,3),(1,3,3),(1,2,3),(1,1,3),(1,1,4),(2,1,4),(3,1,4),(4,1,4),(5,1,4),(6,1,4),(7,1,4),(8,1,4),(8,1,5),(8,2,5),(8,3,5),(8,4,5),(8,4,4),(8,3,4),(8,2,4),(7,2,4),(6,2,4),(5,2,4),(4,2,4),(3,2,4),(2,2,4),(2,2,3),(2,3,3),(2,4,3),(3,4,3),(4,4,3),(5,4,3),(6,4,3),(7,4,3),(8,4,3),(8,3,3),(8,3,2),(7,3,2),(7,2,2),(7,1,2),(8,1,2),(8,2,2),(8,2,3),(8,2,3),(8,1,3),(7,1,3),(7,2,3),(7,3,3),(,3,4),(7,4,4),(6,4,4),(5,4,4),(5,3,4),(6,3,4),(6,3,5),(7,3,5),(7,4,5),(6,4,5),(5,4,5),(4,4,5),(3,4,5),(2,4,5),(1,4,5) End.

On page 153, Start at (1,1,1), go to (1,2,1),(1,3,1),(1,4,1),(1,4,2),(1,3,2),(1,2,2),(1,1,2),(1,1,3),(1,2,3),(1,3,3),(1,4,3),(2,4,3),(2,4,2),(2,3,2),(2,2,2),(2,1,2),(2,2,1),(3,2,1),(3,1,1),(4,1,1),(5,1,1),(6,1,1),(7,1,1),(8,1,1),(8,1,2),(8,2,2),(8,3,2),(8,4,2),(8,4,3),(8,3,3),(8,2,3),(8,1,3),(8,1,4),(8,2,4),(8,3,4),(8,4,4),(8,4,5),(8,3,5),(8,2,5),(8,1,5),(7,1,5),(7,2,5),(7,3,5),(7,4,5),(7,4,4),(7,3,4),(7,2,4),(7,1,4),(7,1,3),(7,2,3),(7,3,3),(7,4,3),(7,4,2),(7,3,2),(7,2,2),(7,1,2),(6,1,2),(6,2,2),(6,2,1),(7,2,1),(7,3,1),(7,4,1),(6,4,1),(6,3,1),(6,3,2),(6,4,2),(5,4,2),(5,3,2),(5,2,2),(5,3,2),(5,1,3),(6,1,3),(6,2,3),(6,3,3),(6,4,3),(6,4,4),(6,3,4),(6,2,4),(6,1,4),(6,1,5),(6,2,5),(6,3,5),(6,4,5),(5,4,5) ,(5,3,5),(5,2,5),(5,1,5),(4,1,5),(3,1,5),(2,1,5),(1,1,5),(1,2,5),(1,3,5),(1,4,5)End.

On page 154, Start at (1,1,1), go to (2,1,1),(3,1,1),(4,1,1)(4,1,2),(5,1,2),(6,1,2)(7,1,2),(8,1,2),(8,1,1)(7,1,1), (6,1,1),(5,1,1),(5,2,1),(6,2,1),(7,2,1)(8,2,1),(8,2,2),(7,2,2)(6,2,2),(5,2,2),(5,2,3)(6,2,3),(7,2,3),(8,2,3)(8,1,3),(7,1,3),(6,1,3),(5,1,3),(5,1,4),(5,2,4)(5,3,4),(5,3,3),(6,3,3)(7,3,3),(8,3,3),(8,4,3)(8,4,4),(8,3,4),(8,2,4)(8,1,4),(7,1,4),(7,1,5)(8,1,5),(8,2,5),(8,3,5),(8,4,5),(7,4,5),(7,3,5)(7,2,5),(6,2,5),(6,1,5),(6,1,4),(6,2,4),(6,3,4)(6,4,4),(5,4,4),(4,4,4)(4,4,3),(4,3,3),(4,2,3),(4,1,3),(4,1,4),(4,2,4)(4,3,4),(4,3,5),(4,2,5)(4,1,5),(5,1,5),(5,2,5)(5,3,5),(6,3,5),(6,4,5)(5,4,5),(4,4,5),(3,4,5),(2,4,5),(1,4,5)End.

On page 155, Start at (1,1,1), go to (1,2,1),(1,3,1),(1,4,1),(2,4,2),(2,4,1),(3,4,1),(4,4,1),(5,4,1),(6,4,1),(6,4,2),(6,3,2),(6,2,2),(6,1,2),(7,1,2),(7,1,1),(8,1,1),(8,2,1),(7,2,1),(7,3,1),(8,3,1),(8,4,1),(7,4,1),(7,4,2),(7,4,1),(7,4,2),(8,4,2),(8,3,2),(7,3,2),(7,2,2),(8,2,2),(8,1,2),(8,1,3),(7,1,3),(6,1,3),(6,2,3),(6,3,3),(6,4,3),(6,4,4),(7,4,4),(7,3,4),(6,3,4),(5,3,4),(5,2,4),(5,1,4),(4,1,4),(4,1,3),(5,1,3),(5,2,3),(5,3,3),(5,4,3),(5,4,4),(4,4,4),(4,3,4),(3,3,4),(3,4,4),(3,4,5),(4,4,5),(5,4,5),(6,4,5),(7,4,5),(7,3,5),(6,3,5),(5,3,5),(4,3,5),(4,2,5),(4,1,5),(3,1,5),(2,1,5),(1,1,5),(1,2,5),(1,3,5),(1,4,5)End.

On page 156, Start at (1,1,1), go to (1,2,1),(2,2,1),(2,1,1),(3,1,1),(3,2,1),(3,2,2),(3,1,2),(2,1,2),(1,1,2) ,(1,2,2),(1,3,2),(1,4,2) , (1,4,3),(1,3,3),(1,2,3),(1,1,3),(2,1,3),(2,2,3),(2,3,3),(2,4,3),(2,4,4),(1,4,4),(1,3,4),(2,3,4),(3,3,4),(3,2,4),(2,2,4),(1,2,4),(1,2,5),(1,1,5),(2,1,5),(2,2,5),(2,3,5),(3,3,5),(3,2,5),(3,1,5),(4,1,5),(5,1,5),(5,2,5),(4,2,5),(4,3,5),(4,3,4),(4,2,4),(4,2,3),(4,3,3),(4,4,3),(3,4,3),(3,3,3),(3,2,3),(3,1,3),(4,,1,3),(5,1,3),(5,2,3),(5,3,3),(5,4,3),(6,4,3),(6,3,3),(6,2,3),(6,1,3),(7,1,3)(8,1,3),(8,2,3),(8,3,3),(8,4,3),(8,4,4),(8,3,4),(7,3,4),(7,4,4),(7,4,5),(6,4,5),(5,4,5),(4,4,5)(3,4,5),(2,4,5),(1,4,5)End.

On page 160, Start at (1,1,1,1), go to (1,2,1,1),(1,3,1,1),(1,3,2,1),(1,2,2,1),(1,1,2,1),(1,1,2,2),(1,2,2,2), (1,3,2,2),(1,3,1,2),(1,2,1,2),(1,1,1,2),(2,1,1,2),(2,2,1,2), (2,3,1,2),(2,3,1,1),(2,2,1,1),3,2,1,1),(3,3,1,1),(3,3,2,1),(2,3,2,1)(2,3,3,1),(3,3,3,1), (3,2,3,1),(3,1,3,1),(3,1,3,2),(3,2,3,2), (3,3,3,2)End.